A Brief History of
Heaven

Blackwell Brief Histories of
Religion

This series offers brief, accessible and lively accounts of key topics within theology and religion. Each volume presents both academic and general readers with a selected history of topics which have had a profound effect on religious and cultural life. The word "history" is, therefore, understood in its broadest cultural and social sense. The volumes are based on serious scholarship but they are written engagingly and in terms readily understood by general readers.

Published

Alister E. McGrath – A Brief History of Heaven
G. R. Evans – A Brief History of Heresy

Forthcoming

Carter Lindberg – A Brief History of Love
Douglas Davies – A Brief History of Death
Dana Robert – A Brief History of Mission
Tamara Sonn – A Brief History of Islam

A Brief History of
Heaven

ALISTER E. MCGRATH

Blackwell
Publishing

© 2003 by Alister E. McGrath

350 Main Street, Malden, MA 02148-5018, USA
108 Cowley Road, Oxford OX4 1JF, UK
550 Swanston Street, Carlton South, Victoria 3053, Australia
Kurfürstendamm 57, 10707 Berlin, Germany

The right of Alister E. McGrath to be identified as the Author of
this Work has been asserted in accordance with the UK Copyright,
Designs, and Patents Act 1988.

First published 2003 by Blackwell Publishing Ltd

Library of Congress Cataloging-in-Publication Data

McGrath, Alister E., 1953–
  A brief history of heaven / Alister E. McGrath.
      p. cm. – (Blackwell brief histories of religion)
  Includes bibliographical references and index.
  ISBN 0-631-23353-9 – ISBN 0-631-23354-7 (pbk.)
  1. Heaven. I. Title. II. Series.
  BT846.3 M34 2002
  236′.24′09–dc21

                                          2002007251

A catalogue record for this title is available from the British
Library.

Set in 9¹/₂/12pt Meridian
by Graphicraft Limited, Hong Kong
Printed and bound in the United Kingdom
by TJ International, Padstow, Cornwall

For further information on
Blackwell Publishing, visit our website:
http://www.blackwellpublishing.com

Contents

List of Illustrations

Picture research by Thelma Gilbert.

Preface

The purpose of this short book is easily stated. It sets out to explore a few aspects of the development of the idea of heaven in Western culture, and the inspiration it has brought to Western literature and personal faith. It is a subject that has long fascinated me, both academically and spiritually, and I hope its readers will find themselves sharing at least something of my excitement as I wrote it.

Unlike some other excellent recent studies of the history of heaven,[1] this book does not attempt to offer a chronological overview of the development of the idea of heaven, but looks at the ways in which Western literature – both Christian and secular – understands this notion, and the difference it makes to human life and thought. Its approach is thus primarily thematic, rather than historical.

---

[1] The best studies currently available in English are Colleen McDannell and Bernhard Lang. *Heaven: A History*. New Haven, CT: Yale University Press, 1988, and Jeffrey Burton Russell. *A History of Heaven: The Singing Silence*. Princeton, NJ: Princeton University Press, 1997.

The origins of the book lie in research I undertook to expand the final chapter of my widely used textbook *Christian Theology: An Introduction*,[2] which deals with the concept of heaven. As I researched this theme, I became aware of two major difficulties. First, there was no way I could include any more than a fraction of that research within the severely limited confines of that chapter. It called out for a book in its own right. And second, the exploration of the idea of heaven in the field of Western literature was far more interesting than anything I found in works of systematic theology. Although care has been taken to ensure that the theological foundations of the ideas are carefully explained, this book therefore focuses on the depiction and discussion of heaven in works of literature, rather than technical works of theology.

Alister McGrath
Oxford, May 2002

---

[2] Alister McGrath, *Christian Theology: An Introduction*. 3rd edn. Oxford: Blackwell Publishing, 2001.

Chapter 1

The City: The New Jerusalem

"I saw the holy city, the New Jerusalem" (Revelation 21:2). These words from the final book of the Bible set out a vision of heaven that has captivated the Christian imagination. To speak of heaven is to affirm that the human longing to *see* God will one day be fulfilled – that we shall finally be able to gaze upon the face of what Christianity affirms to be the most wondrous sight anyone can hope to behold. One of Israel's greatest Psalms asks to be granted the privilege of being able to gaze upon "the beauty of the Lord" in the land of the living (Psalm 27:4) – to be able to catch a glimpse of the face of God in the midst of the ambiguities and sorrows of this life. We see God but dimly in this life; yet, as Paul argued in his first letter to the Corinthian Christians, we shall one day see God "face to face" (1 Corinthians 13:12).

To *see* God; to *see* heaven. From a Christian perspective, the horizons defined by the parameters of our human existence merely limit what we can see; they do not define what there is to be seen. Imprisoned by its history and mortality, humanity has had to content itself with pressing its boundaries to their absolute limits, longing to know what lies beyond them. Can we break through the limits of time and space, and glimpse another realm – another dimension, hidden from us at present, yet which one day we shall encounter, and even enter?

Images and the Christian Faith

It has often been observed that humanity has the capacity to think. Perhaps it is still better observed that we possess the unique capacity to *imagine*. Our understanding of the universe, God, and ourselves is primarily controlled by images, rather than concepts. The concept of heaven is an excellent example of a Christian idea that is fundamentally imaginative in provenance, and that demands an imaginative mode of encounter with the reality that it mediates. This insight lies behind the Orthodox emphasis on the important role of icons in the Christian life, which – when rightly understood and used – act as "windows into heaven." Perhaps this is nowhere so evident as in human reflection on heaven, which is controlled and stimulated by a series of powerful images – supremely, the image of a city and of a garden.

Human language finds itself pressed to its limits when trying to depict and describe the divine. Words and images are borrowed from everyday life, and put to new uses in an attempt to capture and preserve precious insights into the nature of God. The Christian understanding of both the divine and human natures is such that – if it is right – we are unable to grasp the full reality of God. Can the human mind ever hope to comprehend something that must ultimately lie beyond its ability to enfold?

A story is told concerning the great Christian theologian Augustine of Hippo (354–430), who is particularly noted for a massive treatise on the mystery of the Trinity – the distinctively Christian understanding of the richly textured nature of God. Perhaps in the midst of composing this treatise, Augustine found himself pacing the Mediterranean shoreline of his native North Africa, not far from the great city of Carthage. Not for the first time, a theologian found his language and imagery challenged to the utmost, and his intellectual resources exhausted, in his attempt to put into words the greater reality of God. While wandering across the sand, he noticed a small boy scooping seawater into his hands, and pouring as much as his small hands could hold into a hole he had earlier hollowed in the sand. Puzzled, Augustine watched as the lad repeated his action again and again.

Eventually, his curiosity got the better of him. What, he asked the boy, did he think he was doing?. The reply probably perplexed him still further. The youth was in the process of emptying the ocean into the small cavity he had scooped out in the hot sand. Augustine was dismissive: how could such a vast body of water be contained in such a small hole? The boy was equally dismissive in return: how could Augustine expect to contain the vast mystery of God in the mere words of a book?

The story illuminates one of the central themes of Christian theology and spirituality alike – that there are limits placed upon the human ability to grasp the things of God. Our knowledge of God is accommodated to our capacity. As writers from Augustine to Calvin argued, God is perfectly aware of the limitations placed upon human nature – which, after all, is itself a divine creation. Knowing our limits, such writers argued, God both discloses divine truths and enters into our world in forms that are tempered to our limited abilities and competencies. Familiar images from the world around us become windows of perception into the nature and purposes of God. The parables of Jesus are perhaps the most familiar example of this: an everyday event (a sower sowing seed in the fields), or a keenly observed event (a woman's joy on finding a lost coin) become the means by which deeper spiritual truths are disclosed. The woman's joy becomes a powerful symbol of the delight of God when wayward humanity returns home to its tender creator and redeemer. Yet this is not an arbitrary association or connection; it is one that Christians hold to be divinely *authorized.*

This is perhaps best seen in the Old Testament images of God, which are developed and given still greater impact in the New. As the Oxford scholar and theologian Austin Farrer argued, Christianity represents a "rebirth of images," both in terms of the importance assigned to images in conceiving and sustaining the Christian life and the new impetus given to the religious imagery that the church inherited from Israel. To speak of God as "king," "shepherd," or "mother" is to draw upon a richly textured biblical tradition, which authorizes its users to speak of God in this manner, and whose imagery engages both mind and imagination in a sustained process of reflection and internal appropriation. Such analogies were drawn from the ancient Near Eastern world of everyday experience; they nevertheless possessed the capacity to point beyond themselves, signifying something of a greater reality lying beyond them and the world that contained them.

Christian writers have always appreciated the importance of these images, not least because they appealed to both the human reason and imagination. Romanticism may be singled out for its emphasis on the imagination as a faculty of spiritual discernment, and a correspondingly high emphasis on the role of religious imagery. "Vision or Imagination is a Representation of what Eternally Exists, Really and Unchangeably" (William Blake). Where reason, the Romantics argued, kept humanity firmly anchored to the realities of this world, the imagination liberated humanity from bondage to the material order, enabling it to discern transcendent spiritual truths. "While reason is the natural organ of truth, imagination is the organ of meaning" (C. S. Lewis). Yet Romanticism differed merely in its *emphasis* at this point; such insights have nourished Christian theology and spirituality down the ages.

Heaven is perhaps the supreme example of a Christian concept that is mediated directly through images. To speak of "imagining heaven" does not imply or entail that heaven is a *fictional* notion, constructed by deliberately disregarding the harsher realities of the everyday world. It is to affirm the critical role of the God-given human capacity to construct and enter into mental pictures of divine reality, which are mediated through Scripture and the subsequent tradition of reflection and development. We are able to inhabit the mental images we create, and thence anticipate the delight of finally entering the greater reality to which they correspond. Marco Polo (1254–1324), having returned to Italy from the court of Kublai Khan, was able to convey some of the wonders of China by asking his audience to imagine a world they had never visited, but which he could recreate, if only in part, by his narratives and descriptions. The unknown could be glimpsed by comparisons with the known – through *analogies*.

Biblical writers imagined – that is to say, pictured and invited others to picture – heaven in terms of certain types of earthly spaces – spaces that possessed distinct qualities capable of disclosing the unique nature of heaven itself. Three such images are of critical importance: the kingdom, the city, and the garden. Each of these analogies of heaven models an aspect of the greater reality to which they point, however haltingly. Yet analogies are at best imperfect accounts of their referents, modeling only part of a greater whole. They possess an inbuilt propensity to break down, misleading those who press them beyond their intended limits. Above all, these three images mislead us if we regard them as irreducibly spatial or geographical in nature, and thus conveying the notion that heaven is merely a place or region. A spatial analogy does not imply that heaven is a specific physical location, any more than the use of social analogies for God – such as "father" or "king" – implies that God is a physical human being.

To explore the Christian vision of heaven, it is therefore necessary to engage with its controlling images. We shall begin by considering perhaps the most familiar of all: the image of heaven as a city – more specifically, as the New Jerusalem. Many sections of the Old Testament resound with the praise of the city of Jerusalem, which is seen both as a tangible image of the presence and providence of God within its sturdy walls, and also as a pointer to the fulfillment of messianic expectations. The New Testament gives a new twist to this focus, not least in the remarkable reworking of the theme of the "city of God" found in the Revelation of St. John. For this biblical writer, the fulfillment of all Christian hopes and expectations centers upon the new Jerusalem, the city of God within which the risen Christ reigns triumphant. This image has stimulated intense reflection on the part of Christian theologians. For Augustine of Hippo, the conflict between the "city of God" and the "city of the world" underlies the quest for responsible Christian political and social action. The reformer John Calvin (1509–64) saw the city of Geneva as the ideal Christian republic, embodying the core values of the kingdom of God on earth. The early Puritans, founding settlements in the Massachusetts Bay area, found inspiration in the biblical image of the city on the hill. Boston was to become the American Geneva, the city of God which would draw all comers to its powerful and purifying light.

So how did this association between heaven and Jerusalem develop?

The City of Jerusalem in the Old Testament

In turning to consider how a city came to be an image of heaven, we must appreciate that the ancient world saw the city as far more than an aggregate of streets and buildings. A city offered security; its gates and walls protected its population against their enemies, whether these took the form of marauding wild animals or invading armies. One of the great prayers of ancient Israel was that there should be no breaches in the walls of the city of Jerusalem (Psalm 144:14). The security of the city's population depended on the integrity of its walls, towers, and gates.

Yet a city is more than a place of safety. In the ancient world, the "city" designated a community of citizens, united by common origins and sharing common concerns, rather than the physical buildings that they occupied. Greek cities were often destroyed in times of war, but were reconstructed or resettled elsewhere. The core identity of the city – what was transmitted from one generation to another – rested in its citizens, not its physical structures. Cities were understood to be cohesive corporate entities, rather than aggregates of individuals, defined by a definite set of beliefs and values, which in turn determined those of its members.

Yet for Israel, there was a third aspect of the city which was of particular significance. A city was a *settlement*. Where once Israel had been a nomadic people, wandering in the wilderness of Sinai for 40 years, it finally came to settle down in cities. The period of wandering was over; a period of permanent inhabitation of a definite geographical region had begun.

In the Old Testament, one city towers above all others in significance. To the Israelites, Jerusalem was simply *"the* city." The rise of the prominence of Jerusalem is directly linked to David's decision to establish his throne within this ancient Jebusite city, and to make it the resting place of the Ark of the Covenant. These deeply symbolic actions led to Jerusalem being viewed as the chosen habitation of God, "for the glory of the Lord filled the house of the Lord" (1 Kings 8:10–11). The pilgrim who made the long journey to the city could do so in the sure knowledge that God truly dwelt within Jerusalem's sturdy walls (Psalms 9:11, 74:2, 135:21).

This highly idealistic view of Jerusalem was tainted by the prophetic insistence that sin and corruption within its walls would lead to the city losing its unique status. The siege of Jerusalem by the Assyrians, culminating in its capture and the destruction of its temple in 586 BC, was a devastating catastrophe, both for the social and political history of the city and for the hopes and beliefs of its population. Had Jerusalem lost its special status in the sight of God? The prophet Ezekiel had a vision of the "glory of the Lord" departing from the Jerusalem Temple. Would it ever return? It was against this background of despair that the prophetic vision of the New Jerusalem began to take shape.

A new city of God would arise, in which the throne of God would be established, and within which the "glory of the Lord" would once more dwell. The glory of this renewed temple would exceed that of the former temple, destroyed by the Assyrians (Haggai 2:9).

Initially, this prophetic vision of a New Jerusalem was understood to apply to a future earthly city – a reconstructed city of bricks and mortar, which would rise from the ruins of the old city with the return of its people from their exile in Babylon. The Old Testament books of Nehemiah and Ezra document attempts to restore Jerusalem to its former glory, and fulfill the hopes of a renewed presence of the glory of the Lord. Yet with the passing of time, Jewish hopes began to crystallize around the idea of a heavenly Jerusalem – a future city, beyond this world, filled with the "glory of the Lord," in which God is seated on a throne. The city is filled with eternal light, which draws people from afar to the safety and rest that it offers.

The future hopes of Israel, which had once centered on the earthly city of Jerusalem and its temple, now underwent a decisive shift in focus. The calamitous history of Jerusalem led many to look to a future heavenly city, which was somehow represented or foreshadowed in its earthly counterpart. This trend, which was already present in the centuries before Christ, received a massive stimulus as a result of the Jewish revolt of AD 66 against the occupying Roman forces in Palestine. The Roman emperor Titus, in ruthlessly putting down this revolt in AD 70, destroyed the temple at Jerusalem, leaving only small segments of the original edifice standing (such as the western "wailing wall," still a site for Jewish prayers). With the destruction of the earthly focus of Jewish hopes, it was perhaps inevitable that a heavenly alternative would be found. The "New

Jerusalem" now came to refer to a future hope that lay beyond history, rather than to the hope of rebuilding the original Jebusite city of David. While the earthly city of Jerusalem plays an important role for several New Testament writers, it is this vision of a heavenly Jerusalem that dominates its closing pages.

The City of Jerusalem in the New Testament

The image of the "New Jerusalem" has exercised a controlling influence over Christian literature and art down the centuries. The origins of this evocative image lie primarily in the "Revelation of St. John," the closing book of the Christian Bible. Its powerful imagery has saturated Christian hymnody and theological reflection, and perhaps nowhere so clearly as the church's reflection on how heaven is to be visualized. The consolation of heaven is here contrasted with the suffering, tragedy, and pain of life on earth. Revelation – also known as "the Apocalpyse" in some Christian circles – is traditionally held to reflect the conditions of social exclusion or perhaps persecution faced by Christians in this region of the Roman empire in the later years of the reign of the emperor Domitian. Perhaps its most enduring image – and certainly that most relevant to this study – is its portrayal of the New Jerusalem:

> Then I saw a new heaven and a new earth; for the first heaven and the first earth had passed away, and the sea was no more. And I saw the holy city, the new Jerusalem, coming down out of heaven from God, prepared as a bride adorned for her husband. And I heard a loud voice from the throne saying, "See, the home of God is among mortals. He

will dwell with them; they will be his people, and God himself will be with them; he will wipe every tear from their eyes. Death will be no more; mourning and crying and pain will be no more, for the first things have passed away." And the one who was seated on the throne said, "See, I am making all things new." (Revelation 21:1–5)

The theme of the New Jerusalem is here integrated with motifs drawn from the creation account – such as the presence of the "tree of life" (Revelation 22:2) – suggesting that heaven can be seen as the restoration of the bliss of Eden, when God dwelt with humanity in harmony. The pain, sorrow, and evil of a fallen world have finally passed away, and the creation restored to its original intention. The Christians of Asia Minor at this time were few in number, and generally of low social status. There is no doubt that they derived much consolation from the anticipation of entering a heavenly city that vastly exceeded any earthly comforts or security they had known. The holy city was paved with gold and decked with jewels and precious stones, dazzling its inhabitants and intensifying the sense of longing to enter through its gates on the part of those still on earth.

The New Jerusalem – like its earthly counterpart – is portrayed as a walled city. Its security is beyond question. It is perched on the peak of a hill that no invading army could hope to ascend. Its walls are so thick that they could not be breached by any known siege engine, and so high that no human could hope to scale them. Its 12 gates are guarded by angels. Just as return to Eden was once prevented by a guardian angel, so the New Jerusalem is defended against invasion by supernatural forces.

It is important to note that the 12 gates of the New Jerusalem – though guarded by angels – are permanently thrown open. Whereas the classic fortified city of ancient times was designed to exclude outsiders, the architecture of the New Jerusalem seems designed to welcome them within its boundaries. The city is portrayed as perfectly cubical (21:16), perhaps signifying that it is a perfection of the square temple that the prophet Ezekiel envisaged for the rebuilt Jerusalem after the return from exile (Ezekiel 43:16, 48:20).

The careful attention paid to imagery suggests that the New Jerusalem is to be seen in terms of the fulfillment of Israel through the restoration of its 12 tribes (21:12–14). Most significantly of all, the New Jerusalem does not contain a temple (21:22). The cultic hierarchies of the old priestly tradition are swept to one side. All are now priests, and there is no need for a temple, in that God dwells within the city as a whole. In a remarkable transformation of images, the city has itself become a temple, in that God is now all in all. Where Old Testament prophets had yearned for the rebuilding of the temple, Revelation declares that it has become redundant. What it foreshadowed had now taken place. With the advent of the reality of God's presence, its symbol was no longer required. The dwelling place of God is now with the people of God; it can no longer be contained within a physical structure. The New Jerusalem is thus characterized by the pervasive presence of God, and the triumphant and joyful response of those who had long awaited this experience.

This image of heaven resonates strongly with one of the leading themes of Paul's theology – that Christians are to be regarded as "citizens of heaven" (Philippians 3:19–21). Paul makes a distinction between those who "set their minds on earthly things" and those whose citizenship is "in heaven." Paul himself was a Roman citizen, who knew what privileges this brought – particularly on those occasions when he found himself in conflict with the Roman authorities. For Paul, Christians possessed something greater: the "citizenship of heaven," which is to be understood as a present possession, not something that is yet to come. While believers have yet to enter into the full possession of what this citizenship entails, they already possess that privilege. We have no permanent citizenship in this world, in that our citizenship is in heaven (Philippians 3:20). As the author of the letter to the Hebrews puts it, "here we have no lasting city, but we are looking for the city that is to come" (Hebrews 13:14).

The theme of a heavenly city is thus firmly embedded in the New Testament. It proved highly attractive to subsequent Christian writers, who saw the image of the "city of God" as a remarkably fertile means of articulating the basic themes of the Christian hope. Perhaps the most important of these writers is Augustine of Hippo.

Augustine of Hippo on the Two Cities

Augustine's major work *The City of God* was written in a context that could easily be described as "apocalyptic" – the destruction of the great city of Rome, and the collapse of the Roman Empire, which seemed to many to mark the end of civilization as they knew it. A central theme of Augustine's work is the relation between two cities – the "city of God" and the "secular city" (or "the city of the world"). The complexities of the Christian life, especially its political aspects, can be explained in terms of the tensions and interplay between these two cities. The fall of Rome was widely held to be prophesied in the Book of Revelation, which sees

Babylon as a symbol of this great imperial power. It is no accident that Augustine chose to return to the imagery of this New Testament book in his attempt to bring stability and a sense of historical location to the Christian church at this apocalyptic moment.

According to Augustine, believers live "in this intermediate period," separating the incarnation of Christ from his final return in glory. The church is to be seen as in exile in the "city of the world." It is *in* the world, yet not *of* the world. These two cities embody radically different values and aspirations.

> The two cities are shaped by two loves: the earthly by the love of self, even to the contempt of God; the heavenly by the love of God, even to the contempt of self. The former, in a word, glories in itself, the latter in the Lord. For the one seeks glory from people; but the greatest glory of the other is God, the witness of conscience. The one lifts up its head in its own glory; the other says to its God, "You are my glory, and the one who lifts up my head." In the one, the princes and the nations it subdues are ruled by the love of ruling; in the other, the princes and the subjects serve one another in love, the latter obeying, while the former are mindful of the needs of all. The one delights in its own strength, represented in the persons of its rulers; the other says to its God, "I will love you, O Lord, my strength."

There is a tension between the present situation of believers, in which the church is exiled in the world, and somehow obliged to maintain its distinctive ethos while surrounded by disbelief, and their future hope, in which the church will be delivered from the world, and finally allowed to share in the glory of God. Augustine rejects the idea that the church on earth is a pure body of saints (a teaching associated with his bitter opponents, the Donatists). For Augustine, the church shares in the fallen character of the world, and therefore includes the pure and the impure, saints and sinners. Only at the last day will this tension finally be resolved. Although Augustine does not develop this idea quite as far as some of his readers might like, later writers remedied this shortcoming. For John Calvin, a distinction could be drawn between the "visible" and "invisible" church – that is, between the church as an empirical and observable reality in the world, and as a future reality in the heavenly places. While Calvin insisted that there was a genuine continuity between the two, they were not identical.

So what is life in the heavenly city like? Perhaps the most famous aspect of Augustine's reflections on heaven concern the sexual aspects of human life. For Augustine, there will be no sex in heaven. Both male and female will enjoy the beauty of perfect bodies, but there will be no temptation to lust precisely because there will be no temptation of any kind.

> Both male and female will be raised, yet there will be no lust, which is the cause of shame. For they were naked before they sinned, and the man and woman were not ashamed. While all blemishes will be removed from our bodies, their natural forms will remain. The female will not be seen as a defective, but as a natural state, which now experiences neither sexual intercourse nor childbirth. There will be female body parts; these, however, will not be adapted to their former purpose, but to a new beauty, which will not cause lust on the part of anyone looking on. Rather, it will inspire praise of the wisdom and goodness of God.

Augustine's argument here rests on his interpretation of the paradise narrative of Genesis, which he takes to mean that human nakedness was a thing of beauty before sin entered the world and made it a cause of temptation and lustful desire. Heaven, which is supremely characterized by an absence of sin, allows a restoration of the conditions of paradise, in which humans could be naked without shame or fear.

Augustine further argues that life in the New Jerusalem is characterized by the theme of *rest*. Does not the letter to the Hebrews promise rest to believers? It is in the heavenly city that this Gospel promise finds its fulfillment. Eternal life will be like a perpetual Sabbath, in which the saints will dwell in the peace of God. Their earthly labors in the vineyard having ceased at sundown, believers enter into the reward promised them by the Lord of that vineyard (Matthew 20:1–12). The peace enjoyed in the heavenly city is grounded in the final rout and scattering of the enemies of the believer, both outward and inward.

> There is no complete peace as long as we have to govern our own faults. For as long as those faults remain, they threaten us with warfare. Furthermore, we cannot rest in victory over those that have been suppressed, in that we must ensure that they remain suppressed.

For Augustine, the complete tranquillity that heaven alone allows results from all external foes having been vanquished, and human weaknesses and faults transcended in the New Jerusalem.

Influential though Augustine's theological analysis has been on Christian political thinking down the ages, it is important to appreciate that it has failed to have the *iconic* significance one might expect. Augustine developed ideas, rather than images, preferring to extract the conceptual meat from the image of the "heavenly city" rather than develop its iconic potential. The "two cities" thus become little more than convenient pegs on which to hang important theological principles; they are not developed *as images*, with an inbuilt propensity to stimulate and excite the baptized imagination.

Yet it is arguably the *imagery*, rather than the *theology*, of the New Testament that has had the greatest impact on the development of the notion of heaven in Christian literature. The idea of a heavenly city proved to be a remarkably fertile source of stimulation for Christian writers, seeking to depict the future Christian hope in highly visual and memorable terms. What better way was there to stimulate and sustain the Christian hope than anticipating the delight of entering the palatial courts of the New Jerusalem, and savoring its spacious chambers? To develop this theme, we may turn to consider the theme of the "New Jerusalem" in some spiritual writers of the Middle Ages.

The Heavenly City and Medieval Spirituality

A remarkable new period in the history of the Christian church began under Charlemagne (c.742–814), the first Emperor of the Holy Roman Empire. During his long reign – often referred to as the "Carolingian period" – a cultural Renaissance began. Religious iconography was an integral aspect of this Renaissance, as may be seen from the new interest in mosaics and murals in the design of ecclesiastical buildings – such as Charlemagne's palatine chapel – or the illustration of sacred manuscripts. The four surviving ninth-century illuminated manuscripts of the Book of Revelation demonstrate that a certain stylized way of representing the heavenly city had developed, reflecting popular stereotypes of what cities ought to look like. The New Jerusalem is depicted as a collection of buildings enclosed within towered, crenellated walls.

This development is of particular interest when set against the backdrop of what are usually described as "otherworld journeys." Early writings of this genre tend to portray heaven primarily in Edenic terms, representing it as a rich, verdant, and fertile garden. This is particularly clear in the apocryphal "Apocalypse of Paul," dating from the early second century. This writing mingles the images of heaven as city and garden, but focuses primarily on the opulent gardens that surround that city:

> I entered in and saw the city of Christ. And it was all of gold, and twelve walls compassed it about, and there were twelve towers within . . . And there were twelve gates in the circuit of the city, of great beauty, and four rivers that compassed it about. There was a river of honey, and a river of milk, and a river of wine, and a river of oil. And I said to the angel: What are these rivers that compass this city about? And he said to me: These are the four rivers which flow abundantly for them that are in this land of promise, of which the names are these: the river of honey is called Phison, and the river of milk Euphrates, and the river of oil Geon, and the river of wine Tigris.

The imagery here represents an easily recognizable image of Eden, with its four irrigating rivers, mingled with the theme of the city of God. Yet the author's interest clearly focuses on the garden, rather than the city. This focus of interest in the Edenic aspects of heaven continues in later "otherworld journey" literature, particularly those of Celtic origin, such as the "Voyage of Brendan" and "Patrick's

Purgatory." The traditional Celtic Christian emphasis upon the beauty and majesty of nature here impacts upon their conception of heaven.

Yet elsewhere, the motif of the city begins to dominate. The rise of the Italian city state and a new interest in urban architecture led to the image of the heavenly city gaining priority over that of the paradisiacal garden in the twelfth and thirteenth centuries. Great Renaissance cities such as Florence saw themselves as recapturing the glory of ancient Rome, and lent new credibility to conceiving heaven in urban terms. If cities represented the height of human civilization, why should not heaven represent its apotheosis? The "otherworld journeys" of the knight Tondal (1150) and Thurkil of Essex (1206) – to which we shall return presently – thus both place their emphasis upon the city at the center of a garden, rather than dwell on the beauties of those gardens themselves. Heaven now primarily consists of richly jewelled and gilded churches, citadels, or fortresses, with particular attention being paid to their architectural features. These luxuriant buildings are located in the midst of rolling lush parklands; yet the garden now merely sets the context for the city, rather than being the dominant image.

The significance of the New Jerusalem for Christian spirituality was explored most thoroughly within the religious orders of the Middle Ages. The Christian culture of western medieval Europe attached particular importance to the monastic orders. It was clearly understood that those who had renounced the world to enter the great monasteries of Europe were to be regarded as spiritually superior to those who remained within the world, and enjoyed its comforts and pleasures. It is tempting to regard this as a form of spiritual arrogance. Yet the monastic orders saw it otherwise, arguing that the monastic life was based on the beliefs and lifestyle of the primitive Christian community at Jerusalem, as it is described in Acts 4:32: "Now the whole group of those who believed were of one heart and soul, and no one claimed private ownership of any possessions, but everything they owned was held in common." We see here the great themes of unity of heart and soul, common property, and renunciation of the world that were valued and put into practice within the monastic communities. The monastic life was thus seen as a quest for Christian authenticity, marking a recovery of a more biblical way of life in an increasingly corrupt and unstable culture.

Yet leaving behind the delights of the world in order to enter the regimented and disciplined life of the monastery was no easy matter. Works such as Thomas à Kempis's *Imitation of Christ*, written during the fifteenth century, encouraged their readers to develop a "contempt" for the world, cultivating the view that the world was a fallen and sinful sphere of existence, which had to be repudiated if salvation was to be achieved. Several means of encouraging the emergence of a culture of disinterest or disdain for the world were developed. One – particularly associated with Thomas à Kempis himself – was to promote meditation on the life of Christ, particularly Christ's command that his followers should deny themselves, take up their cross, and follow him (Mark 8:34).

A second, and rather more positive, strategy focused on the hope of heaven, which was easily visualized in terms of a triumphant entry into the New Jerusalem, paralleling Christ's entry into the earthly Jerusalem toward the end of his ministry, celebrated on Palm Sunday. Believers were encouraged to anticipate their entry into heaven, and to appreciate how the joy and glory of heaven eclipsed any earthly pleasure or delight. This theme found its way as early as the ninth century into a section of the Requiem Mass. The final part of that Mass – "*In Paradisum deducant te Angeli*," usually abbreviated simply to "*In Paradisum*" – celebrates the hope of the New Jerusalem after earth's struggles and sorrows:

> May angels lead you to paradise;
> May martyrs welcome you on your arrival;
> May they guide you to the holy city of Jerusalem.

This liturgical theme was picked up and developed in the monastic devotional literature of the period, which contrasted the eternal bliss of heaven with the passing joys and sorrows of earth. The deprivations and hardships of the monastic life would seem insignificant in comparison with the joy of entering heaven. In his classic vision of the new Jerusalem, Bernard of Cluny (c.1100–c.1150) vividly depicts the heavenly city in evocative terms, designed to captivate the imagination and galvanize the human longing to enter its portals. The New Jerusalem exceeds in beauty and glory anything that the human heart can desire and hope to embrace. J. M. Neale's well-known translation runs:

> Jerusalem the golden
> With milk and honey blessed,
> Beneath thy contemplation
> Sink heart and voice oppressed.
> I know not, O, I know not
> What joys await us there,
> What radiancy of glory,
> What bliss beyond compare.
>
> They stand, those halls of Zion,
> All jubilant with song,

And bright with many an angel,
And all the martyr throng.
The Prince is ever with them,
The daylight is serene,
The pastures of the blessed
Are decked in glorious sheen.

There is the throne of David,
And there, from care released,
The shout of them that triumph,
The song of them that feast.
And they, who with their Leader,
Have conquered in the fight,
For ever and for ever
Are clad in robes of white.

O sweet and blessed country,
The home of God's elect!
O sweet and blessed country
That eager hearts expect!
Jesu, in mercy bring us
To that dear land of rest;
Who art, with God the Father
And Spirit, ever blessed.

Bernard here celebrates the richness of the New Jerusalem, which is compared to the Promised Land anticipated by Israel. He sets out a vision of what lies ahead as a means of encouraging and sustaining Christian faith at present. Note Bernard's emphasis upon the inability of human language to convey adequately the wonders of heaven, and his insistence that believers can be assured that all these wonderful things are awaiting them. Those who find the life of faith tiring and dispiriting can, according to Bernard, take comfort and encouragement from this vision of the

New Jerusalem, and thus keep going on the road that leads to the celestial city.

Bernard's powerful appeal to the baptized imagination in evoking a mental picture of the heavenly city was echoed throughout the early Middle Ages. The popular depiction of the New Jerusalem is best seen from the famous "Apocalypse tapestries" of the late fourteenth century, now housed at the castle of Angers, the capital of the ancient province of Anjou. In 1373, the French King, Charles V, lent his brother, the duke of Anjou, an illustrated copy of the Apocalypse. The duke was so impressed by the illustrations that he commissioned the master weaver Nicholas Bataille to produce a massive tapestry, to include as many of these scenes as possible. Bataille managed to incorporate 105 apocalyptic vignettes in his 144 meters of tapestry, of which 67 have been partially or completely preserved. One is an illustration of the New Jerusalem, which depicts the city as a classic medieval castle, complete with moat, walls, gate, and towers.

The rise of the medieval city state in Italy led to cities such as Florence becoming models for their heavenly counterparts and archetypes. This process can be seen most clearly in the visionary writings of Gerardesca of Pisa (1212–69), which depict heaven as a city surrounded by seven castles and other minor fortresses, enfolded within a vast uninhabited parkland. Gerardesca clearly recognizes a hierarchy within this celestial paradise. Although she insists that all the saints are inhabitants of the New Jerusalem, her vision places saints of the first rank, including the Virgin Mary, in the central city, and lesser saints in its outlying fortresses.

The *Pelerinage de Vie Humaine* ("Pilgrimage of Human Life"), written by Guillaume de Deguileville in the period 1330–1, opens with the poet describing a vision of the New

Jerusalem, which rapidly becomes the goal of his life. The poem sets out an understanding of human life as a pilgrimage from birth to death, and focuses particularly on the role of the "three summoners" – age, illness, and death. These figures play an important role in the popular devotional literature of the Middle Ages. They are viewed as harbingers of final divine judgment, forcing individuals to evaluate their spiritual states and make appropriate adjustments. The vision of the New Jerusalem thus becomes a stimulus for personal repentance and renewal. To see the heavenly city is one thing; to be allowed to enter it is quite another.

Further medieval speculation focused on the clothes worn by those fortunate enough to enter the celestial city. While some argued that the inhabitants of the New Jerusalem would be naked, most regarded this as undignified and vulgar. The citizens of the New Jerusalem would be clothed, with the precise manner of clothing being in accord with their dignity. Abbess Hildegard of Bingen (1098–1179) insisted that the saints were "dressed in garments of silk, wearing white shoes." Hildegard's reflections on the New Jerusalem are best seen in her canticle *"O Jerusalem, aurea civitas"* ("Jerusalem, the golden city"), which depicts the city as "robed in royal purple." While Hildegard's imagery is clearly derived from Revelation, she effortlessly melds familiar Gospel images with its fabric to yield a rich spiritual tapestry.

Many writings of this period are saturated with the hope of heaven, often coupled with ambitious and occasionally highly experimental reflections on the urban geography of this celestial city – for example, as in Giacomo da Verona's *On the Celestial Jerusalem* (1260), and the "Vision of Thurkil of Essex" (1206), which is probably the work of Ralph of

Coggeshall. Perhaps most importantly, *The Visions of the Knight Tondal* tells the story of a wealthy and errant Irish knight, whose soul goes on a journey through hell to paradise with an angel for a guide. Originally written in Latin at some point around 1150 by Marcus, an Irish monk in Regensburg, the story was later translated into 15 vernacular languages. In several ways, the work can be seen as an anticipation of Dante's *Divine Comedy*. The story of Tondal rapidly became one of the most popular in a long tradition of visionary and moralizing literature. As a result of his experiences, Tondal is spiritually transformed and vows to lead a more pious life. The foretaste of the joys of paradise and the pains of hell are enough to persuade him to amend his life so that he may enjoy the former and evade the latter.

Pearl *and the New Jerusalem*

One of the finest accounts of the New Jerusalem in English literature is found in the fourteenth-century work generally known as *Pearl*. This poem belongs to a group of four fourteenth-century poems, also including *Cleanness, Patience,* and *Sir Gawain and the Green Knight*. These poems, all written in the dialect of the northwest English Midlands, are believed to have been written by the same unknown author. While *Sir Gawain and the Green Knight* has been hailed as one of the most splendid works of medieval English literature, mingling the values of chivalry with more romantic themes, *Pearl* is of especial importance to our explorations of the theme of the New Jerusalem. It contains what is arguably the finest account of the New Jerusalem to have been written in the English language.

The poem opens with the narrator coming to terms with the loss of his "pearl" maiden, and rapidly moves on to offer a meditation on the nature of heaven, and the means by which it is entered. In his vision, the poet finds himself in an Eden-like garden, from which he glimpses the maiden across a river. She seeks to answer his many questions about the new realm in which she finds herself, and console him over her loss.

Pearl opens with the poet mourning his beloved, whom he describes as a "priceless pearl." Her face now sheathed in clay, she has returned to the earth from which she came. The poet cannot bear the thought of her physical decay and disintegration. Yet in a vision, he sees his beloved Pearl once more. She is now a "bride of Christ," adorned with precious pearls. The dreamer is astounded; how could someone who died so young have so elevated a place in heaven? The maiden replies that the same reward was promised by Christ to all, irrespective of how long they labored in the vineyard. Where earthly society is rigorously stratified, there are no such distinctions in the New Jerusalem.

The maiden goes on to tell the dreamer of the two Jerusalems – the historical Jerusalem in which Christ was condemned and martyred, and the heavenly Jerusalem described in the Book of Revelation. A redeemed people must, she argues, live in a redeemed city. Just as those who have been cleansed by the redeeming death of Christ are spotless, so heaven takes the form of a "spotless" New Jerusalem, without the flaws and sins of earthly cities, including Jerusalem itself. "As [Christ's] flock is without a blemish, so is his city without stain." The dreamer asks to be allowed to see Pearl's new home. She gently chides him; only those who have been made perfect can enter the New Jerusalem. At best, he can see it from a distance.

"Spotless maid so meek and mild," I said to that lovely flower, "bring me to that pleasant dwelling and let me see your happy abode." The fair one said, "That God will forbid; you may not enter his stronghold, but I have permission from the Lamb as a special favour for a glimpse of it. From outside, you may see that bright cloister, but you may not place a foot within it; you have no power to walk in the street unless you are clean without stain."

There then follows a scene strongly reminiscent of one of the most dramatic moments in the Old Testament, in which Moses is permitted to catch a glimpse of the Promised Land over the River Jordan. He can never enter it, and will die and be buried outside its sacred bounds. By ascending Mount Nebo, Moses is able to peer into a land he will never enter. *Pearl* consciously develops this imagery, as the dreamer is led up a hill from which he has a clear view of the heavenly Jerusalem – a city that he cannot hope to enter in his present state.

As John the apostle saw it with his own eyes, I saw that city of great renown, Jerusalem so new and royally adorned, as if it were light that had come down from Heaven. The city was all of bright gold, burnished like gleaming glass, adorned below with noble gems; with twelve tiers, each beautifully constructed and garnished with separate precious stones.

The poet then lists these precious stones individually, partly as a paraphrase of the biblical text on which his vision is based, and partly to allow his readers to develop an enhanced appreciation of their significance.

As John named these stones in Scripture, I knew them from his account. The first jewel was called jasper, which I saw on the first base: it glinted green in the lowest tier. Sapphire held the second place; chalcedony without flaw in the third tier showed pale and clear. Fourth was the emerald with surface so green; sardonyx the fifth; the sixth was the ruby. . . .

These precious stones possessed a far greater significance to their medieval readers than is often appreciated. The "lapidaries" of this period offered detailed spiritual inter-pretations of these stones, allowing us to understand at least something of what the *Pearl* poet understood by his vision of the New Jerusalem. Typical spiritual associations of these stones include treating jasper as a symbol of faith, sapphire of hope, chrysolite as the preaching and miracles of Jesus Christ, and beryl as the resurrection.

As the vision unfolds, we find the basic features of the New Jerusalem, as set out in Revelation 21, explored with exquisite care, as if each was charged with spiritual signi-ficance. The poet is clearly captivated by this vision of the heavenly city, and longs to enter its portals.

Beneath the moon might no mortal heart endure so great a wonder, as I saw when I observed that city, so wondrous was its form. I stood still, like a startled quail, in amazement at this spectacle, so that I felt neither rest nor toil, so greatly was I enraptured by its pure radiance. I dare say with clear conscience that if any mortal had experienced that great boon, no doctor could preserve him; his life would end beneath that moon.

Overcome with joy and anticipation, the dreamer throws himself into the river so that he may swim to its far side and enter this beautiful city. With this action, his dream ends; he awakes to find himself in the same place in which he had settled down to mourn his Pearl – but now content in the knowledge that she is safe. His vision moves him to reflect on what he must do if he also is to enter the New Jerusalem in his turn.

The poem is remarkable in many respects, not least in its use of imagery to depict the heavenly realm and its masterly reflection on the theme of consolation in the event of death. While there is no evidence to suggest that John Bunyan knew about, or drew upon, the *Pearl* poet's vision of the New Jerusalem, there are clear affinities between this classic of the fourteenth century and perhaps the most famous English literary depiction of the New Jerusalem – *The Pilgrim's Progress* – to which we now turn.

John Bunyan's Heavenly City

John Bunyan (1626–88) is perhaps one of the best-known Puritan writers of the seventeenth century. He was born in the English county of Bedfordshire, and became involved with the Puritan cause during the English Civil War. With the establishment of the Puritan commonwealth, Bunyan turned his attention to preaching, and became the minister of an independent congregation in Bedford. His Puritan sympathies caused him to be out of favor when the English monarchy was restored in 1660, with the result that he spent many years inside Bedford jail. Bunyan used his time in prison to write his autobiography *Grace Abounding to the Chief of Sinners*, and begin work on his best-known work, *The Pilgrim's Progress*, the first part of which appeared in 1678, and the second in 1684.

The Pilgrim's Progress was read both as an adventure story – foreshadowing the modern novel – and as an allegory of the struggles, temptations, sufferings, and final salvation of the human soul. The central narrative of the book focuses on its hero Christian, initially bowed down with a burden of sin upon his back, who flees from the City of Destruction and seeks eternal life. He thus sets out on a long and arduous pilgrimage, which leads him from the mire of the Slough of Despond up the straight and narrow path of the Hill of Difficulty, down into the Valley of Humiliation, where he battles with the foul fiend Apollyon, and into the terrifying Valley of the Shadow of Death. He passes through Vanity Fair with all its worldly allurements, is held captive by Giant Despair in Doubting Castle, and at last, after crossing the bridgeless River of Death, is received in the Celestial Jerusalem. The characters that Christian meets along the way embody abstract qualities and defects, virtues and vices, each designated by their names – such as "Faithful," "Hopeful," and "Mr. Worldly Wiseman." These are almost certainly modeled on the men and women that Bunyan knew, using the simple, lively, humorous language of ordinary people. Perhaps it is no surprise that the work went on to become one of the most widely read works in the English language, reaching the height of its popularity in the Victorian period.

Although the theme of the Christian life as a pilgrimage had been used by many writers before Bunyan, there are no reasons for suspecting that he was aware of these, or made any use of previous treatments in his own writing. *Pilgrim's Progress* is best regarded as a brilliant and highly original narrative, incorporating biblical ideas and imagery without the mediating filter of previous writers. The only literary source that may be identified with any certainty for Bunyan's masterpiece is the King James translation of the Bible, which appeared in 1611, and is known to have had a deep impact on the shaping of the imagery and vocabulary of modern English.

The tension between two such cities – earthly and heavenly – had been the subject of much reflection within the Christian tradition prior to Bunyan – for example, in Augustine's *City of God*. Yet Bunyan succeeded in establishing the journey from the "city of destruction" to the "heavenly city" as a framework for making sense of the ambiguities, sorrows, and pains of the Christian life. His powerful appeal to imagery, coupled with a masterly use of narrative, ensured that the imagery of the New Jerusalem would have a profound and permanent effect on popular Christian spirituality.

The narrative tells of how Christian and his friends travel through the "wilderness of this world" in search of the heavenly city. The hope of finding and entering this city dominates the narrative. The vocabulary and imagery of Bunyan's narrative draws extensively on the New Jerusalem tradition from the Book of Revelation. This can be seen from the tantalizing description of the heavenly Jerusalem offered by the "Shining Ones" – angelic beings who reassure Christian and his traveling companions concerning the final goal of their quest.

> The talk they had with the Shining Ones was about the glory of the place; who told them that the beauty and glory of it was inexpressible. There, said they, is the "Mount Zion, the heavenly Jerusalem, the innumerable company of angels, and the spirits of just men made perfect" (Hebrews 12:22–24). You are going now, said they, to the paradise of God, wherein you shall see the tree of life, and eat of the never-fading fruits thereof; and when you come there, you shall have white robes given you, and your walk and talk shall be every day with the King, even all the days of

eternity (Revelation 2:7; 3:4; 22:5). There you shall not see again such things as you saw when you were in the lower region upon the earth, to wit, sorrow, sickness, affliction, and death, "for the former things are passed away."

Bunyan's account of the New Jerusalem shows some significant parallels with that of *Pearl*, not least in the fusion of the imagery of the entry into the Promised Land with that of the New Jerusalem. A river separates us from the heavenly city, just as the River Jordan was placed between Israel and its promised land. It is only by crossing this river that access to the city can be gained. In the closing pages of his narrative, Bunyan tells of how Mr. Steadfast prepared to cross the river from this life to the next, trusting that the trumpets would sound for him on the other side:

> This river has been a terror to many; yea, the thoughts of it also have often frightened me. Now, methinks, I stand easy, my foot is fixed upon that upon which the feet of the priests that bare the ark of the covenant stood, while Israel went over this Jordan (Joshua 3:17). The waters, indeed, are to the palate bitter, and to the stomach cold; yet the thoughts of what I am going to, and of the conduct that waits for me on the other side, doth lie as a glowing coal at my heart. I see myself now at the end of my journey, my toilsome days are ended. I am going now to see that head that was crowned with thorns, and that face that was spit upon for me.

Yet the reader of *Pilgrim's Progress* is left with many unanswered questions. What appearance would Mr. Steadfast possess in his new home? Would his friends recognize him when their turn came to cross the cold and bitter waters of the river of death? Such musings have always been part of Christian reflections on the nature of heaven, and we may turn to consider them in what follows.

The Shape of the Heavenly Body

The New Testament affirms that Christians are "citizens of heaven." But what do citizens of heaven look like? If heaven is to be compared to a human city, what are its inhabitants like? The New Testament has remarkably little to say on this, in that it hints at such matters as a mystery, rather than disclosing them as facts. The image of a seed, used by Paul in 1 Corinthians 15, was taken by many writers to mean that there was some organic connection between the earthly and heavenly body. Resurrection could thus be conceived as the unfolding of a predetermined pattern within the human organism. Yet even this image had to be treated with caution. Where some theologians took the view that this obliged them to treat such matters with restraint, others appear to have seen themselves as liberated from the traditional constraints imposed by the biblical text, and launched into the most stratospheric of theological speculations.

One possibility would be to imagine the streets of the New Jerusalem as inhabited by disembodied souls. On this model, the human being consists of two entities – a physical body, and a spiritual soul. Death leads to the liberation of the soul from its material body. This view was commonplace within the Hellenistic culture of the New Testament period. However, this idea was vigorously opposed by most early Christian theologians. The most significant minority voice in this matter belonged to Origen, a highly creative theologian with a strongly Platonist bent, who held that the resurrection body was purely spiritual. This view was contested by most Christian writers, who insisted that the phrase "the resurrection of the body" was to be understood as the permanent resurrection of both the body and the soul of the believer.

But what do citizens of heaven look like? We have already seen above how medieval writers enjoyed reflecting on the clothing of the saints in heaven; this interest also extended to their physical appearance. Many early Christian writers argued that the "citizens of heaven" would be naked, recreating the situation in paradise. This time, however, nakedness would neither give rise to shame nor sexual lust, but would simply be accepted as the natural and innocent state of humanity. Others, however, argued that the inhabitants of the New Jerusalem would be clothed in finery, reflecting their status as citizens of God's chosen city.

It was clear to many writers that the final state of deceased believers was not of material importance to their appearance in heaven. The issue emerged as theologically significant during a persecution of Christians in Lyons around the years 175–7. Aware that Christians professed belief in the "resurrection of the body," their pagan oppressors burned the bodies of the Christians they had just martyred, and threw their ashes into the River Rhône. This, they believed, would prevent the resurrection of these martyrs, in that there was now no body to be raised. Christian theologians responded by arguing that God was able to restore all that the body had lost through this process of destruction.

Methodius of Olympus offered an analogy for this process of reconstitution which would prove highly influential in discussing this question. The resurrection could, he argued, be thought of as a kind of "rearrangement" of the constituent elements of humanity. It is like a statue that is melted down, and reforged from the same material – yet in such a manner that any defects or damage are eliminated.

> It is as if some skilled artificer had made a noble image, cast in gold or other material, which was beautifully proportioned in all its features. Then the artificer suddenly notices that the image had been defaced by some envious person, who could not endure its beauty, and so decided to ruin it for the sake of the pointless pleasure of satisfying his jealousy. So the craftsman decides to recast this noble image. Now notice, most wise Aglaophon, that if he wants to ensure that this image, on which he has expended so much effort, care and work, will be totally free from any defect, he will be obliged to melt it down, and restore it to its former condition. . . . Now it seems to me that God's plan was much the same as this human example. He saw that humanity, his most wonderful creation, had been corrupted by envy and treachery. Such was his love for humanity that he could not allow it to continue in this condition, remaining faulty and deficient to eternity. For this reason, God dissolved humanity once more into its original materials, so that it could be remodelled in such a way that all its defects could be eliminated and disappear. Now the melting down of a statue corresponds to the death and dissolution of the human body, and the remoulding of the material to the resurrection after death.

A similar argument is found in the *Four Books of the Sentences*, the masterpiece of the great twelfth-century theologian Peter Lombard. This book, which served as the core textbook for just about every medieval theologian, took the view that the resurrected body was basically a reconstituted humanity, from which all defects had been purged:

Nothing of the substance of the flesh from which humanity is created will be lost; rather, the natural substance of the body will be reintegrated by the collection of all the particles that were previously dispersed. The bodies of the saints will thus rise without any defect, shining like the sun, all their deformities having being excised.

The twelfth-century *Book of the Dun Cow* (*Leabhar na Uidhre*) – so-called because the vellum upon which it is written is supposedly taken from the hide of St. Ciaran's cow at Clonmacnoise – raises a further question concerning the nature of the resurrection body. What happens if the believer is *eaten*? The *Book of the Dun Cow* – presumably responding to genuine pastoral concerns at this point – argues that the various fragments of humanity, however scattered and variously decomposed they may be, are "recast into a more beautiful form" by the "fire of Doom." However, the work recognizes the locational importance of the precise place at which the believer dies.

Those who have been devoured by wild animals and dispersed in various locations will arise according to the counsel of the Lord, who will gather them together and renew them . . . In this case, they will arise at the place at which they were devoured and dispersed, for this is what is reckoned to be their tomb.

A similar issue arose in the twentieth century, when the practice of cremation became increasingly common in Christian nations, partly on account of the increasingly prohibitive cost of burial, raising the question of whether cremation was inconsistent with belief in the resurrection. Perhaps the most influential answer to this question was offered by the famous American evangelist Billy Graham, who wrote thus in a nationally syndicated newspaper column:

> The aspect of cremation that worries some Christians is the thought of the total annihilation of the body. We need to get our thinking in a right perspective here. The body is annihilated just as completely in the grave as it is in cremation. The graves of our ancestors are no longer in existence, and soil in which they were buried has long since been removed elsewhere. We must therefore accept that what happens to the body or to the grave cannot be of any significance so far as the resurrection is concerned. . . . In Corinthians 5, Paul makes the contrast between living in a tent, a temporary home that can be pulled down and put away, and living in a permanent home that will last forever. Our bodies are our temporary tents. Our resurrected bodies will be our permanent homes. They are similar in appearance but different in substance. Cremation is therefore no hindrance to the resurrection.

A final question that has greatly vexed Christian theologians concerns the *age* of those who are resurrected. If someone dies at the age of 60, will they appear in the streets of the New Jerusalem as an old person? And if someone dies at the age of 10, will they appear as a child? This issue caused the spilling of much theological ink, especially during the Middle Ages. By the end of the thirteenth century, an emerging consensus can be discerned. As each person reaches their peak of perfection around the age of 30, they will be resurrected as they would have appeared at that time – even if they never lived to reach that age. Peter Lombard's discussion of the matter is typical of his age: "A boy who dies immediately after being born will be resurrected in that form which he would have had if he had lived to the age of thirty." The New Jerusalem will thus be populated by men and women as they would appear at the age of 30 (the age, of course, at which Christ was crucified) – but with every blemish removed.

In this opening chapter, we have explored one of the great icons of heaven – the celestial city. Yet alongside the image of the New Jerusalem, Christian theology sets another – an image that evokes a very different set of resonances and associations. The Christian Bible closes with the image of the New Jerusalem; it opens, however, with the image of paradise. We now turn to consider the great theme of paradise as a similitude of heaven.

Chapter 2

The Garden: Heaven as Paradise

The theme of paradise has captivated the literary imagination. While classic accounts – such as Milton's *Paradise Lost* – continue to exercise a controlling influence over the depiction of paradise, more recent writings demonstrate a continuing interest in the image. Where is paradise to be found? How can evil arise in such a paradisiacal context? Novels as diverse as William Golding's *Lord of the Flies* and Alex Garland's *The Beach* continue to tap the rich wellsprings of insight contained in this powerful image. But where does the notion of "paradise" come from? And how does it relate to the Christian idea of heaven?

In the previous chapter, we reflected on the image of the city as a model for heaven. Yet models drawn from nature itself have their place in this discussion. The image of the garden brings together the natural and the cultural – the raw beauty of nature combined with the human desire to allow this beauty to be showcased, presented to its best advantage by framing it in a certain manner. For Henry David Thoreau, nature was "nobody's garden" – a way of looking at the natural order that stressed its beauty, independent of human fabrication or engineering. Yet for others, the idea of a walled garden, enclosing a carefully cultivated area of exquisite plants and animals, was the most powerful symbol of paradise available to the human imagination, mingling the images of the beauty of nature with the orderliness of human construction.

The writings of the blind poet John Milton are probably the best-known English literary accounts of paradise. Having been lost through sin, paradise is restored through the death of Christ. The whole of human history is thus enfolded in the subtle interplay of sorrow over a lost paradise, and the hope of its final restoration.

> I, who erewhile the happy garden sung,
> By one man's disobedience lost, now sing
> Recover'd Paradise to all mankind,
> By one man's firm obedience fully tried
> Through all temptation, and the tempter foil'd
> In all his wiles, defeated and repulsed,
> And Eden raised in the waste wilderness.

Deep within the human soul there nestles a sense that something is wrong with the world as we know it. The world we know is somehow not quite what it ought to be. It seems to cry out for restoration or renewal. Mircea Eliade, the noted scholar of religion, has noted the abiding importance of a "nostalgia for paradise" in human thought and literature. Yet few are content merely to mark and mourn the loss of the past. The history of human culture demonstrates a "repeated attempt to re-establish the paradisical situation lost at the dawn of time" (Eliade). This is often expressed in terms of the interplay of two eras – the paradise that was lost in the early mists of time, and to which we shall one day be restored. This may take the form of a Marxist analysis of the rise and ultimate demise of capitalism, or the Christian belief in the final restoration of all things to God's intended patterning. A sense of "nostalgia for paradise" permeates much Christian writing, particularly during the Middle Ages – yet this is often coupled to a strongly affirmative belief that this paradise will be regained, and perhaps even transcended.

But what is this paradise? And how does it relate to the Christian theme of heaven? Our attention turns immediately to the most famous of all paradisiacal gardens – the "garden of Eden."

The Quest for the Garden of Eden

While much popular literature speaks of the "Garden of Eden," it is perhaps better to think of "Eden" as the region in which the garden is located, rather than the name of the garden itself. Other biblical passages designate the garden in other manners – such as the "Garden of God" (Ezekiel 28:13) or the "Garden of the Lord" (Isaiah 51:3). The garden rapidly became a symbol of innocence and harmony, a place of peace, rest, and fertility. The powerful imagery of the four rivers that permanently watered the rich ground and its opulent plant and animal life served as a stimulus to the imaginations of Christian writers and painters alike.

Jewish and early Christian writers spent much effort and energy in an ultimately vain attempt to track down the four rivers that enfolded Eden, named by Genesis as the Tigris, Euphrates, Pison, and Gihon. The first two of these are easily identified as the great rivers of ancient Mesopotamia. The identity of the others remains unclear. The first-century

Jewish historian Josephus suggested that they were actually the Nile and Euphrates. On the basis of this identification, Eden has been located in as many diverse areas as the fabulous lost city of Atlantis. Some early Christian fathers and late classical authors suggested it could lie in Mongolia, India, or even Ethiopia. Others favored eastern Turkey: the four rivers of paradise could be identified with the Murat River, the Tigris, the Euphrates, and the north fork of the Euphrates, which branches off in this region.

A theory that excited particular attention in the 1980s focused attention on the Persian Gulf. There had long been a degree of consensus that the most promising site for Eden was the ancient region of Sumer, some 200 kilometers (125 miles) north of the present head of the Persian Gulf. In a fascinating piece of historical research, Dr. Juris Zarins argued that Eden – like Atlantis – was lost beneath the waters of the sea. The waters of the Persian Gulf had risen since biblical times, submerging this earthly paradise. Part of Zarins' argument involved the identification of the Pison with the Wadi Riniah and Wadi Batin – the modern Saudi names for a dry river bed in which water no longer flows. Zarins completed his argument by suggesting that the biblical Gihon was actually the Karun River, which rises in Iran and flows to the southwest, entering the head of the Persian Gulf.

Yet the debate over the physical location of Eden per-haps misses the point at issue. The Christian tradition has never seen the precise geography of paradise as being of primary importance; rather, the central question has to do with the identity and nature of humanity, and supremely its final destiny. To speak of paradise is not to hanker after a return to a specific physical place, but to yearn for the restoration of a specific spiritual state. We must therefore turn to explore the biblical witness to the idea of paradise in a little more detail.

Paradise in the Bible

It is in the Old Testament that we are first introduced to the idea of "paradise." The word itself has been borrowed from other languages of the ancient Near East, including the Old Persian word *paradeida*, which probably designates "an enclosed garden" or perhaps "a royal park." The Greek word *paradeisos* – borrowed from the Persian original – is often used in the writings of historians such as Xenophon to refer to the great walled gardens of the royal palaces of Persian kings such as Cyrus. The original "garden of Eden" (Genesis 2) is referred to as "paradise" in Greek translations of the Old Testament; the term is also used at several points in the original Hebrew text of the Old Testament. The word "Eden" itself may derive from the Sumerian word *edinu* ("plain"). It is possible that a traditional Mesopotamian image of "the king as gardener" may underlie some of the themes in this passage, and be taken up and developed in new directions in the New Testament.

From the earliest stage, the word "paradise" came to be imbued with a series of qualities that ensured that it became a central theme in the Christian account of heaven. Paradise was seen, like the Garden of Eden, as a place of fertility and harmony, where humanity dwelt in peace with nature and "walked with God." That idyllic state had been lost at the dawn of human history. Part of Israel's hopes and expectations for the future centered around the nostalgic longing for a restoration of this paradisiacal relationship with the environment and God. This development was

Jan Breugel, *The Garden of Eden*, 1620. Museum of Fine Arts, Budapest.

encouraged by the classic Greek translation of the Old Testament – the Septuagint – which used the phrase "paradise of delight" (Genesis 2:15), translating the Hebrew term for "garden" as "paradise", and interpreting the term "Eden" in terms of the related word *adanim* ("pleasure" or "delight").

Hosea, writing in the eighth century before Christ, looks forward to a future transformation of the human situation, in which human enmity against other humans is ended, along with a restoration of the integrity of the original created order: "I will make for you a covenant on that day with the wild animals, the birds of the air, and the creeping things of the ground; and I will abolish the bow, the sword, and war from the land" (Hosea 2:18). A related theme can be seen in the writings of Joel, in which a series of paradisiacal images are fused with themes taken from the entry of Israel into the promised land.

> In that day the mountains shall drip sweet wine, the hills shall flow with milk, and all the stream beds of Judah shall flow with water; a fountain shall come forth from the house of the LORD and water the Wadi Shittim. (Joel 3:18)

The future state of Israel is depicted in terms of a new Eden: its mountains will flow with wine, its hills will flow with milk, and the dry river beds will be filled with pure clear water – just as Eden was surrounded and watered by its four great rivers. A similar theme is found in Micah 4:4, which offers a vision of a future state in which the vineyard and fig tree serve as symbols of tranquillity and fertility.

One of the most interesting reworkings of the paradise theme is found in the prophecy of Ezekiel, dating from the time of the exile of the people of Jerusalem in Babylon, which seems to envisage the anticipated restoration of Jerusalem in Edenic terms. For Ezekiel, the people of Jerusalem had brought their destruction and exile upon themselves by profaning the temple of the Lord, and failing to live up to their obligations as God's people. Yet Jerusalem will be restored, in a form that transcends the city and temple of earlier times. The land will be renewed and made fertile by a sacred healing river that flows eastward, emptying into the Dead Sea. Ezekiel's vision of the New Jerusalem that will arise to replace the fallen city draws heavily upon paradisiacal imagery, suggesting that a new paradise will be created within the walls of the restored city of God.

The Old Testament book that has had the most impact on the development of the garden as an image of paradise is the Song of Songs. This remarkable love poem has long been seen as an allegory of the great Christian drama of sin and redemption, affirming the love of Christ for both the individual soul and the church. The poem is notable for evoking a series of echoes of the tale of Eden, most notably its reworking of the theme of love within a garden. Yet the most significant aspect of the poem is not its musings on the nature of love, but the imagery that it deploys in so doing – images that Christian theologians and artists found profoundly engaging, particularly during the Middle Ages.

The New Testament employs the paradise motif, but does not appear to develop it significantly beyond the Old Testament's statements. Perhaps most famously, Christ assured the repentant criminal who was being crucified alongside him that he would enter paradise that very day: "today you will be with me in paradise" (Luke 23:43). Access to paradise, which was lost through Adam, has been regained through Jesus Christ, the "new Adam" who brings about a reversal and transformation of the human situation (Romans 5:14–16; 1 Corinthians 15:45–8). This theme is developed in the Pauline letters, which explore the complex interplay between paradise as a future hope for believers, and its anticipation in the present.

Yet there are strong hints of the paradise theme elsewhere in the New Testament. One of the most important resurrection scenes in John's Gospel is set in a garden (John 19:41). It is of no small importance that John – perhaps the most sensitive of the four gospel writers to the place of symbolism – should place this encounter between the risen Christ and Mary Magdalene in such a location. There is evidence that the term "gardener" was used as a title for some ancient monarchs; might Mary's initial belief that Jesus is the gardener be seen as a deeper recognition of the lordship of Christ over his paradise? We shall never know for certain, however fascinating it might be to speculate on this theme.

It is entirely possible that this line of thought may lie behind one of the most famous depictions of this incident – Fra Angelico's *Noli Me Tangere*, painted over the period 1425–30 at the Convent of St Mark, Florence. This fresco shows Christ and Mary in the foreground, with the tomb in which Christ's body was laid to the left. The garden is represented as rich in foliage and vegetation, mirroring some contemporary depictions of the Garden of Eden. It is clear that the garden is enclosed, suggesting the imagery of the *hortus conclusus*, to which we shall return presently.

Early Christian Views of Paradise

The early church found the paradise motif compelling in articulating the Christian hope, not least in stressing the idea of the restoration of Adam's lost inheritance through Christ. Early Christian writers developed a number of ways of interpreting the story of Eden, often choosing to stress the spiritual, rather than the geographical, aspects. Irenaeus (c.130–c.200) identified a common theological strand linking the fall of humanity in Eden with its redemption in Christ and ultimate entry into heaven. For Irenaeus, redemption involved the "recapitulation" in Christ of the history of the human race. Developing the contrast between Adam and Christ that is found in the New Testament letters of Paul, Irenaeus argues that Christ traverses the entire trajectory of human history, correcting Adam's failings and errors. There is thus a correspondence between what was lost by Adam in Eden and what was regained by Christ on the cross. Fascinated by the symbolism of these two histories, Irenaeus

Fra Angelico, *Noli Me Tangere*, 1425–30, fresco, Convent of San Marco, Florence. Photo SCALA

points up the congruity between Adam and Christ. Our innocence was lost by the disobedience of Adam, and restored through the obedience of Christ. Human innocence was lost in one garden (Eden), yet regained in another (Gethsemane). In Eden, the tree of life became a tree of death; in Gethsemane, a tree of death (the cross) became a tree of life. And so on. For Irenaeus, the history of human salvation is shaped by the events of Eden, just as our final place of restoration will bring to perfection the conditions of that paradise.

In his *Symposium*, Methodius of Olympus (died c.311) argued that the Christian gospel makes the fruit of the tree of life available once more; those who pluck and possess it are assured of their re-entry into paradise at the resurrection.

> They have not understood that the tree of life which Paradise once bore, now again the Church has produced for all, even the ripe and lovely fruit of faith. It is necessary that we bring this fruit when we come to the judgment-seat of Christ, on the first day of the feast; for if we are without it we shall not be able to feast with God, nor, according to John, to share in the first resurrection. For the tree of life is wisdom. "She is a tree of life to those that take hold of her" (Proverbs 3:18) . . . Any who have not believed in Christ, or have not grasped that he is the first principle and the tree of life is unable to celebrate this feast, since they cannot show to God their tabernacles adorned with the most lovely of fruits. How shall they rejoice? So do you want to know the lovely fruit of the tree? Consider the words of our Lord Jesus Christ, how pleasant they are. Good fruit came by Moses, that is the Law, but not so lovely as the Gospel. For the Law is a kind of figure and shadow of things to come, but the Gospel is truth and the grace of life. The fruit of the

prophets was indeed delightful, but not as delightful as the fruit of immortality which is plucked from the gospel.

Methodius's argument involves the coupling of the concepts of paradise and the resurrection using the imagery of the re-entry into paradise. The eternal life that was indeed promised by the tree of life in paradise has once more been made available through Christ.

Such ideas formed the common theme of much early Christian preaching. Cyril of Jerusalem (c.315–86) argued that redemption through Christ, embraced and publicly affirmed in baptism, restored the believer to paradise. Yet the imagery of paradise allowed Cyril to explore the darker side of the realities of Christian life in the world. Just as the serpent was able to secure the expulsion of Adam and Eve from their paradise, so believers must be careful not to fall victim to temptation lest they too are expelled from the "meadow of paradise":

So may the gate of paradise be opened to every man and every woman among you. Then you will enjoy the Christ-bearing waters in all their fragrance, and receive the name of Christ, and the power of divine things . . . The baptism that lies before you is truly a great thing – the ransoming of captives, the remission of transgressions, the death of sin, a new birth of the soul, a garment of light, a holy and unbreakable seal, a chariot to heaven and the delights of paradise, a welcome into the kingdom, and the gift of adoption! But there is a serpent by the wayside watching those who pass by. Be alert, in case he stings you with unbelief. He sees so many receiving salvation, and "seeks those who he may devour" (1 Peter 5:8). You are drawing near to the Father of Spirits, but you must first go past that serpent. So how may you get past him? Have "your feet shod with the gospel of peace" (Ephesians 6:15) so that even if the serpent should sting, he may not hurt you. Have an abiding faith within you, a steadfast hope, a strong sandal, that you may pass by the enemy, and enter into the presence of your Lord.

Not all early Christian writers adopted such a literal understanding of paradise. Ambrose of Milan (c.339–97), for example, drew upon the ideas of the Jewish Platonist writer Philo of Alexandria in offering an allegorical reading of the story of paradise. The Garden of Eden is now understood to be a "delightful well-tilled land in which the soul finds pleasure" – in other words, a Platonic world of ideas and values, rather than a physical or geographical entity. To speak of paradise "planted with trees" is a picturesque manner of referring to the human soul with its various virtues. Adam represents the virtues of reason, and Eve the human senses, which are easily led astray by the pursuit of pleasure. Perhaps unsurprisingly, Ambrose interprets the serpent as pleasure, who deflects the human soul from its hitherto steadfast pursuit of virtue into the lesser goal of seeking pleasure.

> The figure of the serpent represents pleasure, and the figure of the woman represents the emotions of the mind and the heart (which the Greeks call *aesthesis*). When the senses are deceived, on this view, the mind (which the Greeks call *nous*) falls into error.

The Christian interpretation of Eden was given a new sense of direction by Augustine of Hippo. For Augustine, Eden was a place of innocence and fulfillment. Irrespective of its geographical or historical location, it was to be seen as a landmark on the long trajectory of humanity from creation to fall, through redemption to final consummation. Augustine's account of Eden is saturated with paradisiacal themes, which he subsequently develops in his doctrines of redemption and final consummation in heaven:

> Humanity dwelt in paradise as they pleased, so long as they desired what God commanded. They lived in the enjoyment of God, living without any want, with the ability to live for ever. They had food so that they might not hunger, drink so that they might not thirst, and the "tree of life" so that they might not be wasted through ageing. . . . They were healthy in body, and peaceful in soul. In paradise, it was neither too hot nor too cold . . . There was no sadness, nor any foolish joy, for true gladness flowed ceaselessly from the presence of God.

Augustine's depiction of paradise has important implications for his concept of heaven, in that the life to come involves the restoration of the conditions of this earthly paradise.

The Millennium as Paradise

One of the most interesting aspects of early Christian reflections concerning the afterlife is its interest in the idea of the millennium – the period of one thousand years which, according to the Book of Revelation, intervenes between the coming of Christ and the final judgment.

> Then I saw thrones, and those seated on them were given authority to judge. I also saw the souls of those who had been beheaded for their testimony to Jesus and for the word of God. They had not worshiped the beast or its image and had not received its mark on their foreheads or their hands.

> They came to life and reigned with Christ a thousand years.
> (Revelation 20:4)

During this period of a millennium, Christ reigns over a restored earth, until the redeemed are finally transferred to their permanent resting place in heaven. The third-century writer Tertullian describes this as follows:

> We also hold that a kingdom has been promised to us on earth, but before heaven: but in another state than this, as being after the resurrection. This will last for a thousand years, in a city of God's own making, the Jerusalem which has been brought down from heaven which the Apostle also designates as "our mother from above" (Galatians 4:26). When he proclaims that "our *politeuma*," that is, citizenship, "is in heaven" (Philippians 3:20), he is surely referring to a heavenly city. . . . We affirm that this is the city established by God for the reception of the saints at the resurrection, and for their refreshment with an abundance of all blessings, spiritual blessings to be sure, in compensation for the blessings we have despised or lost in this age. For indeed it is right and worthy of God that his servants should also rejoice in the place where they suffered hardship for his name. This is the purpose of that kingdom, which will last a thousand years, during which period the saints will rise sooner or later, according to their merit. When the resurrection of the saints is completed, the destruction of the world and the conflagration of judgment will be effected; we shall be "changed in a moment" into the angelic substance, by the "putting on of incorruption" (1 Corinthians 15:52–3), and we shall be transferred to the heavenly kingdom.

Early Christian writers found it irresistible to speculate on what this period of one thousand years might be like. During this era, the earth would be restored to its former status of paradise, and humanity would enjoy the privileges of Adam and Eve. Perhaps the most remarkable account of the millennium is found in the second-century apocryphal "Apocalypse of Paul," which offers the most vivid and detailed description of this new paradise:

> And I looked round about that land and saw a river flowing with milk and honey. And there were trees planted at the brink of the river, heavily laden with fruits. Now every tree bore twelve fruits in the year, and they had many different fruits. And I saw the creation of that place and all the work of God, and there I saw palm-trees of twenty cubits and others of ten cubits: and that land was seven times brighter than silver. And the trees were full of fruits: from the root of each tree up to its heart there were ten thousand branches with tens of thousands of clusters, and there were ten thousand clusters on each branch, and there were ten thousand dates in each cluster. And thus was it also with the vines. Every vine had ten thousand branches, and each branch had upon it ten thousand bunches of grapes, and every bunch had on it ten thousand grapes. And there were other trees there, myriads of myriads of them, and their fruit was in the same proportion.

This immensely rich vision of a fecund and verdant paradise resonated with Christians, who often experienced deprivation of adequate food and drink, partly on account of adverse social conditions resulting from their faith, and partly because of the climate of the region.

Medieval Visions of Paradise

It is widely agreed that the Middle Ages was of immense importance in consolidating both Christian iconography and theology. Where earlier writers had been prepared to acknowledge their conceptual limits, refusing to speculate on matters they believed to lie beyond responsible theological speculation, their medieval successors developed great "cathedrals of the mind" (Etienne Gilson). The theological and artistic elaboration of the theme of heaven that developed around this time is particularly evident in the development of the theme of paradise. Heaven was now situated within a complex system of spheres, whose motions and interconnections governed the entire universe. This is vividly depicted in Hartmann Schedel's *Nuremberg Chronicle* (1493), one of the most popular printed books of the late Middle Ages.

On this grand view of the universe, the earth reposed at the center of a series of concentric spheres, arranged as follows:

The sphere of the moon,
The sphere of Mercury,
The sphere of Venus,
The sphere of the sun,
The sphere of Mars,
The sphere of Jupiter,
The sphere of Saturn,
The sphere of the Zodiac (the fixed stars).

Each of these eight spheres rotates round the earth according to its own predetermined rhythms. Beyond them lies the "empyrean" – a vast, eternal, infinite and formless void in which paradise is to be found, and God and the saints dwell, at least, in popular presentations of the matter, such as that found in the *Nuremberg Chronicle*. Note how the empyrean is here portrayed as being populated by God, seated on a throne, and the saints who surround him.

The medieval cosmos, diagram from Schedel's *Nuremberg Chronicle*, 1493. Photo AKG, London.

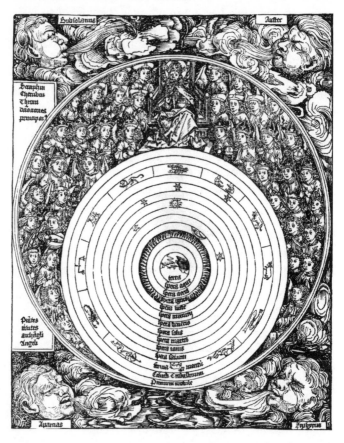

This framework was often supplemented in works of popular devotion. An excellent example of this process of elaboration is found in one of the most interesting works of Girolamo Savonarola (1452–98). In *The Compendium of Revelations*, Savonarola extended his speculation to the precise form of the empyrean, lying beyond the sphere of the fixed stars. The universe, he argued, was enclosed by a wall of precious stones. This wall enclosed a vast extended garden, richly carpeted with fresh green grass, studded with the brilliant flowers of paradise. Within this garden Savonarola located the nine ranks of the angelic hierarchy, paralleling the nine ranks of the physical universe, crowned with the glorious vision of the Trinity.

While the theology of this depiction of the universe was highly speculative, to say the least, it offered a powerful visual means of depicting the location of heaven which the medieval mindset found entirely persuasive. The theories of Nicolaus Copernicus and Johannes Kepler caused the abandonment of this understanding of celestial mechanics in the late sixteenth and early seventeenth centuries, and forced a reconsideration of what some had considered to be the settled question of the physical location of heaven.

Medieval theologians subjected this notion of God "dwelling in heaven" to critical scrutiny. Thomas Aquinas, while conceding that heaven can be said to be a place, insisted that the limitations of this spatial analogy be recognized. While the Lord's Prayer does indeed speak of God being "in heaven," Aquinas argues that this is to be taken as an affirmation of God's pre-eminence over the created order. God cannot be contained by anything; how then can God's presence be said to be limited to heaven? Heaven, for Aquinas, is a boundless realm in which the redeemed can enjoy the vision of God for ever.

Yet the question of the physical location of heaven was generally seen as secondary to its nature. The Middle Ages took great pleasure in conceiving both Eden and heaven primarily in terms of a garden. "Paradise means nothing other than a most pleasant garden, abundant with all pleasing and delightful things – trees, apples, flowers, fresh running water, and the songs of the birds" (Lorenzo de Medici). As we have seen, many English gentry of the seventeenth and eighteenth centuries fashioned their estates after the opulent image of Eden presented in Milton's *Paradise Lost*. Many Renaissance artists inverted this procedure, and portrayed paradise in terms of local landscapes. This is strikingly evident in a famous fresco of Benozzo Gozzoli (c.1420–97). This fresco, painted for the Palazzo Riccardi in Florence, depicts paradise as a Tuscan landscape, heavily populated with angelic beings.

Yet perhaps the most famous Tuscan work of art to deal with the great theme of Paradise is Dante's *Divine Comedy*, to which we now turn.

Dante's Divine Comedy

Dante Alighieri (1265–1321) was born into a well-established family in the city of Florence, which was at that time an independent city state, consciously modeling itself on the great city states of the classical period. We know virtually nothing concerning the first 30 years of his life; it is, however, clear that he established a reputation as a poet during this time. One of the most significant works of this early period in his life was *La Vita Nuova* ("The New Life"), which can be seen as a work in the tradition of "courtly love," focusing on the theme of unrequited love for a woman who lay beyond the reach of her admirers.

Benozzo Gozzoli, *Angels Worshiping*, fresco, Palazzo Medici Riccardi, Florence. Photo SCALA

It is at this point that we need to introduce the figure of Beatrice Portinari (1266–90), a member of the Portinara family who went on to marry into the Bardi family. She died in 1290, at the age of 24. Dante tells his readers that he first saw her and fell in love with Beatrice when he was a mere nine years of age, but that this love came to dominate his thoughts and passions at the age of 18. His love for her could never be requited, because Dante's family was considerably less important and wealthy than either the Portinara or Bardi dynasties. Beatrice features prominently in *La Vita Nuova*, and will later reappear in the *Divine Comedy*.

Beatrice's death in 1290 led Dante to turn his attention from romantic poetry to the world of philosophy and theology, and become embroiled in the complex world of Florentine politics. Florence had been severely shaken by a political crisis in 1293, which had seen the traditional power of the established families shaken by a rising mercantile class. Alongside this tension between established families and the rising middle classes there remained serious tensions between two such families – the Guelfs and Ghibellines – compounded by divisions within the Guelfs, which led to acrimonious infighting between sections of that family. In such a complex and politically unstable situation, it was easy to take a wrong step. To cut a long story short, Dante was unwise enough to ally himself with the wrong faction within the Guelf family. Realizing that his situation was untenable, he fled the city in October 1301. He was initially exiled and then condemned to death in his absence by the Florentine courts.

Exile was an established way of life in the world of the Italian city states, and Dante would hardly have been alone in his situation. Although it is virtually impossible to be sure what happened to Dante after his departure from

Florence in 1301, it is entirely possible that he was able to secure some kind of patronage from the Ghibelline family in another part of Italy, away from his native Tuscany. What we do know is that his exile from Tuscany was of momentous importance to his understanding of his own destiny, and that he regarded it as a turning point in his life. It was at this stage in his life that he conceived and began to write the major work that we now know as the *Divine Comedy*. Dante died at Ravenna in 1321.

The *Divine Comedy*, a vernacular poem in 100 cantos (more than 14,000 lines), was composed during this period of exile. It is the tale of the poet's journey through hell and purgatory (guided by Virgil) and through paradise (guided by Beatrice, to whom the poem is a memorial). Although the work belongs to the same genre as the otherworld journeys of the knight Tondal (1150) and Thurkil of Essex (1206), the sheer imaginative brilliance of Dante's poetic creation completely overshadows them. Written in a complex pentameter form known as terza rima, it is a magnificent synthesis of the medieval outlook, picturing a changeless universe ordered by God. Through it, Dante established his native Tuscan as the literary language of Italy. It must be noted that the title is misleading to English readers, in that the term "comedy" implies something amusing or funny. The Italian term *Commedia* is better translated as "drama." The term "divine" appears to have been added by a Venetian publisher at a later stage.

The *Divine Comedy* takes the form of three major inter-connected poems, respectively entitled *Inferno* ("Hell"), *Purgatorio* ("Purgatory"), and *Paradiso* ("Paradise"). The work makes substantial use of the leading themes of Christian theology and spirituality, while at the same time including comment on contemporary political and social events. The poem describes a journey that takes place in Holy Week 1300 – before Dante's exile from Florence. From the substantial number of clues in the text, it can be worked out that the journey begins at nightfall on Good Friday. After entering hell, Dante journeys downwards for an entire day, before beginning his ascent toward purgatory. After climbing Mount Purgatory, Dante rises further until he eventually enters into the presence of God.

Throughout the journey, Dante is accompanied by guides. The first guide is Virgil, the great Roman poet who wrote the *Aeneid*. It is widely thought that Dante uses Virgil as a symbol of classical learning and human reason. As they draw close to the peak of Mount Purgatory, Virgil falls behind, and Dante finds himself in the company of Beatrice, who leads him through the outer circles of heaven. Finally, he is joined by Bernard of Clairvaux, who leads Dante into the presence of God – the "love which moves the sun and the other stars."

The structure of the poem is immensely intricate, and it can be read at a number of levels. It can, for example, be read as a commentary on medieval Italian politics, particularly the intricacies of Florentine politics over the period 1300–4; or it can be seen as a poetic guide to Christian beliefs concerning the afterlife. More fundamentally, it can be read as a journey of self-discovery and spiritual enlightenment, in which the poet finally discovers and encounters his heart's desire.

Toward the end of *Purgatorio*, Dante describes how he and Virgil finally reach the top of Mount Purgatory. Virgil now bids Dante farewell; he can accompany him no further. This is widely interpreted as a literary reworking of the theological notion that human reason has a limited role in leading the soul to God. At a certain point, human reason fails, and the soul must entrust itself to the love of God – a notion that Dante found conveniently represented by the figure of Beatrice. Dante now enters the sacred forest, widely thought to be modeled on the great pine forest of Chiassi, which Dante knew from his period of exile, and which is explicitly mentioned in Canto 28. Dante completely eschews the traditional image of paradise as a garden. Canto 28 of *Purgatorio* opens with the poet describing his initial encounter with the forest. In Longfellow's translation:

> Eager already to search in and round
>   The heavenly forest, dense and living-green,
>   Which tempered to the eyes the new-born day,
>
> Without more delay I left the bank,
>   Taking the level country slowly, slowly
>   Over the soil that everywhere breathes fragrance.
>
> A softly-breathing air, that no mutation
>   Had in itself, upon the forehead smote me
>   No heavier blow than of a gentle wind,
>
> Whereat the branches, lightly tremulous,
>   Did all of them bow downward toward that side
>   Where its first shadow casts the Holy Mountain;
>
> Yet not from their upright direction swayed,
>   So that the little birds upon their tops
>   Should leave the practice of each art of theirs;
>
> But with full ravishment the hours of prime,
>   Singing, received they in the midst of leaves,
>   That ever bore a burden to their rhymes.

The forest here represents the state of human innocence, which once existed in Eden. In Dante's portrayal of the grand trajectory of redemption, humanity returns to its original state before it advances into the heavenly paradise that lies beyond. The earthly paradise is not an end in itself, but a place of transition and preparation, as Dante prepares to enter into the heavenly paradise which lies beyond. The paradisiacal forest invigorates Dante, creating a longing within him to go further, and reach beyond its limits:

> If, Reader, I possessed a longer space
>   For writing it, I yet would sing in part
>   Of the sweet draught that ne'er would satiate me;
>
> But inasmuch as full are all the leaves
>   Made ready for this second canticle,
>   The curb of art no farther lets me go.
>
> From the most holy water I returned
>   Regenerate, in the manner of new trees
>   That are renewed with a new foliage,
>
> Pure and disposed to mount unto the stars.

In the third part of the work – *Paradiso* – we find Dante setting out his vision of the paradise that awaits the saints. His human language fails him as he attempts to put into words the glories and subtleties of what he beholds. "This passing beyond humanity (*trasumanar*) cannot be set forth in words (*per verba*)." We find a series of verbs used to describe paradise prefixed with *tras*, indicating the need to go beyond conventional human limits in describing heaven: we must *trasmodare*, *trasumanar*, *transvolare*, if we are to fully grasp the glory of the heavenly paradise. The trajectory of Dante's thought in this final part of the *Comedy* leads through the visible heavens to the invisible empyrean that lies beyond. Accommodating himself for the sake of intellectual decency to the cultural conventions of the time, Dante sets out a complex vision of nine interlocking concentric spheres, which are clearly based on contemporary astronomical wisdom. Yet Dante's real concern lies with the need to pass beyond the realm of the human and physical, in order to pass into the presence of God. Dante's vision of paradise is theocentric, and we find little of the traditional paradise imagery in this closing part of his masterpiece.

In marked contrast, other Italian artists of the period were determined to use the traditional garden imagery as a means of depicting heaven. Perhaps one of the most interesting images to be developed in this way is that of the "enclosed garden," which underwent a remarkably transformation during the Middle Ages.

Paradise and the Enclosed Garden

The image of paradise as an "enclosed garden" (*hortus conclusus*) was seen as theologically fecund at the earliest stages in Christian history. Even as early as the second century, the "walled garden" was being interpreted as an image of the Christian church. Irenaeus remarked that "the Church has been planted as a garden (*paradisus*) in this world," and developed a complex account of the life of the church on the assumption that it was a means of bearing and restoring the lost values of Eden to the world. Augustine was one of many Christian theologians to accept and develop this imagery:

> In the Song of Songs the Church is described as "an enclosed garden, my sister and bride, a sealed fountain, a well of living water, an orchard of choice fruit" (Song of Songs 4:12–13). I dare not interpret this except as applying only to the holy and righteous, not to the greedy, the fraudulent, the grasping, the usurers, the drunken, or the envious. Those share a

common baptism with the righteous: they do not, however, share a common charity. . . . How have they penetrated into the "enclosed garden, the sealed fountain?" As Cyprian says, they have renounced the world only in word, not in deed; and yet he admits that they are within the Church. If they are within, and form "the Bride of Christ," is this really that bride "without any blemish or wrinkle?" (Ephesians 5:27). Is that "beautiful dove" (Song of Songs 6:9) defiled by such a part of her members? Are those the "brambles" in the midst of which she is "like a lily?" (Song of Songs 2:2). As a lily, she is the enclosed garden, the sealed fountain.

This imagery was developed throughout the Christian tradition, in both Protestant and Catholic circles. One of its most interesting statements can be found in a neglected hymn by Isaac Watts (1674–1748):

> We are a garden walled around,
> Chosen and made peculiar ground;
> A little spot enclosed by grace
> Out of the world's wide wilderness.
>
> Like trees of myrrh and spice we stand,
> Planted by God the Father's hand;
> And all his springs in Zion flow,
> To make the young plantation grow.
>
> Awake, O, heavenly wind! and come,
> Blow on this garden of perfume;
> Spirit divine! descend and breathe
> A gracious gale on plants beneath.

This approach to the Christian church develops the notion of a closed and protected community, within which faith, hope, and love may blossom, and individuals may live in tranquillity with each other and with God. The church is called out of the world in much the same way as a garden is an enclosed portion of wilderness, which can be watered, cultivated, and tended. The church is thus an Edenic community, seeking to recover the values of paradise within its own bounds. A similar idea is found in the writings of Ephrem the Syrian (died 373), who regularly asserted that the church was not merely the gateway to paradise; in some way, a paradisiacal realm was established within its walls.

It was during the Middle Ages that the image of the "walled garden" (*hortus conclusus*) became widely used in literature, both sacred and secular. Medieval writers often adopted strongly allegorical interpretations of the original text of the Song of Songs, perhaps embarrassed by the eroticism of its language, or its apparent endorsement of secular love. In the hands of biblical interpreters such as Bernard of Clairvaux or Hugh of St. Victor, the work became an affirmation of the cardinal teachings of the Christian church, and a celebration of the love of God for the world. This interpretation, which is not particularly evident on the basis of the text itself, rests upon a series of allegorical construals of the text.

For example, the imagery of a dove is used at several points throughout this work (see Song of Songs 2:14, 5:2, 6:9). What are we to read into this? Hugh of St. Victor was quite clear as to how this image was to be interpreted:

> The dove has two wings, just as the Christian has two ways of life – the active, and the contemplative. The blue feathers of its wings are thoughts of heaven; the less defined shades of its body are the changing colours of a restless sea, an allegory of the ocean of human passions on which the church

sails. And why are the eyes of the dove such a beautiful golden hue? Because yellow is the colour of ripe fruit, of experience and maturity, so that the yellow eyes of the dove are as the wisdom of the church as it contemplates the future. Furthermore, the dove has red feet, just as the church moves through the world with her feet in the blood of the martyrs.

Hugh's interpretation of the image of the dove involves the identification of layers of meaning which are hardly obvious to the untrained reader of the text, and allows him to draw inferences that go far beyond its decidedly modest theological affirmations.

It should therefore come as little surprise to note that the "bride" of the Song of Solomon was widely identified with the Virgin Mary. Mary came to be widely depicted within the formalized context of an enclosed garden. Perhaps the most familiar of these is the setting for the annunciation – that is, the announcement by Gabriel that Mary is to bear a child who will be the savior of the world. This development results from the fusion of two images – the biblical image of the enclosed garden, deriving from the Song of Songs; and the image of the "Garden of Venus," as developed in the fourth-century Latin poet Claudian's *Epithalamion for Honorius Augustus*. Claudian's vision of the garden of perpetual youth, dedicated to Venus, was easily Christianized to become the enclosed garden within which Mary received the good news of the coming of eternal life to humanity. The imagery of the enclosed garden also became a potent symbol of Mary's virginity. None could enter to violate her chastity.

The power of this imagery is perhaps best appreciated from Domenico Veneziano's fifteenth-century *Annunciation*. Veneziano's illustration is part of the Magnoli altarpiece, which had five predella panels. This famous panel painting depicts Gabriel greeting Mary in front of an enclosed garden. Yet the central focus of the picture is not Gabriel or Mary – both of whom are displaced – but a closed gate at the far end of the garden, on which the lines of perspective converge. The symbol is taken from the Song of Songs, and was widely used by medieval spiritual writers as a symbol of the perpetual virginity of Mary. Mary in her walled garden thus became a symbol of the doctrine of the immaculate conception.

Just as the image of the "walled garden" fused biblical and pagan themes, so it was often used for secular purposes. Writings such as the *Roman de la Rose* and Chaucer's *Parliament of Fowles* developed the theme of courtly love, often set in the context of wooing the beloved in a highly stylized walled garden. The most famous example of this iconographical transformation is Botticelli's *Primavera*, in which the imagery normally associated with Mary and the

Domenico Veneziano, *Annunciation*, Fitzwilliam Museum, University of Cambridge.

annunciation is transposed to represent the spring of a secular Eden, in which "Flora adorns the world with flowers."

It will be clear even from this brief analysis of Christian literature that the notion of the "restoration of Eden" forms an important aspect of the proclamation of the gospel. So how is this idea developed in relation to the idea of heaven?

Heaven as the Restoration of Eden

Important through such theological reflections on Eden were to the life and thought of the church, the most influential depictions of Eden are to be found in works of literature, rather than sermons and doctrinal treatises. John Milton's *Paradise Lost* depicts a vernal paradise, bathed in the exquisite moist heat of a gentle spring day, untroubled by any external concerns. Milton's rich prose draws extensively on classic sources, such as Homer's Garden of Alcinous and Hesiod's account of the "Isles of the Blessed." Milton here set a trend that others would follow. Later works such as Thomas Burnet's *Sacred Theory of the World* develop the notion that pagan fables of paradise were dim and distorted recollections of Eden, thus laying the foundation for the incorporation of the rich classical paradisiacal legacy into the literature of Christianity. Milton's epic transfigures the elements of the biblical account of Eden, as the potent imagery of Renaissance gardens interplays with its more modest biblical counterpart.

> Southward through Eden went a River large,
> Nor chang'd his course, but through the shaggie hill
> Pass'd underneath ingulft, for God had thrown

That Mountain as his Garden mould high rais'd
Upon the rapid current, which through veins
Of porous Earth with kindly thirst up drawn,
Rose a fresh Fountain, and with many a rill
Water'd the Garden; thence united fell
Down the steep glade, and met the neather Flood,
Which from his darksom passage now appeers,
And now divided into four main Streams,
Runs divers, wandring many a famous Realme
And Country whereof here needs no account,
But rather to tell how, if Art could tell,
How from that Sapphire Fount the crisped Brooks,
Rowling on Orient Pearl and sands of Gold,
With mazie error under pendant shades
Ran Nectar, visiting each plant, and fed
Flours worthy of Paradise which not nice Art
In Beds and curious Knots, but Nature boon
Powrd forth profuse on Hill and Dale and Plaine,
Both where the morning Sun first warmly smote
The open field, and where the unpierc't shade
Imbround the noontide Bowrs.

This fantastic and detailed elaboration of Eden struck a deep chord of sympathy with many of Milton's wealthier readers, who reorganized their estates to reflect the glories of this vision of Eden. Milton's vivid depiction of Eden as a place of delight, harmony, and joy inspired his readers to create their own paradise. Notice how the rose is described as "without thorn"; in Eden, it has no enemies, and thus requires no defence against them:

> Thus was this place,
> A happy rural seat of various view;
> Groves whose rich Trees wept odorous Gumms and
> Balme,

Others whose fruit burnisht with Golden Rinde
Hung amiable, Hesperian Fables true,
If true, here onely, and of delicious taste:
Betwixt them Lawns, or level Downs, and Flocks
Grasing the tender herb, were interpos'd,
Or palmie hilloc, or the flourie lap
Of some irriguous Valley spread her store,
Flowers of all hue, and without Thorn the Rose:
Another side, umbrageous Grots and Caves
Of coole recess, o're which the mantling Vine
Layes forth her purple Grape, and gently creeps
Luxuriant; mean while murmuring waters fall
Down the slope hills, disperst, or in a Lake,
That to the fringed Bank with Myrtle crownd,
Her chrystall mirror holds, unite their streams.
The Birds their quire apply; aires, vernal aires,
Breathing the smell of field and grove, attune
The trembling leaves.

Although Alexander Pope's noted poem *Windsor Forest* (1713) is probably more celebrated for its celebration of the controversial Treaty of Utrecht, signed in July of that year, than its reworking of the paradise motif, there is no doubting the importance Pope attached to this theme. Pope's own interest in gardening led him to compare the elegance of Windsor to the fabled Garden of Eden:

The Groves of Eden, vanished now so long,
Live in description, and look green in song.
These, were my breast inspired with equal flame,
Like them in beauty, should be like in fame.
Here hills and vales, the woodland and the plain,
Here earth and water seem to strive again;
Not chaos-like together crushed and bruised,
But, as the world, harmoniously confused:

Where order in variety we see,
And where, though all things differ, all agree.

The poem is notable for the manner in which it integrates the theme of ordering with that of the primal beauty of nature. A garden melds the glories and raw splendor of nature with the symmetry and precision of human enterprise. Eden may have been tamed; its beauty can still be appreciated, even in its tempered form.

The rise of the scientific revolution of the seventeenth and eighteenth centuries saw a gradual erosion of the popularity of the Eden motif in English literature and preaching. Over a period of time, Eden gradually came to be seen not as history but as a symbol of the human condition, and supremely its longings. Alternative visions were increasingly adopted and explored. While Robert Browning's *Sordello* offers a disparagement, rather than a sustained critique, of the "Eden tale," others were more direct in their criticisms. Shelley's *Queen Mab: A Philosophical Poem* (1812) represents a ferocious attack on organized religion. Dismissing the "fabled Eden," Shelley offers a secular alternative which retains some of the imagery, but not the doctrinal content, of traditional Christian visions of heaven.

This poem takes the form of a dream-vision allegory in which the fairy Queen Mab takes the mortal maiden Ianthe on an extraterrestrial excursion in order to show her the past, present, and future states of the human world. The past is irrational, the record of one mistake after another. The present has been irreversible corrupted by the institutions of kings, priests, and statesmen. But the future will be a supremely glorious affair of apocalyptic renovation. Shelley's version of this event is not religious but secular, with the "Spirit of Necessity" replacing divine providence as the agent of redemption. Nevertheless, despite Shelley's evident secularism, his anticipation of a "taintless" humanity in a renovated world seems to be for the most part directly derived from traditional Christian writings, especially the Book of Revelation. As is so often the case, religious images survive, while their attending ideas have faded into obscurity.

In the opening two chapters of this work, we have explored two images that have exercised a controlling influence over Christian reflection on heaven. Yet the iconography of heaven highlights another question. How is access to paradise to be gained? How may the gates of the New Jerusalem be opened, in order that we may enter? In the following chapter, we turn to explore these issues.

Chapter 3

Opening the Gates of Heaven: Atonement and Paradise

To visualize heaven is one thing; to be welcomed within its portals is quite another. The Christian visualization of heaven marks, at least in one respect, a radical inversion of existing literary conventions. In traditional Jewish writings, heaven is conceived as a spatially extensive realm to which pious individuals must ascend. This is best seen from the extensive *hekhalot* and *merkavah* literature, which recount the journeys of Jewish sages – such as Rabbis Akiba and Ishmael – into the heavenly realms. These writings depict individuals as ascending through the six outer "palaces" of heaven, before entering the final palace, and beholding the glory of God. Yet the Book of Revelation envisions the New Jerusalem as *descending* to believers. No longer is ascent required; heaven has entered into the realm of human possibilities.

There is a clear parallel here with the Christian doctrine of the incarnation, which affirms that God descended and entered into the realm of human history, rather than demand that humanity extricate itself from that realm and reach heaven through its own limited resources. The descent of the New Jerusalem is a powerful iconographic affirmation of the Christian understanding of the accessibility of heaven, as a consequence of the life, death, and resurrection of Christ.

So in what way is access to heaven linked with the person of Jesus Christ? The area of Christian theology that deals with how individuals may hope to enter heaven is traditionally known as "the doctrine of the atonement." This unusual term, which can be traced back to the fourteenth century, was used by William Tyndale in his groundbreaking English translation of the New Testament (1526). Tyndale found himself encountering some difficulty in conveying the idea of "reconciliation" to his readers (in that this now-familiar English word had yet to be invented). The idea, however, was clearly present in the New Testament, which spoke of sinners being reconciled to God through Christ. How could this idea be rendered in English?

Tyndale thus used the word "atonement" to express the state of "at-one-ment" – that is, reconciliation. Tyndale's translation was so influential that this hitherto unfamiliar word gained growing acceptance, and was used in perhaps the most celebrated English Bible of all time – the King James Bible of 1611, better known in Britain as the "Authorized Version." Its rendering of Romans 5:11 proved highly influential. "We also joy in God through our Lord Jesus Christ, by whom we have now received the atonement." More recent translations offer a more recognizable interpretation of this verse: "we also rejoice in God through our Lord Jesus Christ, through whom we have received reconciliation." Yet this pivotal translation served to persuade generations of English-speaking theologians that the benefits won by Christ through his cross and resurrection could be summarized in the terse phrase "the atonement."

Before exploring the Christian understanding of how humanity is restored to paradise, we must pause to consider the corollary of this theme – namely, that humanity *needs* to be restored to its Eden. Salvation presupposes a state from which humanity must be delivered. As we shall see, an integral aspect of the Christian understanding of sin is that humanity has become alienated as much from God as from Eden, prompting the question of how restoration is to be achieved.

The Genesis account of the expulsion of Adam and Eve from Eden seems to have a clear note of finality stamped upon it. "At the east of the garden of Eden [God] placed

The Expulsion from Eden, seventeenth-century engraving.
Historical Picture Archive/Corbis.

the cherubim, and a sword flaming and turning to guard the way to the tree of life" (Genesis 3:24). A seventeenth-century engraving of this event brings poetic license to bear upon it, depicting a suitably chastised Adam and Eve being led down the steps from paradise, and forced into the harshness of a godless world.

Humanity having been expelled from paradise, the way back is permanently closed. From this point onwards, it seems, humanity must seek and create its own paradise. Yet for writers such as Augustine or C. S. Lewis, the memory of Eden lingers, haunting humanity with its longing to regain entrance to this forbidden realm. Nature itself becomes a parable, charged with a divinely imbued potential to recreate the memory of Eden, and make us long to return to its now-deserted meadows. We shall be exploring how the shadow of Eden has impacted on the human longing for the transcendent in more detail in the next chapter. At this stage, our concern focuses on the themes of separation and restoration that are evoked by the biblical narrative of the expulsion from Eden.

Christian theology characterizes the nature and destiny of humanity in terms of having been created for the specific purpose of relating to God, as the supreme joy that this world can bring. This intimate relationship has been disrupted and attenuated through sin. It is perhaps not surprising that the biblical metaphors of sin are dominated by the theme of separation or alienation from God. Paul reminds his readers that they were once "without Christ, aliens from the commonwealth of Israel and strangers to the covenants of promise, having no hope and without God in the world" (Ephesians 2:12). Sin is a barrier between humanity and their intended paradise. If that redemption can be thought of as the reversal and restoration of the human situation resulting from "man's first disobedience" (Milton), it follows that an integral element of Christian thought is the restoration of humanity to paradise through redemption. If sin excludes us from paradise, redemption hastens to invite us within its portals.

This naturally raises the question of how access to paradise is related to the death of Christ, a central theme both of Christian theology and the body of literature that has been inspired by it. In what follows, we shall move on to consider the question of how access to heaven is to be achieved. In what way do the death and resurrection of Christ relate to the hope of heaven? What models were developed to express Christian understandings of the manner in which Christ was able to throw open the once barred gates of paradise, and welcome believers within its bounds? In what follows, we shall explore some of the most important models of atonement, and their classic literary embodiments.

Christ the Victor

"Thanks be to God, who gives us the victory through our Lord Jesus Christ" (1 Corinthians 15:57). The early church gloried in the triumph of Christ upon the cross, and the victory that he won over sin, death, and Satan. The gates of heaven had been thrown wide open through the conquest of Calvary. The powerful imagery of the triumphant Christ rising from the dead and being installed as "ruler of all" (*pantokrator*) seized the imagination of the Christian east. The cross was seen as the site of a famous battle, comparable to the great Homeric epics, in which the forces of good and evil engaged, with the good emerging victorious.

The early church was more concerned to affirm Christ's victory over the enemies of humanity than to speculate over precisely how it came about. Christ's resurrection and his triumphant opening of the gates of heaven to believers was something to be proclaimed and celebrated, rather than subjected to the desiccations of theological analysis. Early Christian liturgies were saturated with the thought of the cosmic victory achieved by Christ on the cross. A fourth-century homily, traditionally ascribed to Hippolytus, takes great pleasure in pointing out the cosmic dimensions of the redemption achieved by Christ on the cross, without feeling the need to explore the mechanics of how this redemption is accomplished.

> This tree is for me a plant of eternal salvation. By it I am nourished, by it I am fed. By its roots, I am firmly planted. By its branches, I am spread out, its perfume is a delight to me, and its spirit refreshes me like a delightful wind. I have pitched my tent in its shadow, and during the heat I find it to be a haven full of perfume . . . This tree of heavenly proportions rises up from the earth to heaven. It is fixed, as an eternal growth, at the midpoint of heaven and earth. It sustains all things; it is the support of the universe, the base of the whole inhabited world, and the axis of the earth. Established by the invisible pegs of the Spirit, it holds together the various aspects of humanity in such a way that, divinely guided, its nature may never again become separated from God. By its peak which touches the height of the heavens, by its base which supports the earth, and by its immense arms subduing the many spirits of the air on every side, it exists in its totality in every thing and in every place.

This homily eloquently witnesses to the powerful amalgam of imagery that came to be attached to the cross as the basis of the hope of heaven.

The note of triumph struck by this homily was echoed in other contexts, and led to the appropriation of a cultural icon of the period in Christian depictions of the benefits won by Christ on the cross. The Roman cultural context led to the theme of the victory of Christ being depicted as a triumphant procession, comparable to those of ancient Rome. In its classical form, the triumphal parade proceeded the *triumphator* from the Campus Martius through the streets of Rome, finally ending up at the temple of Jupiter on the Capitoline Hill. The parade was led by the general's soldiers, often carrying placards with slogans describing the general and his achievements (e.g., Julius Caesar's troops carried placards which bore the words: *Veni, Vidi, Vici*) or showing maps of the territories he conquered. Other soldiers led carts containing booty that would be turned over to Rome's treasury. A section of the parade included prisoners, often the leaders of the defeated cities or countries, bound in chains.

It was a small step for Christian writers to transform this imagery into the liturgical proclamation of *Christus Triumphator*. This powerful symbolism was firmly grounded in the New Testament, which spoke of the victorious Christ as "making captivity a captive" (Ephesians 4:8). While this theme can be seen in some Christian art of this early period, its most dramatic impact was upon the hymnody of the period. One of the greatest hymns of the Christian church, dating from this period, portrays Christ's triumphant procession and celebrates his defeat of his foes.

Venantius Honorius Clementianus Fortunatus (c.530–c.610) was born in Ceneda, near Treviso, in northern Italy. He became a Christian at an early age, and went on to study at Ravenna and Milan. He gained a reputation for excellence in poetry and rhetoric, and went on to become elected bishop of Poitiers around 599. He is chiefly remembered for his poem, *Vexilla regis prodeunt* – "the royal banners go forth." According to a well-established tradition, in the year 569, St. Radegunde presented a large fragment of what was believed to be the true Cross to the town of Poitiers, in southern Gaul. Radegunde had obtained this fragment from the Emperor Justin II. Fortunatus was the one chosen to receive the relic on its arrival at Poitiers. When the bearers of the holy fragment were some two miles distant from the town, Fortunatus, with a great gathering of believers and enthusiasts – some of whom were carrying banners, crosses, and other sacred emblems – went forth to meet them. As they marched, they sang this hymn, which Fortunatus had composed for the occasion. This was soon incorporated within the passiontide office of the western church, and is still widely used today in marking Holy Week within western Christianity. The English translation is taken from the *Mediaeval Hymns and Sequences* (1851) of the great Victorian hymnologist and medievalist John Mason Neale (1818–66).

> The royal banners forward go,
> The cross shines forth in mystic glow;
> Where he in flesh, our flesh Who made,
> Our sentence bore, our ransom paid.
>
> There whilst He hung, His sacred side
> By soldier's spear was opened wide,
> To cleanse us in the precious flood
> Of water mingled with His blood.
>
> Fulfilled is now what David told
> In true prophetic song of old,
> How God the heathen's King should be;
> For God is reigning from the tree.

O tree of glory, tree most fair,
Ordained those holy limbs to bear,
How bright in purple robe it stood,
The purple of a Saviour's blood!

Upon its arms, like balance true,
He weighed the price for sinners due,
The price which none but He could pay,
And spoiled the spoiler of his prey.

To Thee, eternal Three in One,
Let homage meet by all be done:
As by the cross Thou dost restore,
So rule and guide us evermore.

Christ the Hero

The cult of the hero can be traced back to the classical period, which celebrated the achievements of individuals whose daring and bravery resulted in glory and prosperity for their people. It reached a new level of development in Old and Middle English literature, in which works such as *Beowulf* and *The Song of Roland* portrayed the hero as the savior of his people. While the hero may possess many outstanding moral qualities, the supreme quality demanded of him is valor and victory in battle. Perhaps it was natural that Christ should be thought of as the greatest hero, doing glorious battle with the forces of darkness, death, and despair and emerging triumphant.

Heroic ideals were deeply embedded in Anglo-Saxon culture, both in Germany and subsequently in England. The great stories of heroes such as Beowulf and Ingelt were related with enthusiasm, and served to keep alive the heroic ideas of that culture. So great was the influence of these writings that in 797 Alcuin wrote to bishop Higbald, asking that Scripture and the works of the Christian fathers – not pagan myths – should be read aloud at meals in the monastic refectories. So what better way to counter the influence of pagan heroes than to portray Christ himself as the hero above all heroes?

This literary transformation of Christ to conform to the heroic ideals of the age is best seen in the famous Old English poem *The Dream of the Rood* (the word "rood" means a "cross"), thought to have been written about the year 750. This dramatic and highly original work offers an account and interpretation of Christ's death and resurrection that represents a significant change of emphasis from the original biblical accounts of these events. In order to emphasize the momentous triumph of the crucifixion, the author depicts Christ as a bold and confident warrior who confronts and defeats sin in a heroic battle. This depiction make a direct appeal to the high esteem in which the virtues of honor and courage were held in Anglo-Saxon culture of this period.

The structure of the poem is complex and suggestive. It opens with an address, in which the poet identifies himself, and relates how he dreamt a most wonderful dream in the middle of the night: "I saw a wondrous tree spreading aloft, spun about with light." A description of the cross follows, in which the poet relates how he sees a richly jeweled and gilded cross, perhaps similar to the highly ornamented crosses carried in church processions at this time. Yet as the poet gazes on the cross, it seems to change its appearance. Blood makes its appearance, as the dual aspects of the cross begin to impact upon the poet's imagination. At one time, it is studded with jewels; at another, it is drenched with blood: "At times, it was soaked with wetness, drenched by the coursing of blood; at times adorned with treasure." The poet then hears the cross tell its own story. There are three major elements to this: the crucifixion itself, Christ's deposition and burial, and the final deposition and rediscovery of the Cross.

The most distinctive feature of the poem is its deliberate and systematic portrayal of Christ as a hero, who mounts the cross in order to achieve a magnificent victory. The words used to describe Christ's approach to the cross reveal the poet's deliberate decision to portray Jesus as a purposeful courageous warrior: "The young man, who was almighty God, stripped himself, strong and unflinching. He climbed upon the despised gallows, courageous under the scrutiny of many, since he willed to redeem mankind. I quaked, then, when the man embraced me." Christ did not passively accept the cross; he actively embraced it, as a hero seeks out and engages his foe. The poet depicts Christ as enthusiastically preparing for combat, longing to engage with his enemies, rather than endorsing the more traditional imagery of Christ being led passively to the cross. Where the Gospel passion narratives hold that Christ was stripped of his clothes by the Roman soldiers, the *Dream of the Rood* has Christ stripping *himself* in readiness for action. "The young warrior, God our Saviour, valiantly stripped before the battle." At a later point in the poem, the poet even suggests that Christ actually initiates the battle to redeem humanity.

This active role on the part of Christ the hero is echoed by language used by the cross itself in the poem. The poet hears the cross tell its own story, particularly how it saw "the Lord of all mankind hasten with much fortitude, for he meant to mount upon me." These words tend to suggest a much more active and purposeful image of Christ than the more passive language of certain biblical passages, such as those which speak of the "Passover lamb which has been sacrificed," implying activity on the part of those who killed Christ and passivity on his part as a victim.

The poet regularly styles Christ as "the young hero" or "the warrior," avoiding the traditional language of Christian theology. Christ is portrayed as a heroic, fair, young knight in terms that echo the description of Beowulf, a much-admired mythical hero of the same era. In Beowulf, the central figure of the narrative is acclaimed as a "king," "hero," and "valiant warrior," possessed of "strength and vigor," "daring," and a "determined resolve." When Beowulf prepares to go to battle against Grendel's mother, he shows no concern for his own life or safety, but is eager to plunge into battle.

The *Dream of the Rood* is also reluctant to allow that Christ died of wounds incurred by the process of crucifixion. For the poet, death is something that Christ actively and purposefully chose, not something that he suffered passively. Whereas the Gospel passion narratives present Christ as so exhausted by the scourging he has received from Pilate's soldiers that a passer-by has to be pressed into carrying the cross, the *Dream of the Rood* presents the cross as already raised, waiting for Christ to embrace it. "Men carried me upon their shoulders until they set me up on a hill." Christ *eagerly mounts* the cross; the exhausted and wounded Christ of the Gospel narratives is set to one side, in order to heighten the triumph Christ secures by his death.

In a further dramatic inversion of imagery, the poet transfers *to the cross* the wounds that traditionally were ascribed to the person of Christ himself. Apparently reluctant to allow that the Christ who died was in any way physically disfigured, the poet allows the cross to tell of how *it* was wounded: "They pierced me with dark nails; the wounds are visible upon me, gaping malicious gashes." As the poet depicts the events of Calvary, the cross itself almost becomes a hero, endowed with the virtues of courage and perseverance. To pick up on some of the imagery of the poem, the cross endures being hewed, severed, pierced, and bound. It permits the enemy to use it as a gallows and to be mocked and spattered with blood. Throughout the crucifixion, the cross was conscious of the heavy burden, physical and theological, which it bore, as it struggled to remain upright, holding its king, daring not to bow or break until the moment when it meekly relinquished its precious burden to the "hands of men."

The Dream of the Rood is a remarkable piece of poetry, establishing a firm link between the heroic ideals of Anglo-Saxon culture and the achievement of Christ on the cross. The closing lines of the poem establish the critical link between the cross and entry into heaven, secured and safeguarded by Christ himself:

> May the Lord be a friend to me, who here on earth once suffered on the gallows-tree for the sins of men. He redeemed us and gave us life, and a heavenly home. Hope was renewed with dignity and with happiness for those who had once suffered burning. The Son was victorious in that undertaking, powerful and successful, when he came with a multitude, the company of souls, into God's kingdom, the one almighty Ruler, to the delight of the angels and of all the saints who had previously dwelt in glory in heavens, when their Ruler, almighty God, came where his home was.

A further development of the theme of "Christ the victor" depicts Christ as extending the triumph of the cross and resurrection to the netherworld. The medieval idea of "the harrowing of hell" holds that, after dying upon the cross, Christ descended to hell, and broke down its gates in order that the imprisoned souls might go free. The idea rests (rather tenuously, it has to be said) upon 1 Peter 3:18–22, which makes reference to Christ "preaching to the spirits in prison." However, the text that proved the most significant stimulus to the development of this idea was the apocryphal Gospel of Nicodemus. While the final version of this work is generally thought to date from the fifth century, the specific section dealing with the "harrowing of Hell" may date from as early as the second century.

> Then there was a great voice like thunder, saying: Lift up your gates, O rulers; and be lifted up, you everlasting gates; and the King of glory shall come in. When Hades heard this, he said to Satan: Go forth, if you are able to, and stand up to him. Satan therefore went forth outside. Then Hades said to his demons: Secure well and strongly the gates of brass and the bars of iron, and attend to my bolts, and stand in order, and see to everything; for if he come in here, woe will seize us. . . .
>
> There came, then, again a voice saying: "Lift up the gates." Hades, hearing the voice the second time, answered as if he did not know who it was, and said: "Who is this King of glory?" The angels of the Lord said: "The Lord strong and mighty, the Lord mighty in battle." And immediately with these words the brazen gates were shattered, and the iron bars broken, and all the dead who had been bound came out of the prisons, and we with them. And the King of glory

entered in the form of a man, and all the dark places of Hades were lighted up.

Immediately Hades cried out: "We have been conquered: woe to us! But who art you, that you possess such power and might? And what are you, who comes here without sin, apparently insignificant and yet of such great power, lowly and exalted, the slave and the master, the soldier and the king, who has power over the dead and the living? You were nailed to the cross, and placed in the tomb; and now you are free, and hast destroyed all our power. Are you the Jesus about whom the chief satrap Satan told us, that through cross and death you are to inherit the whole world?"

Then the King of glory seized the chief satrap Satan by the head, and delivered him to His angels, and said: "Bind his hands and his feet, his neck and his mouth, with iron chains." Then He delivered him to Hades, and said: "Take him, and keep him secure till my second appearing."

The dramatic power of this scene was such that, despite its slightly questionable theological and literary provenance, it was picked up and incorporated into countless popular accounts of the cycle of events at Easter. The hymn "You Choirs of New Jerusalem," written by Fulbert of Chartres (c.970–1028), expresses this theme in two of its verses, picking up the theme of Christ, as the "lion of Judah" (Revelation 5:5), defeating Satan, the serpent (Genesis 3:15):

> For Judah's lion bursts his chains
> Crushing the serpent's head;
> And cries aloud through death's domain
> To wake the imprisoned dead.
>
> Devouring depths of hell their prey
> At his command restore;
> His ransomed hosts pursue their way
> Where Jesus goes before.

The idea rapidly became established in popular English literature of the Middle Ages. One of the most important pieces of Christian literature of this period is usually known simply as the "Junius Codex" or the "Junius Manuscript," held in the Bodleian Library, Oxford. The text gained its name through having being owned by Francis Junius (1589–1677), an antiquarian who was a close personal acquaintance of John Milton. Indeed, some writers have suggested that similarities between Milton's *Paradise Lost* and parts of the material in this codex may rest on Milton having had access to this source through his friend.

This manuscript consists of two books: the first of which consists of commentaries on Genesis, Exodus, and Daniel; the second of which consists of a complex work focusing on Christ and Satan. The Junius Codex appears to have been written in four different hands at some point in the late tenth or early eleventh century. However, it seems clear that the manuscript brings together older sources into a single compilation. It is possible that the works were brought together by a religious community, to meet their needs for an appropriate series of readings during the Lenten and Easter seasons. The second of these two texts deals with the final conflict between Christ and Satan, and offers a highly dramatic understanding of the significance of Christ's death and resurrection, reflecting the importance attached to the theme of the "harrowing of hell" in popular Christian culture.

This remarkable work of popular theology offers a vivid and highly realistic account of Satan's rebellion against God, and his final defeat when Christ stormed into his citadel and set his captives free. The writer pictures the eager anticipation of those condemned to hell as they realize that their savior is at hand, and exults in the thought of the ransomed host being welcomed into heaven by their Lord:

> It was indeed a beautiful occasion when that throng came up into the homeland, and the eternal God, the ordaining Lord of mankind, with them, into the renowned citadel. . . . The Lord himself had conquered death then, and put the fiend to flight.

In a highly speculative section, Christ is depicted as musing over the fate of those in hell, and his longing to restore them to heaven through his cross:

> I kept in remembrance that the multitude in this evil dwelling-place was longing that I should lead them home out of their shackles up to their own land, so that they should enjoy the splendours of the Lord and the glory of the heavenly host. They shall have heaven's riches in their thousands. I atoned for you when men pierced me on the tree, with spears on the gallows.

A similar idea is found in *Piers Plowman*, one of the most important English-language poems of the fourteenth century, traditionally attributed to William Langland. In this poem, the narrator tells of how he falls asleep, and dreams of Christ throwing open the gates of Hell, and speaking the following words to Satan:

> Here is my soul as a ransom for all these sinful souls, to redeem those that are worthy. They are mine; they came from me, and therefore I have the better claim on them. . . . You, by falsehood and crime and against all justice, took away what was mine, in my own domain; I, in fairness, recover them by paying the ransom, and by no other means.

> What you got by guile is won back by grace. . . . And as a
> tree caused Adam and all mankind to die, so my gallows-
> tree shall bring them back to life.

It is clear that this highly dramatic understanding of the
way in which Christ threw open the gates of death and
hell, allowing their imprisoned masses to escape and enter
into the joys of heaven, made a potent appeal to the imagination of the readers of *Piers Plowman*.

The theme of the "harrowing of hell" delighted artists of
the Middle Ages. One such depiction of the harrowing of
Hell may be noted here. A fifteenth-century English alabaster panel, held in the Museum of Carcassonne, depicts Christ
as a warrior liberating grateful souls from their imprison-
ment in Hell.

Such is the power of the image that it lingers, often
unrecognized, in later writings. A particularly powerful
example of this can be found in C. S. Lewis's childrens' tale
The Lion, the Witch and the Wardrobe. The book tells the story
of Narnia, a land that is discovered by accident by four
children rummaging around in an old wardrobe. In this
work, we encounter the White Witch, who keeps the land
of Narnia covered in a perpetual wintry snow. As we read
on, we realize that she rules Narnia not as a matter of right,
but by stealth. The true ruler of the land is absent; in his
absence, the witch subjects the land to oppression. In the
midst of this land of winter stands the witch's castle, within
which many of the inhabitants of Narnia have been imprisoned as stone statues.

As the narrative moves on, we discover that the rightful
ruler of the land is Aslan, a lion. As Aslan advances into
Narnia, winter gives way to spring, and the snow begins
to melt. The witch realizes that her power is beginning to

The Harrowing of Hell, fifteenth-century English alabaster. CMN, Paris.

fade, and moves to eliminate the threat posed to her by Aslan. Aslan surrenders himself to the forces of evil, and allows them to do their worst with him – yet by so doing, disarms them. Lewis's description of the resurrection of Aslan is one of his more tender moments, evoking the deep sense of sorrow so evident in the New Testament accounts of the burial of Christ, and the joy of recognition of the reality of the resurrection. Lewis then describes how Aslan – the lion of Judah, who has burst his chains – breaks into the castle, breathes upon the statues, and restores them to life, before leading the liberated army through the shattered gates of the once-great fortress to freedom. Hell has been harrowed, and its inhabitants liberated from its dreary shades.

Christ the Redeemer: Atonement as Satisfaction

An interpretation of the cross that gained considerable influence at the time of the Renaissance may be traced back to the eleventh century. Anselm of Canterbury, seeking to offer a logically and morally persuasive construal of the crucifixion and resurrection, appealed to the legal conventions of his day. Christ's death on the cross could be interpreted as a *satisfaction* offered to God for human sin. The value of the satisfaction thus offered had to be equivalent to the weight of human sin. Anselm argued that the Son of God became incarnate in order that, as the God-man, Christ would possess both the human *obligation* to pay the satisfaction, and the divine *ability* to pay a satisfaction of the magnitude necessary for redemption. This idea is faithfully reproduced by Mrs. Cecil F. Alexander in her famous nineteenth-century hymn *There is a Green Hill Far Away*:

There was no other good enough
To pay the price of sin;
He only could unlock the gate
Of heaven, and let us in.

Much the same theme is developed centuries earlier by George Herbert. Herbert spent the final part of his life as rector of the parish of Fugglestone with Bemerton near Salisbury. At Bemerton, George Herbert conducted what is widely regarded as an exemplary parish ministry. He rebuilt the parish church at his own expense; he visited the poor, consoled the sick, and sat by the bed of the dying. "Holy Mr. Herbert" became the talk of the countryside in the three short years before he died of consumption on March 1, 1633.

While on his deathbed, Herbert sent the manuscript of a collection of poems to his friend Nicholas Ferrar, and requested him to arrange for their publication. The resulting volume of poems, now entitled *The Temple*, was published later in the year of Herbert's death. It met with popular acclaim, and had run to seven editions by 1640. The poem known as "Redemption" is a particularly important exploration of the associations of the Old Testament notion of "redeeming land." Herbert here develops the idea of the death of Christ as the price by which God takes legitimate possession of a precious piece of land. While also exploring the idea of the shame and humility of the cross, Herbert is able to bring out the legal and financial dimensions of redemption.

Having been tenant long to a rich Lord,
    Not thriving, I resolved to be bold,
And make a suit unto Him, to afford
    A new small-rented lease, and cancell th'old.

In heaven at His manour I Him sought:
  They told me there, that He was lately gone
About some land, which he had dearly bought
  Long since on Earth, to take possession.
I straight return'd, and knowing His great birth,
  Sought Him accordingly in great resorts –
In cities, theatres, gardens, parks, and courts:
  At length I heard a ragged noise and mirth
Of thieves and murderers; there I Him espied,
  Who straight, "Your suit is granted," said, and died.

The central image here is the "lease" – that is to say, the right to inhabit a certain place. Herbert wants to "afford" – for he cannot at present hope to pay the high cost – a lease on a new property, and cancel his old. The transition implied is theological as much as physical; Herbert wants to dwell in heaven, not remain on earth. Yet the cost of this transition is immense. The basic theme enunciated by Herbert in this poem is that of the costliness of redemption; that is to say, that the admission-price of the believer to heaven is the death of the Son of God.

A similar point is made by Herbert's fellow-poet Richard Crashaw (1612–49) in *Charitas Nimia; or the Deare Bargain*:

> Lord, what is man? Why should he cost thee
>   So deare? What hath his ruine lost thee?
> Lord, what is man, that thou hast over-bought
>   So much a thing of nought?

Christ the Lover: Atonement and the Enkindling of Love

A leading theme of the New Testament understanding of the death of Christ is that it demonstrates the love of God for humanity, and elicits a matching love in response. This theme is developed within Christian theology in terms of God stooping down to enter the created world, becoming incarnate in Christ. The love of God for wounded humanity is thus focused on the act of divine humility in leaving the glory of heaven to enter the poverty and suffering of the created order, and finally to suffer death upon the cross.

Such thoughts have proved a powerful stimulus to the Christian imagination. John Donne offers what is widely regarded as one of the most significant poetic reflections on the love of God in Holy Sonnet XV.

> Wilt thou love God, as he thee? then digest
> My soul, this wholesome meditation,
> How God the Spirit, by angels waited on
> In heaven, doth make his temple in thy breast.
> The Father having begot a Son most blessed,
> And still begetting (for he ne'er begun)
> Hath deigned to choose thee by adoption,
> Coheir to his glory, and Sabbath's endless rest;
> And as a robbed man, which by search doth find
> His stol'n stuff sold, must lose or buy it again:
> The Son of glory came down, and was slain,
> Us whom he had made, and Satan stol'n, to unbind.
> T'was much, that man was made like God before,
> But, that God should be made like man, much more.

The poem engages with the entire process of incarnation and atonement, focusing on the divine determination to redeem humanity, whatever the cost might be. It develops the idea that humanity has unjustly come under the power and authority of Satan, obliging God to act justly in order to deliver us from this Satanic thrall. Not only did the "Son of Glory" come down from heaven, entering into this world of sin and death; he "was slain" on our behalf, in order to secure our freedom.

One of the most celebrated literary explorations of the love of God is the third poem in George Herbert's collection *The Temple*, which we considered earlier. The closing poem of this remarkable collection – entitled "Love" – can be seen as an extended musing on how it can be that Christ can possibly love sinners, and welcome them to the heavenly banquet.

> Love bade me welcome, yet my soul drew back,
>   Guilty of dust and sin.
> But quick-ey'd Love, observing me grow slack
>   From my first entrance in,
> Drew nearer to me, sweetly questioning
>   If I lack'd anything.
>
> "A guest," I answer'd, "worthy to be here";
>   Love said, "You shall be he."
> "I, the unkind, the ungrateful? ah my dear,
>   I cannot look on thee."
> Love took my hand and smiling did reply,
>   "Who made the eyes but I?"
>
> "Truth, Lord, but I have marr'd them; let my shame
>   Go where it doth deserve."
> "And know you not," says Love, "who bore the blame?"
>   "My dear, then I will serve."
> "You must sit down," says Love, "and taste my meat."
>   So I did sit and eat.

Throughout the poem, Christ himself is personified as "Love." The first verse of the poem invites its readers to imagine themselves approaching Christ, at once attracted to him yet at the same time aware of their weakness and failings. Why should such a Christ want to receive, still less welcome, anyone who was "guilty of dust and sin." Why should the creator stoop down to greet the creature, or the savior to embrace the sinner? Yet Herbert asks us to imagine Christ noticing our hesitation, and moving swiftly to greet and reassure us.

Is there anything that we would like? Herbert's answer to Love's question was simple yet profound: he wanted to be worthy to be Love's guest at the heavenly banquet, the marriage supper of the Lamb. Yet the request seemed utterly beyond his reach. How could someone so insignificant and guilty ever be welcomed into the presence of the glorious Son of God? Herbert believes himself to be so unworthy that he should not even be allowed to gaze upon Christ from a distance, let alone be welcomed into his presence. Yet Love reassures him once more – this time, through *taking him by the hand*. The words instantly evoke a series of Gospel images – as in the healing of a blind man or the raising of a dead young girl – in the language of the King James Bible that Herbert knew so well: "And *he took the blind man by the hand*, and led him out of the town; and when he had spit on his eyes, and put his hands upon him, he asked him if he saw ought" (Mark 8:23); "And *he took the damsel by the hand*, and said unto her, Talitha cumi; which is, being interpreted, Damsel, I say unto thee, arise" (Mark 5:41). Just as Christ was willing to touch and hold these unfortunates, so he takes hold of Herbert. Christ "bore the blame" for his sin, so that it need no longer be a barrier between sinner and savior. And having taking him by the hand, Christ leads him to sit down at table with him – as a guest.

In the third verse of the poem, we find a deeply moving reflection on the sense of unworthiness felt by Herbert.

Even though he knows that Christ loves him, and has willingly borne his guilt, he believes that he has been welcomed into Christ's presence as a *servant* – as one who is to *wait upon* Christ. The poem ends with an exquisite portrayal of Herbert, the hesitant believer, being welcomed as an honored guest, not as an attendant servant, in the portals of the New Jerusalem.

One of the finest pieces of writing to explore the link between the love of God, the death of Christ, and the hope of heaven is Henry Vaughan's poem "Peace." Vaughan's vision of a realm of tranquillity stands in sharp contrast to the turbulent events that took place around him. Vaughan was born in Wales, and went on to study at Jesus College, Oxford, where he became an ardent supporter of Charles I. Personal illness and the death of a brother accentuated his distress over the total defeat of the Royalist cause in England under the Parliamentarian forces. He took solace in the thought of heaven, a "country far beyond the stars," to which his entry had been secured through his savior, who "did in pure love descend to die here for [his] sake."

> My soul, there is a country
>   Far beyond the stars,
> Where stands a wingèd sentry
>   All skillful in the wars,
> There above noise, and danger
>   Sweet peace sits crown'd with smiles,
> And one born in a manger
>   Commands the beauteous files,
> He is thy gracious friend,
>   And (O my soul awake!)
> Did in pure love descend
>   To die here for thy sake,
> If thou canst get but thither,

There grows the flower of peace,
The rose that cannot wither,
   Thy fortress and thy ease;
Leave then thy foolish ranges;
   For none can thee secure
But one who never changes,
   Thy God, thy life, thy cure.

Vaughan's reflections bring out the importance of the hope of heaven. However, to declare that the gates of heaven have been thrown open invites further discussion of how entry is secured – that is, of what we are required to do in order to enter paradise. In what follows, we shall consider two general approaches to this question that developed in Christian history, the one stressing the importance of the institution of the church and its sacraments, and the other placing the emphasis upon the personal response of the individual believer. We begin by considering the role of the church in securing entry to paradise.

The Institutionalization of Atonement: The Church as the Gateway to Heaven

The Christian hope of salvation rests upon the death and resurrection of Christ. Yet there remains the question of how that salvation is mediated and appropriated. In the third century of the Christian era, Cyprian of Carthage penned a slogan that would have a decisive impact on Christian understandings of the role of the church as the mediator and guarantor of redemption: "Outside the church, there is no salvation." This pithy maxim was open to a number of interpretations. That which predominated throughout the Middle Ages can be argued to result directly from the growth in the institutional authority of the church after the collapse of the Roman Empire. Salvation was only to be had through membership of the church. Christ may have made the hope of heaven possible; only the church could make it available. There was an ecclesiastical monopoly on the dispensation of redemption.

This theological position was undergirded by new approaches to biblical interpretation that gained ground after the fall of Rome. Increasingly, Western theologians argued that the Bible had four "senses" or meanings. In addition to the *literal* sense of a passage, three deeper *spiritual* meanings could be discerned: the allegorical sense of the passage, referring to a matter of doctrine; the tropological sense, concerning matters of ethics; and the anagogical sense, which pointed to the Christian hope. For Bede, the great early historian of English Christianity, this approach to the interpretation of biblical passages was pregnant with meaning when applied to passages dealing with the Old Testament Temple.

> The temple of the Lord in the literal sense is the house which Solomon built; allegorically, it is the Lord's body or his church . . . tropologically, it is each of the faithful . . . anagogically, it is the joys of the heavenly mansion.

Each of these senses was reflected in medieval reflections on the nature and significance of the church, particularly in developing the connection between the physical structure of a church building and the theological truths which that institution sought to proclaim.

The insight that the institution of the church was the guarantor of the hope of heaven was rapidly assimilated into church architecture. The great portals of Romanesque churches were often adorned with elaborate sculptures depicting the glory of heaven as a tactile affirmation that it was only by entering the church that this reality could be experienced. Inscriptions were often placed over the great west door of churches, declaring that it was only through entering the church that heaven could be attained. The portal was allowed to be identified with Christ for this purpose, speaking words directed to those passing by, or pausing to admire its magnificent ornamentation. An excellent example is provided by the Benedictine priory church of St.-Marcel-lès-Sauze, which was founded in 985 and extensively developed during the twelfth century. The portal to the church depicts Christ addressing these words to all who draw near:

> *Vos qui transitis, qui crimina flerae venitis,*
> *Per me transite quoniam sum ianua vitae.*
> (You who are passing through, you who are coming to weep for your sins, pass through me, since I am the gate of life.)

Although the words are clearly to be attributed to Christ (picking up on the image of Christ as the "gate of the sheepfold" from John 10), a tactile link has been forged with the building of the church itself. This is often reinforced visually through the physical location of the baptismal font close to the door of the church, thereby affirming that entrance to heaven is linked with the sacrament of baptism.

A similar theme is found in the inscription placed over the portal of the Benedictine church of Santa Cruz de la Serós, located close to the main pilgrimage route from Jaca to Puente la Reina in Spain.

Ianua sum perpes; per me transite, fideles.
Fons ego sum vitae; plus me quam vina sitite.
(I am the eternal door; pass through me, faithful ones.
I am the fountain of life; thirst for me more than for
wine.)

The door of the church of San Juan de la Peña, possibly
dating from the twelfth century, bears the following message:

Porta per hanc caeli fit pervia cuique fideli.
(Through this gate, the heavens are opened to every
believer.)

Perhaps the most famous literary variant on this theme
actually constitutes an ironic inversion of its contents. The
third canto of Dante's *Inferno* – the first of the three books
of his *Divine Comedy* – includes a famous description of the
portal of hell, on which are inscribed the words *"Lasciate
ogni speranza voi ch'entrate"* (Abandon hope, all you who
enter here). Dante's description clearly assumes familiarity
with the conventions of ecclesiastical architecture of the
period, and playfully parodies its leading theme.

Once inside the physical body of the church, the relation
between the institution and heaven continued to be em-
phasized. Having declared itself to be the gateway to heaven,
the church now represented heaven to those within its
portals. The rise of Gothic architecture is usually traced
back to the twelfth century, a period of relative political
stability in western Europe which encouraged the rebirth
of art and architecture. Within a period of a century (1130–
1230) some 25 Gothic cathedrals were built in France. One
of the most distinctive features of this architectural style is
its deliberate and programmatic use of height and light to

generate and sustain a sense of the presence of God and heaven on earth. The extensive use of buttresses allowed the weight of the building to be borne by outside supports, thus allowing the external walls to have large glass windows, which ensured that the building was saturated with the radiance of the sun. The use of stained glass helped generate an other-worldly brilliance within the cathedral, while simultaneously allowing Gospel scenes to be depicted to worshipers. The use of tall, thin internal columns created an immense sense of spaciousness, again intended to evoke the hope of heaven. The cathedral thus became a sacred space, bringing the vast spaciousness and brilliance of heaven within the reach of believers. Its worship was seen as an anticipation of the life of heaven, allowing the worshiper to step into another world, to savor its delights, before returning to the dull routines of everyday life.

While it might be a little ambitious to speak of a coherent "theology of the Gothic cathedral," there can be no doubt of the spiritual aspirations of their designers and the importance of their sacred spaces in anticipating their heavenly counterparts. The theological importance of these tactile values is perhaps best explored by considering the ideas of Abbot Suger (1080–1151), who devoted much of his later life to the restoration of the abbey church of Saint-Denis, near Paris. This early example of the classic Gothic style embodies many of its characteristic emphases. Yet perhaps most importantly, Suger's three books of commentary on the renovation process allow us insights into both the physical process of construction, along with the spiritual and aesthetic principles that governed his design. The inscription he placed above the great bronze doors of the church point to his theological interpretation of the sense of radiance and spaciousness he had created within the building:

> *Nobile claret opus, sed opus quod nobile claret*
> *Clarificet mentes, ut eant per lumina vera*
> *Ad verum lumen, ubi Christus ianua vera.*

(The work shines nobly, but the work which shines nobly should clear minds, so that they may travel through the true lights to the true light, where Christ is the true door.)

Although the density of Suger's lines may detract from the points he hoped to make, their general import is unmistakeable: the human mind is to be drawn upward through the light of the building to the true light, who is the enthroned Christ in heaven.

While not all were persuaded by this theology, which placed such emphasis upon the role of the church – considered both as institution and physical structure – as guarantor and visualization of the hope of heaven, there is no doubting its massive impact upon the culture of the Middle Ages and beyond. Yet there were alternatives, and it is important to note their impact upon Western culture. It should cause no surprise that many Protestant writers reacted against what they regarded as an improper emphasis upon the institution of the church, and sought to regain a genuine theological role for the individual soul in the process of salvation. This is best seen in the movement known as "Pietism," to which we now turn.

The Privatization of Atonement: Personal Faith as the Gateway to Heaven

The Pietist movement is usually regarded as having been inaugurated with the publication of Philip Jakob Spener's

Pia desideria ("Pious Wishes," 1675). In this work, Spener lamented the state of the German Lutheran church in the aftermath of the Thirty Years' War (1618–48), and set out proposals for the revitalization of the church of his day. Chief among these was a new emphasis upon personal Bible study. The proposals were treated with derision by academic theologians; nevertheless, they were to prove influential in German church circles, reflecting growing disillusionment and impatience with the sterility of orthodoxy in the face of the shocking social conditions endured during the war. For Pietism, a reformation of doctrine must always be accompanied by reformation of life.

Pietism developed in a number of different directions, especially in England and Germany. Among the representatives of the movement, two in particular should be noted. Nikolaus Ludwig Graf von Zinzendorf (1700–60) founded the Pietist community generally known as the "Herrnhuter," named after the German village of Herrnhut. Alienated from what he regarded as the arid rationalism and barren religious orthodoxy of his time, Zinzendorf stressed the importance of a "religion of the heart," based on an intimate personal relationship between Christ and the believer. A new emphasis was placed upon the role of "feeling" (as opposed to reason or doctrinal orthodoxy) within the Christian life, which may be regarded as laying the foundations of Romanticism in later German religious thought. Zinzendorf's emphasis upon a personally appropriated faith finds expression in the slogan "a living faith," which he opposed to the dead credal assent of Protestant orthodoxy.

These ideas were developed in England by John Wesley (1703–91) and his brother Charles. Convinced that he "lacked the faith whereby alone we are saved," John Wesley discovered the need for a "living faith" and the role of experience in the Christian life through his conversion experience at a meeting in Aldersgate Street, London, in May 1738, in which he felt his heart to be "strangely warmed." Wesley's emphasis upon the experiential side of Christian faith, which contrasted sharply with the dullness of contemporary English Deism, led to a major religious revival in England. His brother Charles underwent a similar conversion experience a day before John, and published a hymn in which he set out his experience. This is widely believed to be the hymn now known as "Where shall my wondering soul begin?", the final verse of which reads as follows:

> For you the purple current flowed
> In pardons from His wounded side,
> Languished for you the eternal God,
> For you the Prince of glory died:
> Believe, and all your sin's forgiven;
> Only believe, and yours is heaven!

The hymn sets out with great clarity the basic conviction that underlies the Pietist worldview – that it is the individual's free decision to repent and admit Christ into the soul that secures the hope of heaven. Wesley thus sees the human heart as the ultimate "gateway to heaven," in that individuals have the final decision as to whether they enter into the heavenly realms. The institution of the church plays no critical role in this process whatsoever, however valuable it may subsequently be as a means of pastoral support and spiritual nourishment.

For those who stand in this tradition, the door through which people enter heaven is not the institution of the church and its attending sacramental system, but personal conversion – a deliberate decision on the part of individuals to throw open the doors of their lives, and admit Christ as a living presence within them – a presence which may be experienced and *felt*. The experience of Christ in the believer's soul serves both as a reassurance of faith, and an anticipation of finally being with Christ in heaven. As Charles stated this point in an often-omitted verse of his famous hymn "O for a thousand tongues":

> In Christ, your head, you then shall know,
> Shall feel your sins forgiven,
> Anticipate your heaven below,
> And own that love in heaven.

Heaven is thus *anticipated* here on earth, but *entered into* in all its fullness only in the life to come.

A similar theme echoes in the conversion poetry of the great American Pietist writer Fanny J. Cosby (1820–1915). For Cosby, heaven was but a distant dream, something whose music was constantly drowned and distorted by the noise of the world and the sinful human inability to love God. In her poem "The Valley of Silence" – written in the year of her death – she set out her experience of receiving a "second blessing" which gave her a new assurance of salvation, reinforcing her hope of heaven. Once more, her new experience of heaven is framed in terms of a personal response to the call of God, which broke down the barriers she had placed in the path of the love of God. The institution of the church is marginalized; her new faith was a matter between her and God alone.

In the present chapter, we have explored some under-standings of how the human longing to see and possess heaven may be satisfied. But why should any such desire arise in the first place? One possible answer, which we shall explore in chapter 5, concerns the consolation that the idea of heaven offers to those who are suffering, bereaved, or in distress. Yet the Christian understanding of the nature of things also offers another explanation – that in some way, we are hard-wired to long for heaven. It is an integral Christian doctrine of creation that humanity is created with an inbuilt longing to re-enter the paradise from which Adam and Eve were dispossessed. We shall explore something of this idea in what follows.

Chapter 4

The Signposting of Heaven: Signals of Transcendence

Christianity offers an account of the world, a *grand récit* that enfolds human history within the ample girth of the story of the creation, fall, redemption, and final consummation of all things. This framework points to a double signposting of heaven in human experience – both in the interior world of longing, in which we are conscious of yearning for something better and deeper than anything we currently know, and in our reflections on the world around us, in which nature seems to hint at another world and another country, presently inaccessible to our senses, yet whose possession alone can satisfy the restless human heart.

One of the most fundamental themes of the Christian worldview is that humanity has been created "in the image of God" (Genesis 1:27), with the endowed capacity to relate to the God who thus created them, and who subsequently redeemed them in Christ. It is not surprising that many theologians – among them, Augustine of Hippo – should draw attention to the consequent human sense of longing, interpreting this as the memory of a lost paradise, and the anticipation of that paradise regained in heaven. As Anselm of Canterbury pointed out during the eleventh century, God purposefully created humanity with the explicit intention of leading them into eternal blessedness, and has therefore made them yearn for that final goal.

Yet the external world of nature also offers a rich tapestry of hints and rumors of a lost paradise and its potential restoration. In an article entitled "Nature as a Parable," Malcolm Muggeridge points out how a Christian understanding of creation is intimately linked to the notion of nature as a sign of the transcendent, pointing beyond itself, conveying something of its creator.

> Everything that happens to us or in connection with us, all the happenings in the world, great and small, the whole exterior phenomenon of nature and of life – all that amounts to God speaking to us, sending out messages in code, and faith is the key whereby we may decipher them. It sounds very simple, but it's somehow difficult to convey exactly . . . Nature is speaking to us. It is a parable of life itself, a revelation of fearful symmetry.

Paradise is thus not merely a misty memory of an event at the dawn of history, nor a distant promised hope; it is something that engages the imagination here and now, partly through the promptings of a richly signed natural order, and partly through the divinely inspired human yearning for transcendence.

This chapter explores the idea of "heaven in ordinarie" (George Herbert), particularly the way in which the baptized imagination is stimulated and controlled by the stimuli of creation. We begin by considering the idea that nature itself offers an anticipation of heaven.

Nature as an Anticipation of Heaven

The New Testament book of the Acts of the Apostles records a sermon preached by Paul before the Athenian Areopagus, possibly around the year 55. It is clear that Luke – widely regarded as the author of Acts – saw this as highly significant, marking the encounter between the Christian gospel and the intellectual capital of the ancient world. Athens had, by this stage, entered into a period of gentle yet seemingly irreversible decline. The once-proud nation of Greece itself had become little more than a province within the Roman empire, having lost its former glory and importance. Nevertheless, the city retained an iconic significance, even if the reality no longer quite matched up to the image that it sought to project.

Yet the Areopagus address can still be seen as representing the confrontation of two understandings of wisdom and knowledge, which would find themselves in conflict for at least a further three hundred years. Noting that the Athenians were well-known for their religiosity, Paul sought to develop an approach to commending the Christian faith that exploited the religious and philosophical curiosity of the Athenians through an appeal to the "sense of divinity" present in each individual, mirrored both in nature and human consciousness. Paul makes particular reference to an altar dedicated "to an unknown god" (Acts 17:23). There are certainly classical precedents for this, especially according to the writings of Diogenes Laertius. Numerous Christian writers of the early patristic period explained Paul's meaning at this point by appealing to the "anonymous altars" that were scattered throughout the region at that time. The fundamental point Paul makes here is that a deity of whom the Greeks had some implicit or intuitive awareness is being made known to them by name and in full. The god who is known *indirectly* through the creation may be known *fully* in redemption. Paul thus explicitly appeals to the creation – to *nature* – as a basis for his apologetic approach. This found a deep resonance with later Christian writers, especially those concerned to make an appeal to nature as a means of gaining insights about God and the riddle of human destiny.

The poetic importance of this theme is particularly clearly set out in the eighth book of Milton's *Paradise Lost*, which describes Adam reflecting on his own origins and destiny. In theologically careful language, Milton broaches the difficult subject of Adam's sense of connection with God, long before this is confirmed by God himself through revelation. The basic idea is that set out in Paul's Areopagus sermon, in which he spoke of a sense of divinity within every human being. For Milton, this sense of divinity was sufficient to allow Adam to perceive that he is not self-generated, but owes his origin to God:

> Not of myself; by some great Maker, then
> In goodness and in power pre-eminent.

Yet it is to the natural order that Adam turns for inspiration and guidance. In a powerful entreaty to nature itself – echoing the language of Acts 17 – Adam begs it to disclose to him his true nature and destiny:

> Tell me, how may I know him, how adore,
> From whom I have that thus I move and live,
> And feel that I am happier than I know.

This specific formulation of an appeal to nature is Milton's; its general features may be found throughout the long history of Christian thought. In some way – and to some extent – the natural order can point to its culmination in heaven.

Others were wary of any such direct appeal to nature, holding that nature had to be viewed in a certain manner in order for its connection with God as its creator to be appreciated. For John Donne, nature and the Christian Bible were as two books with a single author; the former, however, was to be read in the light of the latter. As he put it in *Sermon 8*:

> The voice of the Creature alone is but a faint voice, a low voice; nor any voice, till the Word of God inanimate it; for then when the Word of God hath taught us any mystery of our Religion, then the Book of Creatures illustrates and establishes, and cherishes that which we have received by faith, in hearing the Word.

The longing for heaven that is evoked by nature is held to rest on the anticipation of seeing the creator of the world, who may be dimly glimpsed through the wonders of the created order. The American theologian and preacher Jonathan Edwards made this point in his famous sermon "The Christian Pilgrim," preached in September 1733:

> God is the highest good of the reasonable creature, and the enjoyment of him is the only happiness with which our souls can be satisfied. To go to heaven fully to enjoy God, is *infinitely* better than the most pleasant accommodations here. Fathers and mothers, husbands, wives, children, or the company of earthly friends, are but shadows. But the enjoyment of God is the substance. These are but scattered beams, but God is the sun. These are but streams, but God is the fountain. These are but drops, but God is the ocean.

The intellectual foundations of such approaches had been laid centuries earlier, and rest on the fundamental idea that nature – as God's creation – mirrors the beauty and wisdom of its creator. Thomas Aquinas argues that the beauty of the creation brings about a longing to contemplate the greater beauty of its creator. If we are capable of being deeply moved by the beauty of nature, how much more will we be overwhelmed by the sight of the one who created it.

> Meditation on [God's] works enables us, at least to some extent, to admire and reflect on God's wisdom . . . This consideration of God's works leads to an admiration of God's sublime power, and consequently inspires reverence for God in human hearts . . . If the goodness, beauty and wonder of creatures are so delightful to the human mind, the fountainhead of God's own goodness (compared with the trickles of goodness found in creatures) will draw excited human minds entirely to itself.

Taking delight in nature is thus seen as nourishing our anticipation of beholding God face to face – of satisfying a desire that owes its origins to God, and can only be fulfilled by God. Paradoxically, nature generates a longing that it cannot itself satisfy, and thus leads us to find God and heaven. While this theme is developed by many theologians, perhaps its most systematic application is found in Romanticism and New England Transcendentalism. It is also a significant element in the writings of the metaphysical poets of the seventeenth century. We shall explore both these matters later in this chapter. Yet our attention is now claimed by the intriguing notion that the internal tensions of human love offer a signpost to heaven.

How may humanity transcend itself? One of the most fundamental of human emotions is that of love – the passionate longing for another. For many writers, this profound human emotion is laden with philosophical significance, not least in relation to the perennial question of how humanity may transcend its own limitations, reaching out to embrace something that presently lies beyond its grasp.

The philosophical importance of the idea of the "ascent of love" has been explored in detail by Martha Nussbaum, most recently in her major work *Upheavals of Thought* (2001). Where most philosophers have studiously evaded the philosophical significance of the human emotions, Nussbaum offers a critical exploration of the notion. One of her most central claims is that emotions such as love and grief, far from constituting irrational distractions to the real business of philosophical analysis, are actually to be seen as "intelligent responses to the perception of value."

In an early paper entitled "Augustine and Dante on the Ascent of Love," Nussbaum contrasts the Platonic characterization of the ascent of love, perhaps best known through the Platonic tradition and some of the early writings of Augustine of Hippo, with Christian accounts of the love of God, especially as these are found in Augustine's later writings, such as the *Confessions*. Platonists, according to Nussbaum's account, aim to ascend by means of their intellectual activity to a tranquil, nonerotic state of contemplation. This contrasts with the Augustinian notion of love, in that Christians, being always conscious of their sinful state and of their complete dependence on divine grace, feel more passive and receptive – in other words, experience something that is much closer to the dynamics of a recognizably human love.

Nussbaum clearly has misgivings about the ultimate validity of any human attempt to transcend itself. This is particularly clear from her approbation of James Joyce's *Ulysses*, which she regards as embodying a thoroughly mundane approach to love, which eschews all pretensions to self-transcendence. Joyce, Nussbaum argues, invites his readers "to climb the ladder and yet, at times, to turn it over. . . . Only in that way do we overcome the temptation, inherent in all ideals, to despise what is merely human and everyday."

Yet others have found the human emotion of love to be laden with transcendental import, illuminating both the complexity of the human situation and the means by which it may be transcended. The "ascent of love" is ultimately an invitation to ascend to heaven, in which all that is good about humanity will be at one and the same time retained, yet transfigured. The origins of this quest may indeed be found in Plato, yet its most powerful statements are to be found within the Augustinian tradition.

We may begin by considering an episode from Plato's *Symposium*, which Nussbaum regards as definitive for the human quest for transcendence. This dialogue contains a remarkable speech by Diotima, which explores how a fundamentally erotic notion of love may be transfigured into something more sublime. The passionate human erotic longing for another begins by focusing on the beauty of a human body. Then, by a complex process of abstraction, the lover is invited to turn from the erotic contemplation of the human body to a more elevated contemplation of the "good" and the "beautiful," which the human body imperfectly reflects. Erotic desire mingles a genuine love of beauty with the more base matters of human relationships, such as jealousy, grief, and betrayal. Surely, Diotima argues, it must be possible to abstract what is good and beautiful from human love, and leave its negative aspects behind? More than that: cannot the ultimate human longing for goodness and beauty not be dissociated from the particularities of time and space, in order to allow the mind to rise upwards, toward the contemplation of what is eternally good and beautiful, rather than its imperfect and transitory manifestations?

Plato thus argues for the need to rise upward, moving from the human experience of love toward its true perfection in the eternal world of forms. Nussbaum is critical of Plato at this point, noting that Plato has a pronounced tendency to omit everything about the beloved that is less than ideal, and consequently espoused "an illiberal perfectionist politics." For Nussbaum, the strikingly earthy and fleshly love between Molly and Leonard Bloom is greatly to be preferred, precisely because it is willing to accept – perhaps even to celebrate – the absence of any transcendent referent to love. Yet many have found Plato's notion of an intellectual ascent through love as a defensible and compelling idea, demanding careful examination.

It is not difficult to see how this Platonic ascent of the mind can be developed within a Christian framework. Augustine's concept of Christian love is fundamentally a reworking of this theme, adapted to the distinctive themes of the Christian tradition. A "redeemed love" exists, which can be dissociated not merely from the particularities of the created order – such as time, space, and physical location – but also from the vicissitudes of the sinful human situation. Human flaws and faults, the specifics of history and culture – these can be left behind, as the human heart soars above an erotic longing for another, and finds its true source and goal in God. Human loves are signposts, signals of a transcendent order, which bid humanity to transcend itself intellectually in the present, in order that it may anticipate its ultimate transfiguration in the heavenly city of God. This process of contemplation, triggered off by the complexities of human love, is seen by Augustine as a God-given means through which the human heart may be prepared for its final entry into heaven.

On Augustine's doctrine of creation, there is a clear link between love and a sense of longing. The sighs of the lovesick soul can be compared to the human longing to be with God, as the true object of human desires and passions – an idea that is developed by Dante, with particular reference to his beloved Beatrice. In the *Divine Comedy*, Beatrice acts as the personification of divine grace; Dante's love for her is explicitly described as "a sign of the old flame," pointing to both continuity and transfiguration in a Christian account of the ascent of love. Again, present human experience is to be interpreted as a signal of transcendence, a hint of the lure of heaven to the human soul. This idea has been explored by countless writers; in what follows, we shall consider two seventeenth-century English responses to this theme.

Experience and the Sense of Heaven: Herbert and Traherne

George Herbert's important poem "The Pulley" uses a mechanical analogy to explore the lingering sense of the divine within human experience, and indicate how it may be transformed. The poem draws extensively on a single biblical image for heaven – that of "rest." In view of the importance of this image for Herbert, we may explore it in a little more detail at this point. God, according to the Genesis creation accounts, "rested" on the seventh day, and ordained that humanity should also rest every seventh day as a Sabbath. This idea was developed within the Bible as an image of heaven, which finally provided the eternal "rest" that had been promised to the people of God. The idea is developed with particular force by the Letter to the Hebrews, which affirms that God has promised a "rest" into which believers can hope to enter (Hebrews 4:2–10).

The human longing for rest can thus be interpreted as a secret longing to enter into the promised rest of heaven, in which weary humans can "rest from their labors" (Revelation 14:13). Herbert's basic premise here is that God has created humanity "restless for heaven"; until that goal is achieved, humanity will remain unsatisfied and dislocated. The poem opens by affirming that, in the creation of humanity, God bestowed all manner of blessings upon them, including strength, beauty, wisdom, honor, and pleasure. Yet one gift was withheld – that of rest. God "made a stay" – that is, held back from giving humanity the gift that would have allowed them to become completely self-sufficient and autonomous. Herbert argues that the bestowal of the full complement of gifts would have led to humanity adoring the gifts of God, rather than the God who had given them. The gift of rest remained "in the bottome" (presumably of the treasure-chest from which the others were taken).

At this point, Herbert introduces the analogy of the pulley – a mechanical device that allows a heavy load to be lifted by relatively little force through the use of an often complex series of ropes and wheels. Human exhaustion will be the force that moves the entire human person to the rediscovery of God, rather than the mere taking pleasure in the gifts of God. The human yearning for rest thus becomes the engine that drives the human quest for God, and the final securing of rest in heaven.

> When God at first made man,
> Having a glasse of blessings standing by;
> Let us (said he) poure on him all we can:
> Let the world's riches, which dispersèd lie,
>   Contract into a span.
>
> So strength first made a way;
> Then beautie flow'd, then wisdome, honour, pleasure:
> When almost all was out, God made a stay,
> Perceiving that alone, of all his treasure,
>   Rest in the bottome lay.
>
> For if I should (said he)
> Bestow this jewell also on my creature,
> He would adore my gifts instead of me,
> And rest in Nature, not the God of Nature:
>   So both should losers be.
>
> Yet let him keep the rest,
> But keep them with repining restlesnesse:
> Let him be rich and wearie, that at least,
> If goodnesse leade him not, yet wearinesse
>   May tosse him to my breast.

The linking of the themes of heaven, paradise, childhood innocence, and a sense of the transcendent is particularly well illustrated in the works of Thomas Traherne (1636–74). Traherne's works were not discovered until 1896, two centuries after his death, when a collector browsing through a London bookshop came across the notebook in which they had been scribbled, and realized the importance of what he had discovered. The works were published in two volumes during the years 1903–8. In his *Centuries of Meditations*, Traherne sets out a sequence of perceptions, garnered from the memory of his childhood, in which the imagery of paradise is subtly transformed into a lament for the lost innocence of childhood:

> The corn was orient and immortal wheat, which never should be reaped, nor was ever sown. I thought it had stood from everlasting to everlasting. . . . The city seemed to stand in Eden, or be built in heaven. . . . Certainly Adam in Paradise had not more sweet and curious apprehensions of the world than I when I was a child.

Traherne's poem "Innocence" offers a more subtle and beautiful exploration of this theme. Traherne here describes a glimpse of the transcendent, which overturns and transforms his perceptions of himself and the world in which he lives. The language in which Traherne expresses this experience is saturated with the traditional imagery of heaven, linked with the theme of the restoration of a lost Eden:

> What ere it is, it is a light
> So endless unto me
> That I a world of true delight
> Did then and to this day do see.
> That prospect was the gate of Heav'n, that day
> The ancient light of Eden did convey
> Into my soul: I was an Adam there
> A little Adam in a sphere
> Of joys! O there my ravish'd sense
> Was entertain'd in Paradise,
> And had a sight of innocence

Which was beyond all bound and price.
An antepast of Heaven sure!

Nature as a Signpost of Heaven: Romanticism and Transcendentalism

The origins of Romanticism lie partly in a reaction against a mechanical view of human nature and the world in general. The Scientific Revolution led increasingly to nature being seen as a mechanism. An older view of nature, which held that it possessed an intrinsic status of privilege and dignity, was swept aside. Secularization eliminated both any special divine status of nature, and any human responsibility towards it. This is brought out in C. S. Lewis's perceptive essay entitled "The Empty Universe." Lewis here argued that the secularization of nature led to it being viewed as nothing but the projection of human ideals and longings. There was nothing special about nature, save our subjective perceptions of how it was to be viewed.

> At the outset the universe appears packed with will, intelligence, life and positive qualities; every tree is a nymph, and every planet a god. Man himself is akin to the gods. The advance of knowledge gradually empties this rich and genial universe, first of its gods, then of its colours, smells, sounds and tastes, finally of solidity itself as solidity was originally imagined. As these items are taken from the world, they are transferred to the subjective side of the account; classified as our sensations, thoughts, images and emotions.

Henceforth, human attitudes to nature would be defined on utilitarian grounds – exploit nature while you can; when your own existence is threatened by its degradation, start treating it with greater respect. Humanity has become the measure of all things.

The overall impact of this new understanding of nature was to eliminate any sense that humanity and nature belonged together, or that their destinies were interlocked. Nature was "the other," something to be quantified as one might count coins, weigh out grain, or measure the distance between towns. It was not something to which humans could relate. Nature is a thing, and is "living" only in the sense that a machine generates activity. And the model that seemed to sum up this worldview was to see nature as a clockwork mechanism.

It was against this mechanical view of nature that Romanticism protested. William Blake wrote scathingly of "Bacon, and Newton, sheath'd in dismal steel" – a critical allusion to the cold mechanical ideology of mechanism. In reacting against this view of the world, Blake and his contemporaries viewed nature in vastly elevated terms as the moral and spiritual educator of humanity. In seeking to recover something they believed to have been lost, they inverted the insights of the new mechanical philosophy. This romanticization of nature began in earnest in the late eighteenth century, initially in the writings of German Romantics such as Goethe and Novalis. Yet the trend is probably seen at its most pronounced in English Romanticism. A good example is found in the famous lines from William Wordsworth's "The Tables Turned" (1798):

> One impulse from a vernal wood
> May teach you more of man,
> Of moral evil and of good,
> Than all the sages can.

In his later works, Wordsworth develops the theme of the ability of the natural world to evoke an aching sense of longing for something which ultimately lies beyond it – as in "Tintern Abbey," which uses the poet's experience of a natural landscape to evoke deeper questions about the mystery of human nature and destiny. It seemed as if there was an ecstatic desire for union with nature, or some "sweet melancholy" which seems to have no rational cause, yet is saturated with spiritual meaning.

> The sounding cataract
> Haunted me like a passion: the tall rock,
> The mountain, and the deep and gloomy wood,
> Their colours and their forms, were then to me
> An appetite: a feeling and a love.

There is a strong sense of the loss of connectedness here, a deep and passionate feeling that individuals have become alienated, not merely from nature, but from their true destiny which nature somehow has the capacity to declare – at least in part. The Romantic poets knew a sense of melancholy, wonder, and yearning, which they believed had its basis in the fundamental human displacement or alienation from its true objects of desire. Humanity had become disconnected with its true goals and longings.

In his important work "Intimations of Immortality," composed between March 27, 1802 and March 6, 1804, Wordsworth suggests that the idea of heaven is best appreciated in the innocence of youth, yet is weakened as one grows in cynicism and scepticism.

> Our birth is but a sleep and a forgetting:
> The Soul that rises with us, our life's Star,

Hath had elsewhere its setting,
And cometh from afar:
Not in entire forgetfulness,
And not in utter nakedness,
But trailing clouds of glory do we come
From God, who is our home:
Heaven lies about us in our infancy!
Shades of the prison-house begin to close
Upon the growing Boy,
But He beholds the light, and whence it flows,
He sees it in his joy;
The Youth, who daily farther from the east
Must travel, still is Nature's Priest,
And by the vision splendid
Is on his way attended;
At length the Man perceives it die away,
And fade into the light of common day.

The poem constitutes a complex and evocative exploration of the idea of immortality. Wordsworth himself was quite explicit on the poem's theme. "When I was impelled to write this poem on the immortality of the soul, I took hold of the notion of pre-existence as having sufficient foundation in humanity for authorizing me to make for my purpose the best use of it I could as a poet." God is both the source and destiny of humanity, whose minds are capable of intuiting the sense of liminality that this engenders – that is to say, the idea of standing on the threshold of a new transcendent realm, which is somehow signified by the natural world and yet exceeds anything it can provide.

Nature thus *evokes an anticipation of the transcendent*. This deeply evocative idea is embedded throughout Shelley's "Hymn to Intellectual Beauty," which posits the idea of an intuited higher power, which saturates nature with its presence and beauty:

> The awful shadow of some unseen Power
> Floats though unseen among us, – visiting
> This various world with as inconstant wing
> As summer winds that creep from flower to flower.

The human experience of this beauty may be sporadic, rather than continual; it is, nevertheless, an integral aspect of the phenomenon of nature. Nature is not simply to be investigated and understood as "the other" by detached observers; it is to be encountered and it is to evoke wonder at its sheer beauty by humanity. Nature elicits the memory or knowledge of "some unseen power," whose shadow or reflection can be discerned within its order and structures.

Matthew Arnold (1822–88) hints at this enshrouded memory of heaven in his poem "The Buried Life" (1852). A yearning for heaven, and the immense sense of sadness which its absence evokes, lies only just beneath the surface of human existence, and breaks through from time to time, challenging the settled materialist assumptions of the era.

> But often, in the world's most crowded streets,
> But often, in the din of strife,
> There rises an unspeakable desire
> After the knowledge of our buried life;
> A thirst to spend our fire and restless force
> In tracking out our true, original course;
> A longing to inquire
> Into the mystery of this heart which beats
> So wild, so deep in us – to know
> Whence our lives come and where they go.

Heaven is like a distant land, whose music and fragrance occasionally wafts into our consciousness, and evokes a painful examination of our goals and desires.

> Yet still, from time to time, vague and forlorn,
> From soul's subterranean depth upborne
> As from an infinitely distant land,
> Come airs, and floating echoes, and convey
> A melancholy into all our day.

As Arnold had it in his essay *On the Study of Celtic Literature*, humanity knows a "wistful, soft tearful longing," shrouded in a misty vagueness, yet bringing about emotional turbulence and intellectual passion, in that it impels a quest for its true origins and goals. Where does this yearning come from? And where is this sense of longing leading us? For Arnold, the transcendent origins and ultimate goals of this longing could only lie in God.

Similar themes are developed within New England Transcendentalism, particularly the writings of Ralph Waldo Emerson (1803–82). "Every natural fact is a symbol of some spiritual fact." The human imagination, according to Emerson, is raised to new heights through the impulses it receives from nature.

> One might think the atmosphere was made transparent with this design, to give man, in the heavenly bodies, the perpetual presence of the sublime . . . If the stars should appear one night in a thousand years, how would men believe and adore; and preserve for many generations the remembrance of the City of God which had been shown! . . . But all natural objects make a kindred impression, when the mind is open to their influence.

Nature thus acts as a signpost to the transcendent, evoking human awareness of the sublime hand of God which fashioned the created order itself.

Longing for Heaven: C. S. Lewis

The theme of a "longing for heaven," which is galvanized yet never satisfied by the world around us, saturates the writings of C. S. Lewis. Clive Staples Lewis was born in Belfast, Northern Ireland on November 29, 1898. His father was a solicitor, who was sufficiently successful to allow the family to move to a large house ("Little Lea") on the outskirts of Belfast in 1905. Shortly afterwards, Lewis's mother died, leaving his father to look after Lewis and his elder brother Warren. The two brothers spent hours alone in the vast attic of the old house, inhabiting imaginary worlds of their own making.

After a period serving in the British Army during World War I, Lewis went up to Oxford. He was a student at University College in the period 1919–23, taking first class honors in Greats (classics and philosophy) in 1922, and first class honors in English the following year. After a period during which his future seemed uncertain, he was elected a fellow of Magdalen College in the spring of 1925. He would remain at the college until 1954, when he was invited to take up the newly created chair of Medieval and Renaissance English at Cambridge.

During the 1920s, Lewis had time to reconsider his attitude to Christianity. The story of his return to the faith he abandoned as a boy is described in great detail in his autobiography, *Surprised by Joy*. After wrestling with the clues concerning God that he found in human reason and experience, he eventually decided that intellectual honesty compelled him to believe and trust in God. He did not particularly want to; he felt, however, that he had no choice. The last paragraph of the chapter entitled "Checkmate" in *Surprised by Joy* describing this great moment of decision merits study:

> You must picture me alone in that room at Magdalen, night after night, feeling, whenever my mind lifted even for a second from my work, the steady unrelenting approach of Him whom I so earnestly desired not to meet. That which I greatly feared had at last come upon me. In the Trinity Term of 1929 I gave in, and admitted that God was God, and knelt and prayed: perhaps, that night, the most dejected and reluctant convert in all England.

After his conversion, Lewis began to establish his reputation as a leading authority on medieval and Renaissance English literature. *The Allegory of Love*, published in 1936, is still regarded as a masterpiece, as is his *Preface to Paradise Lost*. Alongside his scholarly writings, however, Lewis wrote books of a very different nature. Aiming at clarity and conviction, Lewis produced a series of works aimed at communicating the reasonableness of Christianity to his own generation. The works brought him popular acclaim, but seemed to some to destroy his scholarly reputation. This was especially the case with *The Screwtape Letters*, which alienated many of his academic colleagues on account of their "populist" or "vulgar" tone. In 1946, he was passed over for the Merton professorship of English Literature at Oxford.

Lewis's first popular book was *The Pilgrim's Regress*, based loosely on John Bunyan's *Pilgrim's Progress*. It was not a great publishing success. Nevertheless, it contained brilliant insights into the human longing for heaven. As Lewis says in the Preface to the Third Edition:

> The experience is one of intense longing . . . This hunger is better than any other fullness; this poverty better than all other wealth. And thus it comes about, that if the desire is long absent, it may itself be desired, and that new desiring becomes a new instance of the original desire . . . The human soul was made to enjoy some object that is never fully given – nay, cannot even be imagined as given – in our present mode of subjective and spatio-temporal experience.

Undeterred by his lack of commercial success, Lewis continued writing at this popular level. *The Problem of Pain*, which appeared in 1940, was well received, and on the basis of its clarity and intelligence of argument, Lewis was invited to give a series of radio talks by the British Broadcasting Corporation. In 1942, these were published as *The Case for Christianity*. Such was their success that Lewis combined them with two other short works – *Christian Behaviour* (1943) and *Beyond Personality* (1944) – to yield the composite work *Mere Christianity*. 1942 also saw the publication of *The Screwtape Letters*, whose wit and insight firmly established Lewis's reputation as a leading defender of the Christian faith, at the cost of estranging many of his academic colleagues in Oxford.

That reputation was consolidated by further works, including *Miracles* (1947) and *The Four Loves* (1960). His seven-volume *Chronicles of Narnia* brought his ideas about Christianity to a wide audience, and opened his writings up to a new generation of readers. Outspokenly critical of "Christianity-and-water" (as he dubbed liberal versions of Christianity), he struck a deep chord of sympathy with his readers. Professional theologians were irritated at Lewis's success, and accused him of simplifying things; Lewis responded by suggesting that, if professional theologians had done their job properly, there would be no need for lay theologians such as himself. His death in 1963 did nothing to stem the growing tide of interest in his writings. In April 1980, *Time* magazine reported that Lewis was unquestionably "this century's most-read apologist for God."

Lewis was deeply aware of the power of the human imagination, and the implications of this power for our understanding of reality. Perhaps one of the most original aspects of Lewis's writing is his persistent and powerful appeal to the religious imagination. Lewis was aware of certain deep human emotions that pointed to a dimension of our existence beyond time and space. There is, Lewis suggested, a deep and intense feeling of longing within human beings, which no earthly object or experience can satisfy. Lewis terms this sense "joy," and argues that it points to God as its source and goal. Its origins lie *in* heaven, and it is intended to draw us *to* heaven. Lewis develops these ideas with particular clarity in his autobiography, *Surprised by Joy*, which is, in part, an extended meditation on the theme of "joy" – as Lewis understands that term – in the imaginative life of humanity.

Lewis explains to his readers how he stumbled across the idea of nature and human experiences as pointers to the transcendent. "Now, for the first time, there burst upon me the idea that there might be real marvels all about us, that the visible world might only be a curtain to conceal huge realms uncharted by my very simple theology." While still a boy, playing around in the vast attics of the family home, Lewis was encountering the idea of a realm beyond experience that was nevertheless signalled by that experience. At this early stage, he found the Wagnerian vision of the cold and clear northern realms of Valhalla a stimulus to his thinking. It would be some time before its Christian counterpart transformed his thinking on the matter.

> Pure "Northernness" engulfed me: a vision of huge, clear spaces hanging above the Atlantic in the endless twilight of Northern summer, remoteness, severity . . . and almost at the same moment I knew that I had met this before, long, long ago . . . And with that plunge back into my own past there arose at once, almost like heartbreak, the memory of Joy itself, the knowledge that I had once had what I had now for years, that I was returning at last from exile and desert lands to my own country; and the distance of the *Twilight of the Gods* and the distance of my own past Joy, both unattainable, flowed together into a single, unendurable sense of desire and loss, which suddenly became one with the loss of the whole experience, which, as I now stared round that dusty schoolroom like a man recovering from unconsciousness, had already vanished, had eluded me at the very moment when I could first say *It is*. And at once I knew (with fatal knowledge) that to "have it again" was the supreme and only important object of desire.

Lewis is clearly reluctant to speculate on the precise character and appearance of heaven. Although his *Great Divorce* offers some reflections on the nature of heaven, his most suggestive accounts of this theme are found in his science fiction trilogy – *Out of the Silent Planet, Perelandra,* and *That Hideous Strength* – published during the period 1938–45, and especially in the *Chronicles of Narnia* (1950–6). Here, we find heaven explored using two controlling metaphors. In *Perelandra*, Lewis asks us to imagine a world without a Fall. Here, there is no fundamental separation between "heaven" and "earth." Paradise has not been lost, so cannot be regained. Heaven can thus be depicted in terms of an innocent and chaste world.

Perhaps more significantly, Lewis develops a second metaphor, grounded in the famous analogy of the cave, found in Plato's dialogue *The Republic*. In *The Silver Chair*, the fourth volume of the Narnia cycle, Lewis develops the idea of an underground kingdom, whose inhabitants have never seen the light of day, or experienced the fresh air and brilliant colors of the natural world. Lewis depicts the re-entry of the two children Jill and Eustace from the subterranean gloom of the Underland to the beauty of the natural world as a paradigm of passing from earth to heaven. As the children "took in great depths of the free midnight air," they experience a transformation of their situation. And for Lewis, this seems to be the most that can responsibly be said about heaven – that it represents the world changed, and made more than real. Lewis put it like this in his sermon "The Weight of Glory."

> At present, we are on the outside of the world, the wrong side of the door . . . We cannot mingle with the splendours we see. But all the leaves of the New Testament are rustling with the rumour that it will not always be so. Some day, God willing, we shall get *in*.

The hope that Lewis sets out is profoundly attractive and consoling. Yet Lewis was hesitant over stressing the comfort that heaven offered. "Most of us find that our belief in the future life is strong only when God is at the centre of our thoughts; that if we try to use the hope of heaven as a compensation (even for the most innocent and natural misery, that of bereavement) it crumbles away." Yet it is undeniable that many find the idea of heaven attractive precisely for the reason that Lewis critiques – namely, that it offers a profound consolation for those who have lost family and friends. In what follows, we shall offer a brief history of this specific aspect of heaven.

Chapter 5

The Consolation of Heaven

Heaven intrigues, consoles, and inspires. On a May morning, possibly in 1362, a poet lay down on a grassy bank, close to England's Malvern Hills. He was already weary with wandering. The gentle babbling of the nearby brook and the soft radiance of the late spring sun soon made him drowsy, and he fell fast asleep. He "began to dream a marvellous dream," in which he was transported from the harsh realities of fourteenth-century English life to another more wonderful realm, far removed from the war-ravaged, plague-ridden, and politically corrupt England that he knew. The vision of heaven set out in William Langland's *Piers Plowman* captured the imagination of city merchants, country gentry, and ecclesiastical reformers. Langland's vision of heaven accentuated the tension between the real world of everyday experience and another world, which was to come – something of which he could dream and for which he could hope, but which lay in the distant future. It consoled his many readers, and spurred some of them to action. Might not at least some of the values of heaven be realized on earth by those who had the vision to pursue them?

Langland's famous dream made a direct appeal to the deep human longing for something better than the world known to the senses. Surely there must be more than this? The vision of heaven that so entranced Langland and his many readers proved to have the power to console those who feel overwhelmed by the sorrow and pain of this life. The great African American spirituals of the 1860s are a powerful and deeply moving witness to the intense consolation derived from dreaming and singing of a better life, which served both as an emotional compensation for present sufferings and grievances, and a stimulus to hope for the future.

To those who feel overwhelmed by "the grey, gritty hopelessness of it all" (D. H. Lawrence), the idea of heaven is as liberating as it is enthralling. Might there not be another country beyond our vision, yet whose distant music we faintly hear in the depths of the night? Or whose fragrance is carried to us by a passing breeze, leaving us longing to know more of this far-off land? And even dare to hope to enter it? Western culture would be immeasurably impoverished without the imaginative stimulus that these lines of thought have provided to countless generations of poets, writers, and thinkers.

The present chapter explains the manner in which the hope of heaven offers a consolation to those facing loss, death, or pain. An integral aspect of the Christian vision of heaven is the absence of the great enemies of humanity: suffering, sorrow, and death will be banished from the new empire into which the faithful will enter. The basic themes of this hope are set out toward the end of the Book of Revelation:

> I saw the holy city, the new Jerusalem, coming down out
> of heaven from God, prepared as a bride adorned for her

husband. And I heard a loud voice from the throne saying, "See, the home of God is among mortals. He will dwell with them; they will be his peoples, and God himself will be with them; he will wipe every tear from their eyes. Death will be no more; mourning and crying and pain will be no more, for the first things have passed away." (Revelation 21:2–4)

So how has this great theme of the consolation of heaven been explored in the Christian tradition, and beyond? We begin by exploring the impact of the Christian vision of heaven on classical Roman culture.

Reunion with Family in Heaven in Early Roman Christianity

The human longing for consolation in the face of death may be traced back to classical times. Perhaps the most distressing aspect of death is that of *separation* – being forcibly, and it might seem irreversibly, cut off from close friends and relatives, never to see them again. Classic mourning rites and funeral ornaments point to the sense of desolation that traditionally accompanied the death of a significant other. The Hellenistic world had become accustomed to the Hades myth, which portrayed Charon as ferrying the dead across the river Styx to the underworld for the fee of one obol – a coin which was placed in the mouth of a dead person for this purpose. Once on the other side, the dead person took part in a family reunion.

This basic belief undergirds two of Cicero's more important dialogues, *On Old Age* and perhaps more importantly *Scipio's Dream*. In this latter work, Cicero portrays Scipio meeting prominent Roman citizens in paradise, who take advantage of the occasion to lecture him on political ethics.

Yet the work takes on a new tone as Cicero describes Scipio's reunion with his father.

> I now saw my dead father, Paulus, approaching, and I burst into tears. My father put his arms around me and kissed me, urging me not to weep. When, with effort, I held back my tears, I managed to say, "Since this, my dear father, is the true life, . . . why must I remain on earth? Why can I not join you?" "That cannot happen," my father replied, "unless God, who rules all you see around you here, frees you from your confinement in the body. Only then can you gain entrance to this paradise. You see, human beings are brought into existence in order to inhabit the earth, which is at the centre of this holy place, this paradise."

This classic scenario of a family reunion in the world to come impacted on Christian writings of the era. Cyprian of Carthage, a martyr-bishop of the third century, tried to encourage his fellow Christians in the face of suffering and death at times of persecution by holding before them a vision of heaven, in which they would see the martyrs and apostles, face to face. More than that; they would be reunited with those who they loved and cherished. Heaven is here seen as the "native land" of Christians, from which they have been exiled during their time on earth. The hope of return to their native land, there to be reunited with those who they knew and loved, was held out as a powerful consolation in times of trial and suffering.

> We should consider that we have renounced the world, and are in the meantime living here as guests and strangers. Let us greet the day which assigns each of us to his own home, which snatches us from this place and sets us free from the snares of the world, and restores us to paradise and the

kingdom. Anyone who has been in foreign lands longs to return to his own native land . . . We regard paradise as our native land. Why do we not hasten and run, that we may behold our country, that we may greet our parents? There a great number of our dear ones is awaiting us, and a dense crowd of parents, brothers, children, is longing for us, already assured of their own safety, and still longing for our salvation. What gladness there will be for them and for us when we enter their presence and share their embrace!

Cyprian himself was martyred for his faith in 258, presumably consoled by precisely the ideas with which he sought to console others.

The motif is also found in Ambrose of Milan's funeral eulogy for the emperor Theodosius, who died in Milan in January 395. Theodosius had earlier had a serious altercation with Ambrose as a result of his decision in 390 to order the slaughter of seven thousand citizens of Thessalonica to avenge the murder of the Roman governor Butheric. Ambrose, having consulted with his fellow bishops, informed Theodosius that he must do severe public penance before being allowed again to receive the sacraments. Theodosius eventually stripped himself of every sign of royalty and publicly repented of his sin. In his funeral oration, Ambrose asked his listeners to imagine the scene in heaven, in which Theodosius embraces his wife Flaccila and his daughter Pulcheria, before being reunited with his father and his predecessor as a Christian Roman emperor, Constantine.

Heaven as an Encounter with God

Attractive though many found the idea of being reunited with colleagues and family in heaven, the concept that began to dominate Christian thinking about heaven in the Middle Ages was that of entering into the glorious and unsurpassable beauty of God. This strongly theocentric conception of heaven did not deny that Christians would be reunited with family and colleagues; rather, it held that such reunions would be overshadowed by the greater beauty and glory of God.

This idea is present in many early Christian writers. Augustine, for example, argued that heaven was characterised by *caritas*, not *cupiditas* – by a spiritual, rather than a physical, love, which drew its inspiration from God. The love of another person was ultimately grounded in a love of God. These ideas were developed further during the Middle Ages. Thomas Aquinas, perhaps the greatest medieval theologian, argued that even if there was only one person in heaven, that person would still be perfectly happy: enjoying God eclipses everything.

Similar lines of thought are developed by Christian mystical writers. Hildegard of Bingen (1098–1179) argued that "God has established heaven in the full joy of heavenly things" in order to bring to perfection the human experience and love of God available in this life. God "wished to bring humanity back to the bliss of heaven" through redemption; yet this "bliss of heaven" could only be experienced to the full in heaven. At best, life on earth could provide an anticipation of the greater joy that the soul experiences on encountering and beholding God to the full. Echoing such thoughts, Jan van Ruysbroeck (1293–1381) wrote that in "meeting the light, the heart experiences so much delight that it cannot contain itself but bursts out in a cry of joy." The human heart already "swims in a state of bliss" when it encounters God in this life, but transcends even this bliss in the rapturous and fuller encounter that awaits believers in heaven.

It was, however, at the time of the Reformation in Western Europe that this theocentric vision of heaven came to dominate Christian thinking. The rise of Calvinism in the sixteenth and seventeenth centuries witnessed the triumph of a God-centered vision of the Christian life, both in the present and future. The *Shorter Westminster Catechism* sets out this vision succinctly with its opening question, which asks: "What is the chief end of man?" Its response? "To glorify God and enjoy him for ever." The present life of faith is thus focused on knowing and glorifying God; this emphasis is carried over into beliefs concerning the life to come.

A classic statement of this strongly theocentric vision of heaven is found in a treatise of the leading Puritan writer Richard Baxter (1615–91). In his *The Saints' Everlasting Rest*, Baxter set out what he regarded as a compelling account of the glories that awaited believers in heaven. Baxter – himself no mean musician or composer of hymns – saw the worship of God as the supreme activity of the saints in heaven. Nothing could distract them from the adoration of the God who had created and redeemed them, and had finally brought them to eternal rest in the heavenly places.

> O blessed employment of a glorified body! to stand before the throne of God and the Lamb, and to sound forth for ever, "Thou art worthy, O Lord, to receive glory, and honour, and power. Worthy is the Lamb that was slain, to receive power, and riches, and wisdom, and strength, and honour, and glory, and blessing; for thou hast redeemed us to God, by thy blood, out of every kindred, and tongue, and people, and nation; and hast made us unto our God kings and priests. Alleluia; salvation, and glory, and honour, and power, unto the Lord our God. Alleluia, for the Lord God omnipotent reigneth." O Christians! this is the blessed rest;

a rest, as it were, without rest; for "they rest not day and night, saying, Holy, holy, holy Lord God Almighty, who was, and is, and is to come." And if the body shall be thus employed, O how shall the soul be taken up! As its powers and capacities are greatest, so its actions are strongest, and its enjoyments sweetest. As the bodily senses have their proper actions, whereby they receive and enjoy their objects, so does the soul in its own actions enjoy its own objects, by knowing, remembering, loving, and delightful joying. This is the soul's enjoyment. By these eyes it sees, and by these arms it embraces.

For Baxter, the human soul is transformed in heaven, equipped to make full use of heaven's sumptuous spaciousness, and liberated from all earthly bondage to lesser goods. At last, humanity is free to do what it was created to do – sing the praises of God for eternity.

As God will have from them a spiritual worship, suited to his own spiritual being, he will provide them a spiritual rest, suitable to their spiritual nature. The knowledge of God and his Christ, a delightful complacency in that mutual love, an everlasting rejoicing in the enjoyment of our God, with a perpetual singing of his high praises; this is heaven for a saint. Then we shall live in our own element. We are now as the fish in a vessel of water, only so much as will keep them alive; but what is that to the ocean? We have a little air let in to us, to afford us breathing; but what is that to the sweet and fresh gales upon Mount Sion? We have a beam of the sun to lighten our darkness, and a warm ray to keep us from freezing; but then we shall live in its light, and be revived by its heat for ever.

Yet not all English spiritual writers of the period were as easily persuaded as Baxter that the saints would be totally overwhelmed by the radiance of God. For Bishop Jeremy Taylor, an integral aspect of the consolation offered by heaven had to do with the fellowship it offered with other Christians. It would indeed be excellent to be able to gaze upon God. However, the Christian with intellectual aspirations could also look forward to some learned theological discussions with Paul and others, presumably in the ample leisure time afforded them by their new surroundings. Heaven would be like an Oxford high table, offering wit, wisdom, and fellowship, while feasting in the presence of God.

If thou wilt be fearless of death endeavour to be in love with the felicities of saints and angels, and be once persuaded to believe that there is a condition of living better than this; that there are creatures more noble than we; that above there is a country better than ours; that the inhabitants know more and know better, and are in places of rest and desire; and first learn to value it, and then learn to purchase it, and death cannot be a formidable thing, which lets us into so much joy and so much felicity. And, indeed, who would not think his condition mended if he passed from conversing with dull tyrants and enemies of learning, to converse with Homer and Plato, with Socrates and Cicero, with Plutarch and Fabricius? So the heathens speculated, but we consider higher. "The dead that die in the Lord" shall converse with St. Paul, and all the college of the apostles, and all the saints and martyrs, with all the good men whose memory we preserve in honour, with excellent kings and holy bishops, and with the great Shepherd and Bishop of our souls, Jesus Christ, and with God himself.

Taylor's vision of heaven was clearly intended to console those who were dying, and who would find solace in the thought of joining the saints in heaven. It was possible to find great consolation in contemplating the future "peace and joy, and all that good which dwells within the house of God and eternal life."

But what if all this were simply a delusion, a fond dream, an invention designed to soften the harsh hopelessness of life? This was the view that came to dominate some circles in the nineteenth century, as the criticism of religion gained pace.

Heaven as a Dream: Feuerbach, Marx, and Freud

The concept of heaven – whether this takes orthodox forms, or their reworked variants – is profoundly consoling. Those who knew only poverty and hunger on earth may anticipate spiritual riches and feasting in heaven. Death may be the great leveler; heaven continues this theme, while reworking it in the most positive of directions. The humble peasant may hope to be clad in the finest silk, and dwell in the opulent courts of the New Jerusalem.

For many skeptical writers of the early nineteenth century, this was pure nonsense, designed to protect the human soul from the threat of extinction and discourage people from changing their situation on earth. Ludwig Feuerbach (1804–72) argued that the human fear of death and longing for immortality was the driving force behind the notion of heaven. The longings were real enough; they were simply objectified or "projected" to give a totally spurious idea of heaven.

Karl Marx took this approach further, arguing that the human longing for eternal life was the result of socioeconomic alienation. This point is set out succinctly in the opening paragraphs of his *Contribution to the Critique of Hegel's Philosophy of Law* (1844):

> Man, who looked for a superhuman being in the fantastic reality of heaven and found nothing there but the *reflection* of himself, will no longer be disposed to find but the *semblance* of himself, only an inhuman being, where he seeks and must seek his true reality. The basis of anti-religious criticism is: *Man makes religion*, religion does not make man. Religion is the self-consciousness and self-esteem of man who has either not yet found himself or has already lost himself again.

Agreeing with Feuerbach that humanity generates religion, Marx insists that the social causes of religion must be identified. The ultimate origins of religion lie in human alienation from their proper mode of existence. To eliminate religious belief, it is necessary to eliminate its cause, which involves the radical change of the world's economic and social systems.

> But *man is* no abstract being encamped outside the world. Man is *the world of man*, the state, society. This state, this society, produce religion, an *inverted world-consciousness*, because they are an *inverted world*. Religion is the general theory of that world, its encyclopaedic compendium, its logic in a popular form, its spiritualistic *point d'honneur*, its enthusiasm, its moral sanction, its solemn complement, its universal source of consolation and justification. It is the *fantastic realisation* of the human essence because the *human essence* has no true reality. The struggle against religion is therefore indirectly a fight against *the world* of which religion is the spiritual *aroma*.

The hope of heaven is thus a spiritual narcotic, dulling humanity to the pain and sorrow of the world. Instead of encouraging people to fight an unjust social order, religion offers them consolation within its existing structures. Religion is thus a socially constructed notion, reflecting the interests and agendas of the ruling classes, which actively discourages the masses from liberating themselves from their tyranny. Heaven enslaves, and dulls the human appetite for radical social change.

This theme was developed by Stalin, in a speech marking the death of Lenin in January 1924.

Slaves and slaveholders, serfs and sires, peasants and landlords, workers and capitalists, oppressed and oppressors – so the world has been built from time immemorial, and so it remains to this day in the vast majority of countries. Scores, nay, hundreds of times in the course of the centuries have the labouring people striven to throw off the oppressors from their backs and to become the masters of their own destiny. But each time, defeated and disgraced, they have been forced to retreat, harbouring in their breasts resentment and humiliation, anger and despair, and lifting up their eyes to an inscrutable heaven where they hoped to find deliverance. The chains of slavery remained intact, or the old chains were replaced by new ones, equally burdensome and degrading. Ours is the only country where the oppressed and downtrodden labouring masses have succeeded in throwing off the rule of the landlords and capitalists and replacing it by the rule of the workers and peasants.

Yet perhaps a more powerful critique of the notion of heaven was set out in the writings of Sigmund Freud. For Freud, ideas such as heaven or God were wish-fulfillments, originating in the unsatisfied longings of the human heart. Religious ideas such as heaven were "illusions, fulfilments of the oldest, strongest and most urgent wishes of mankind," whose origins lay in the hidden psychoses of the human mind. In particular, Freud held that the origins of religion lay in the projection of an ideal father figure – an idea he developed in some detail in *The Future of an Illusion*. Religion is here held to represent the perpetuation of a piece of infantile behavior in adult life. It is fundamentally an immature response to the awareness of helplessness, by going back to childhood experiences of paternal care: "my father will protect me; he is in control." Belief in a personal God is thus little more than an infantile delusion. Religion is wishful thinking, an illusion. Freud's vigorous atheism appears to have preceded rather than followed his analysis of the origins of religious ideas, so that they can in some ways be seen as *post hoc* explanations of his own atheism.

Intellectually, there is a direct continuity from Feuerbach to Freud through Marx, in that all agree that religious ideas are generated by humanity by processes that are scientifically explicable, and are designed to offer humanity a false hope against the bleakness of life. Other writers offered additional reasons for accepting this Feuerbachian critique of religion in general, and heaven in particular. The hope of heaven, it was argued, led to war among the nations; abandoning belief in heaven would lead to a more peaceful and stable world. That, at least, was the judgment of John Lennon (1940–80), whose song "Imagine" invited its audiences to envisage an ideal world, devoid of conflict and with no heaven or hell. By eliminating religious, political, social, and economic differences, humanity would finally be able to achieve unity. The song was released on 9 September 1971 in the United States, and achieved an instant resonance with the *Zeitgeist*, then dominated by the Vietnam conflict and the rise of the Peace Movement. Beliefs were firmly identified as the enemy of peace. Sadly, Lennon was shot dead in New York on December 8, 1980, a victim of his own fame, rather than of any specific religious beliefs.

Intellectually and politically important though this Feuerbachian line of thought proved to be, it was not one that was universally accepted, either in the nineteenth century or beyond. For many, the thought of heaven continued to be a true source of comfort for those in the "valley of death." Yet if the nineteenth century saw the retention of the vision of heaven as a consolation for earth's sorrows, it did not articulate that vision in terms of the Puritan notion of a God-centered heaven. The classic Roman theme of reunion with family and close colleagues began to enjoy a new lease of life, as we shall see.

Heaven as an Encounter with Loved Ones

Richard Baxter's thoroughly theocentric vision of heaven commanded wide respect throughout English and American Puritan circles, and was highly influential in shaping mainstream Protestant understandings of the matter in the nineteenth century. Yet there were many who found this vision of heaven to be unattractive, even repellent. This is especially evident from a remarkable new genre of literature that emerged in the United States in the aftermath of the American Civil War, which witnessed unprecedented casualties and provoked scenes of distress and mourning throughout the nation. A new interest in spiritualism flourished, as anguished families sought to re-establish contact with relatives who had died on the field of battle.

One of the most influential examples of this new "consolation literature" was penned by Elizabeth Stuart Phelps (1844–1911) at the age of 24 years. *The Gates Ajar* (1868) tells of Mary Cabot, a New England woman who is trying to come to terms with the death of her brother, Roy, in the Civil War. While believing that Roy has gone to heaven, she finds herself repelled by the predominant Puritan doctrine of the form he assumes in this new abode, and consequently her altered relation to him:

> I know nothing about heaven. It is very far off. In my best and happiest days, I never liked to think of it. If I were to go there, it could do me no good, for I should not see Roy. Or if by chance I should see him standing up among the grand, white angels, he would not be the old dear Roy.

What Mary longs for is a restoration of her relationship with Roy. She initially seeks help from her Calvinist pastor – who bears the glorious name of Dr. Bland – but is thoroughly dissatisfied with the consolation he offers. Dr. Bland offered Mary "glittering generalities, cold commonplace, vagueness, unreality, a God and a future at which I sat and shivered." What appears to have distressed Mary was the emotional frigidity and impersonal nature of the New Jerusalem promised by Protestant Orthodoxy:

> There was something about adoration, and the harpers harping with their harps, and the sea of glass, and crying "Worthy the Lamb!" And a great deal more than that bewildered and disheartened me so that I could scarcely listen to it. I do not doubt that we shall glorify God primarily and happily, but can we not do it in some other way than by harping and praying?

Who can miss the echoes of Baxter in this critique?

Mary's dissatisfaction with this strongly theocentric conception of heaven is both crystallized and resolved by her aunt, Winifred Forceythe. Upon being told by the well-meaning Deacon Quirk that heaven amounts to the eternal singing of God's praises, Aunt Winifred unleashes a withering barrage of common sense against the idea of disembodied souls and against the literal reading of the Book of Revelation. Heaven, she is quite clear, is fundamentally an extension of the manners and modalities of the present age, including its network of human relationships.

> [Eternity] cannot be the great blank ocean which most of us have somehow or other been brought up to feel that it is, which will swallow up, in a pitiless glorified way, all the little brooks of our delight. So I expect to have my beautiful home, and my husband, and [my daughter] Faith, as I had them here; with many differences, and great ones, but *mine* just the same.

Aunt Winifred went on to portray heaven in terms of an intensification of the beauties of nature ("glorified lilies of the valley, heavenly tea bud roses, and spiritual harebells") and of human culture ("whole planets turned into works of art"). Heaven, it turns out, is like an extended nineteenth-century family, in which little children are busy "devouring heavenly gingersnaps" and playing rosewood pianos, while the adults listen to learned discourses from glorified philosophers and the symphonies of Beethoven.

Phelps's account of what she believed to lie beyond the gates of Heaven clearly captivated her readers, if the sales of the book are anything to go by. *The Gates Ajar* can be seen to mirror a deepening disquiet within an increasingly sophisticated North American culture concerning the traditional images of heaven, which seemed – at least, to this public – to be cold, impersonal, and unattractive. The materialist vision of heaven she offered in its place retained many aspects of the traditional Christian doctrine, while subtly altering it at critical junctures – not least, in stressing the continuity of individuals, relationships, and environments between this life and the next.

Yet Phelps's highly populist alternative vision of heaven had its rivals, not least from those who believed that the focus of the heavenly life was neither the praise of God nor the reconnection with family and friends, but with the reunion of lost lovers. Dante Gabriel Rossetti's poem *The Blessed Damozel* (1850) represents a remarkable reworking of the traditional Christian vision of paradise, based partly on Dante's *Vita Nuova*. A further influence upon Rossetti at this point were the writings of Edgar Allen Poe. Poe's poem "The Raven" was cited by Rossetti as an influence in 1881: "I saw that Poe had done the utmost it was possible to do with the grief of the lover on earth, and so I determined to reverse the conditions, and give utterance to the yearning of the loved one in heaven." However, the poem may also owe something to Poe's "To One in Paradise," which deals with the grief of the lover on earth.

Where Plato saw heaven as the realm of a nonerotic and idealized love, Rossetti was quite clear that heaven is about the erotic reunion of lovers. *Damozel* opens with its heroine leaning out "from the gold bar of heaven," looking and longing for her beloved. The "gold bar" is here seen both as a support for the damozel (an archaic form of "damsel," by the way) as she looks downward, and a barrier that separates her from her beloved, and prevents her from seeing or touching him.

> It was the rampart of God's house
>   That she was standing on;

By God built over the sheer depth
　　The which is Space begun;
So high, that looking downward thence
　　She scarce could see the sun.

Though in heaven, the damozel is lonely and despond-
ent. The presence of God and the saints is not enough to
console her. The pain of separation from the "heart-
remembered name" is unbearable, and her thoughts turn
to anticipating the restoration of both her love and lover.
Mingling Edenic and Dantean themes, she visualizes their
joyful reunion. Although the presence of God shapes the
context in which that love is expressed, the love is primarily that of the two persons for each other, whose mutual
care overshadows the opulence of their surroundings and
the (implied and assumed) love of God for them.

I wish that he were come to me,
　　For he will come, she said.
Have I not pray'd in Heaven? – on earth,
　　Lord, Lord, has he not pray'd?
Are not two prayers a perfect strength?
　　And shall I feel afraid?

When round his head the aureole clings,
　　And he is clothed in white,
I'll take his hand and go with him
　　To the deep wells of light,
And we will step down as to a stream,
　　And bathe there in God's sight.

As the poem draws to its close, the damozel sets out
the prayer she hopes to bring to the risen Christ, as she
approaches the heavenly throne. The prayer is simply that

the couple may know the same bliss they experienced on earth – but this time, without the fear of separation.

There will I ask of Christ the Lord
   Thus much for him and me: –
Only to live as once on earth
   At peace – only to be
As then awhile, for ever now
   Together, I and he.

Consolation is thus to be had through the anticipation of joy in heaven – but a joy that is not occasioned primarily by the glory of God or the risen Christ. The damozel is lonely, sad and restless until the love of her life is restored to her.

Rossetti went on to express this poetic vision in his famous painting *The Blessed Damozel* (1879). His sketches of some of the finer details of the work have survived, allowing an appreciation of the sensuousness of his conception of the heavenly reunion. The lovers come together in an amorous embrace that clearly goes beyond what many orthodox writers would regard as a proper celestial activity. Far from being lost in the praise of God, the lovers are absorbed in and with each other. Consolation thus arises through being reunited with loved ones in God's presence, rather than entering into the divine presence itself.

African American Spirituals

Finally, we must turn from the rather comfortable world of middle-class Victorian London to another situation, in which the theme of the consolation of heaven played a major

Dante Gabriel Rossetti, detail of sketch for background of *The Blessed Damozel*, 1876. Fogg Art Museum, Harvard University, Cambridge, Massachussets.

cultural role. The immense hardships and deprivations faced by the Black population of the southern American states in the period before the American Civil War and in its immediate aftermath are well known. We have already noted how this context gave rise to a highly significant "consolation literature," affirming that heaven was about the restoration of personal relationships. Yet out of this deep encounter with pain, suffering, and poverty also arose one of the world's most valued art forms – the spiritual.

These spiritual songs reassured their communities of their identity as a people chosen by the Lord. Just as the Lord fought for Moses and the Israelites and brought them out of their land of captivity, so the Lord would deliver them, and force their overseers to let his people go. And if they were not delivered from bondage while still living and suffering in this world, there remained the great hope of freedom and delivery from pain and sorrow in the heavenly Promised Land, which was where they believed they were headed. Their songs set out in simple words the genuine spiritual realities and hopes of an unseen world, which lay in the future yet impacted upon their hopes and fears in the present. Noting this, James Weldon Johnson commented: "The Negro took complete refuge in Christianity, and the Spirituals were literally forged of sorrow in the heat of religious fervor. They exhibited, moreover, a reversion to the simple principles of primitive, communal Christianity."

In June 1867, Thomas Wentworth Higginson penned an article for the *Atlantic Monthly*, in which he wrote of the songs that emerged from this long-suffering people.

> Often in the starlit evening I have returned from some lonely ride by the swift river, or on the plover-haunted barrens,

and, entering the camp, have silently approached some glimmering fire, round which the dusky figures moved in the rhythmical barbaric dance the negroes call a "shout," chanting, often harshly, but always in the most perfect time, some monotonous refrain.

Higginson found the words of these songs deeply moving. It was as if they offered a balm, a consolation for sorrow, often closely linked with the articulation of the hope of heaven. He drew particular attention to "an infinitely quaint description of the length of the heavenly road" which he found in a song known as "O'er the Crossing":

> Yonder's my old mudder,
>   Been a-waggin' at de hill so long.
> It's about time she'll cross o'er;
>   Get home bimeby.
> Keep prayin', I do believe
>   We're a long time waggin' o'er de crossin'.
> Keep prayin', I do believe
>   We'll get home to heaven bimeby.
>
> Hear dat mournful thunder
>   Roll from door to door
> Calling home God's children;
>   Get home bimeby.
> Little chil'en, I do believe
>   We're a long time, &c.
> Little chil'en, I do believe
>   We'll get home, &c.
>
> See dat forked lightnin'
>   Flash from tree to tree
> Callin' home God's chil'en;
>   Get home bimeby.

True believer, I do believe
  We're a long time, &c.
O brudders, I do believe
  We'll get home to heaven bimeby.

Like some of the great medieval hymns celebrating the joys of the New Jerusalem, this spiritual song reassured its audience of the certainty of heaven, and the bringing to an end of this life of sorrow and tears.

Higgington also drew attention to the song "Walk 'em easy," which he described as one of the "most singular pictures of future joys":

O, walk 'em easy round de heaven,
Walk 'em easy round de heaven,
Walk 'em easy round de heaven,
  Dat all de people may join de band.
Walk 'em easy round de heaven. (*Thrice*)
  O, shout glory till 'em join dat band!

Once more, the song sets out a confident and positive vision of the future, in which the future hope of heaven is seen as compensating for the sadnesses of the present.

Yet a criticism may be noted here. Is not the spirituality set out in these spirituals precisely that critiqued by Karl Marx – namely, that the consolation offered by heaven served as a disincentive to action on earth? That the hope of a promised land in the future discouraged engagement with political issues here on earth? While this might well constitute a potential weakness, the development of the African American tradition strongly suggests that it need not. Many of the sermons of the great African American civil rights leader Martin Luther King (1929–68) illustrate – *contra* Marx – how the theme of the Christian hope can be linked with a call to direct political action. King's final sermon was delivered on April 3, 1968, the day before his assassination, at the Mason Temple in Memphis, Tennessee (the headquarters of the largest African American pentecostal denomination in the United States). The sermon is saturated with calls to action, coupled with a strong affirmation of the importance of the hope of heaven in the future, linked with the imagery of the promised land. The sermon ends as follows:

> We've got some difficult days ahead. But it doesn't matter with me now. Because I've been to the mountaintop. And I don't mind. Like anybody, I would like to live a long life. Longevity has its place. But I'm not concerned about that now. I just want to do God's will. And He's allowed me to go up to the mountain. And I've looked over. And I've seen the promised land. I may not get there with you. But I want you to know tonight that we, as a people will get to the promised land. And I'm happy, tonight. I'm not worried about anything. I'm not fearing any man. Mine eyes have seen the glory of the coming of the Lord.

It will be clear from the brief discussion presented in this chapter that the hope of heaven is – and is meant to be – immensely consoling in the face of life's pain and sadness. Yet this raises a question, which we must address in the final chapter of this book. If this hope of heaven is so important to Christian life and thought, how can it be sustained?

Chapter 6

Journey's End: Heaven as the Goal of the Christian Life

For the theologians and spiritual writers of the Christian tradition, the fragrance of the "hope of heaven" saturates the routines of everyday life, and injects a sense of anticipation and expectation into our thoughts and hopes. Joseph Addison (1672–1719), the noted eighteenth-century Anglican poet, journalist, and fellow of Magdalen College, was well aware of the importance of this sense of something that lies beyond our experience, yet somehow breaks through. It comes from God, and points to God.

> It must be so – Plato, thou reason'st well!
> Else whence this pleasing hope, this fond desire,
> This longing after immortality?
> Or whence this secret dread, and inward horror,
> Of falling into naught? Why shrinks the soul
> Back on herself, and startles at destruction?
> 'Tis the divinity that stirs within us;
> 'Tis heaven itself, that points out an hereafter,
> And intimates eternity to man.
> Eternity! thou pleasing, dreadful thought!

Addison suggests that this "longing after immortality" is itself a pointer to the hereafter – and in doing so, picks up one of the great themes of Christian theology from Augustine through Pascal through to a more recent theologian associated with Magdalen College – the literary critic and novelist C. S. Lewis. Our theme in this final chapter concerns how the hope of heaven – that is, the fundamental Christian conviction that this "longing after immortality" is no delusion, no fantasy, but is rather something that corresponds to a reality that awaits us – is maintained and developed in the everyday life of faith.

Inevitably, this means turning our attention briefly to the whole area of spirituality, which figures prominently in this final chapter.

The Concept of Spirituality

The word "spirituality" draws on the Hebrew word *ruach* – a rich term usually translated as "spirit," yet which includes a range of meanings that certainly includes "spirit," yet extends far beyond to embrace such ideas as "breath" and "wind." To talk about "the spirit" is to discuss what gives life and animation to someone. "Spirituality" is thus about the life of faith – what drives and motivates it, and what people find helpful in sustaining and developing it. It is about that which animates the life of believers, and urges them on to deepen and perfect what has at present only been begun.

Spirituality is the outworking in real life of a person's religious faith – what a person *does* with what they believe. Christianity is not just about ideas, although the basic ideas of the Christian faith are of no small importance to Christian spirituality. It concerns the way in which the Christian life is conceived and lived out, with its ultimate goal being the full apprehension of the reality of God. Christian spirituality is reflection on the whole Christian enterprise of achieving and sustaining a relationship with God, which includes both public worship and private devotion, and the results of these in actual Christian life.

The term "spirituality" has gained wide acceptance recently as the preferred way of referring to aspects of the devotional practices of a religion, and especially the interior individual experiences of believers. It is often contrasted with a purely academic, objective, or detached approach to religion, which is seen as merely identifying and listing the key beliefs and practices of a religion, rather than dealing with the manner in which individual adherents of the religion experience and practice their faith. The term is resistant to precise definition, partly due to the variety of senses in which the term is used, and partly due to controversy within the community of scholars specializing in the field over the manner in which the term ought to be used.

Traditional Christian theology draws a distinction between two senses of the term "faith." On the one hand, there is the "faith which is believed" – that is, the body of Christian doctrines to which the individual Christian gives assent. This can be regarded as the domain of Christian theology, which makes its appeal to the mind. On the other, there is the "faith which believes" – in other words, the human activity of trusting, longing, and accepting, which can fluctuate in its intensity from day to day. Spirituality aims to sustain and support faith in this second sense of the word, and does so through an appeal to the reason, emotions, and imagination.

Before moving on to explore the relation between heaven and spirituality, we shall lay down briefly some theological foundations for sustaining this celestial hope.

The Hope of Heaven: Theological Foundations

Christianity is a religion of hope, which focuses on the resurrection of Jesus as the grounds for believing and trusting in a God who is able to triumph over death, and give hope to all those who suffer and die. The word "eschatology" is used to refer to Christian teachings about the "last things" (Greek: *ta eschata*). Just as "Christology" refers to the Christian understanding of the nature and identity of Jesus Christ, so "eschatology" refers to the Christian understanding of such things as heaven and eternal life.

The eschatology of the New Testament is complex. However, a leading theme is that something that happened in the past has inaugurated something new, which will reach its final consummation in the future. The Christian believer is thus caught up in this tension between the "now" and the "not yet." In one sense, heaven has not yet happened; in another, its powerful lure already impacts upon us in a dramatic and complex fashion, in which we are at one and the same time excited at its prospect and rendered dejected through knowing that we are not yet there.

The term "heaven" is used frequently in the Pauline writings of the New Testament to refer to the Christian hope. Although it is natural to think of heaven as a future entity, Paul's thinking appears to embrace both a future reality and a spiritual sphere or realm that coexists with the material world of space and time. Thus "heaven" is referred to both as the future home of the believer (2 Corinthians 5:1–2, Philippians 3:20) and as the present dwelling-place of Jesus Christ, from which he will come in final judgment (Romans 10:6, 1 Thessalonians 1:10, 4:16). One of Paul's most significant statements concerning heaven focuses on the notion of believers being "citizens of heaven" (Philippians

3:20), and in some way sharing in the life of heaven in the present. The tension between the "now" and the "not yet" is evident in Paul's statements concerning heaven, making it very difficult to sustain the simple idea of heaven as something that will not come into being until the future, or that cannot be experienced in the present.

Probably the most helpful way of conceiving the modest New Testament affirmations concerning heaven is to see it as a consummation of the Christian doctrine of salvation, in which the presence, penalty, and power of sin have all been finally eliminated, and the total presence of God in individuals and the community of faith has been achieved. Some such idea underlies the vision of heaven set out in the *Catechism of the Catholic Church*:

> Heaven is the ultimate end and fulfilment of the deepest human longings, the state of supreme, definitive happiness. . . . this consummation will be the final realization of the unity of the human race, which God willed from creation and of which the pilgrim Church has been "in the nature of sacrament." Those who are united with Christ will form the community of the redeemed, "the holy city" of God, "the Bride, the wife of the Lamb." She will not be wounded any longer by sin, stains, self-love, that destroy or wound the earthly community. The beatific vision, in which God opens himself in an inexhaustible way to the elect, will be the ever-flowing well-spring of happiness, peace, and mutual communion.

It should be noted that the New Testament parables of heaven are strongly communal in nature, for example, heaven is portrayed as a banquet, a wedding feast, or as a city – the new Jerusalem. Eternal life is thus not a projection of an individual human existence, but is rather to be seen as sharing, with the redeemed community as a whole, in the community of a loving God.

Yet as we have stressed, the Christian concept of heaven is iconic, rather than intellectual – something that makes its appeal to the imagination, rather than the intellect, which calls out to be visualized rather than merely understood. It is for this reason that the place of Christian worship is of such importance in connection with Christian understandings of heaven.

The Appeal to Worship: Heaven on Earth

It is impossible to understate the place of worship in sustaining the Christian life. Especially within the Greek Orthodox tradition, the public worship of the church represents a drawing close to the threshold of heaven itself, and peering through its portals to catch a glimpse of the worship of heavenly places. The Orthodox liturgy celebrates the notion of being caught up in the worship of heaven, and the awesome sense of mystery that is evoked by the sense of peering beyond the bounds of human vision.

A biblical text that has played no small part in shaping this immense respect for mystery in worship may be noted here. The sixth chapter of the prophecy of Isaiah relates the call of the prophet, portraying him as undergoing a liminal experience as he enters the "holy of holies":

> In the year that King Uzziah died, I saw the Lord sitting on a throne, high and lofty; and the hem of his robe filled the temple. Seraphs were in attendance above him; each had six wings: with two they covered their faces, and with two they covered their feet, and with two they flew. And one

called to another and said: "Holy, holy, holy is the LORD of hosts; the whole earth is full of his glory." The pivots on the thresholds shook at the voices of those who called, and the house filled with smoke. And I said: "Woe is me! I am lost, for I am a man of unclean lips, and I live among a people of unclean lips; yet my eyes have seen the King, the LORD of hosts!" (Isaiah 6:1–5)

The central insight that many theologians gleaned from this passage is that human beings are simply not capable of beholding the worship of heaven itself; it must be accommodated to their capacity through being reflected in created things – such as the created order, the sacramental bread and wine, or the liturgy itself.

To share in worship is thus to stand in a holy place (Exodus 3:5) – a place in which humanity, strictly speaking, has no right to be. Whenever the divine liturgy is celebrated on earth, the boundaries between heaven and earth are removed, and earthy worshipers join in the eternal heavenly liturgy chanted by the angels. During these moments of earthly adoration, worshipers have the opportunity of being mystically transported to the threshold of heaven. Being in a holy place and about to participate in holy things, they on the one hand become aware of their finitude and sinfulness, and on the other gain a refreshing glimpse of the glory of God – precisely the pattern of reflection set out in Isaiah's vision.

The association between worship and heaven is often enhanced musically. Just as Gothic churches embodied a sense of the spaciousness of heaven, allowing and encouraging worshipers to visualize the worship of heaven, so the judicious use of music has widely been held to bring about a corresponding effect. It is difficult to make this point purely verbally, without listening to the music itself. However, to listen to the *Vespers* (1915) of Sergei Rachmaninoff (1873–1943), or the motets "*Assumpta est Maria*" and "*Missa Assumpta est Maria*" of Giovanni Pierluigi da Palestrina (c.1525–94) is to gain something of an appreciation of how the vision of heaven can be mediated musically in worship.

The idea of liminality – that is, being on the threshold of the sacred, peering into the forbidden heavenly realms – is represented visually in the structure of Orthodox churches, especially the way in which the sanctuary and the altar are set apart from the people on account of a deep sense of the awesomeness of the mystery of God. In their treatises on worship, Chrysostom and other Greek patristic writers repeatedly draw attention to the liturgical importance of this sense of the sacred. The altar is the "terrifying table"; the bread and the wine are "the terrifying sacrifice of the body and blood of Christ which worshippers must approach with fear and trembling." For the Orthodox, there is an especially close link between the eucharist – the sacrament celebrated with and through bread and wine – and the experience of the worship of heaven. To explore this further, we may turn to explore the first of a series of biblical images of central importance to Christian spirituality, as it engages with the hope of heaven – the image of a feast.

Feasting in the Kingdom

Reading the biblical text and meditation upon it has been of central importance to Christians down the ages. It should therefore be no surprise to learn that many biblical images have exercised a controlling influence over Christian spirituality. It is much easier to reflect upon an image than upon an idea. In what follows, we shall explore four biblical images of heaven that have been of central importance to Christian spirituality, and note the way in which they have been deployed and developed within the tradition.

Jesus frequently compared the kingdom of God to a feast – perhaps like a great banquet thrown in celebration of a marriage (Luke 14:15–24). When the prodigal son returned to his father (Luke 15:11–24), the father threw a feast in celebration of the safe return of the son who he had believed to be lost. This theme is of importance to spirituality, partly on account of the light that it casts on the Christian faith itself, and partly on account of what it suggests needs to be done to advance in that faith.

The image of a feast suggests a number of interlocking themes. In the first place, the image points to an abundance of food and drink, which are capable of meeting and satisfying human hunger. A leading theme of the Christian understanding of human nature is that it has been created for fellowship with God, and is empty until and unless this relationship with God has been established. The image also points to the notion of invitation. A feast is something to which people have to be *invited* before they can share in the rejoicing and feasting. Jesus Christ himself ate at table with those who contemporary Jewish society regarded as social outcasts, making the point that these unfortunate people were welcomed and accepted into his presence. Feasting is about being wanted and welcomed into the presence of someone of dignity and importance. It is a profoundly affirming matter. Finally, feasting is about celebration and rejoicing. A feast is arranged to mark an occasion of importance, such as a wedding, so that all those who know and love those who are to be married may share in and express their joy and delight.

Each of these themes is developed within Christian spirituality, especially in relation to the eucharist. While the bread and the wine remind us of both a human need (spiritual hunger and thirst) and the manner in which the gospel is able to identify and meet those needs, it is important to note the eschatological elements of this sacrament. The eucharist is directed toward the Christian hope. The "feasting" image finds its fulfillment in the vision of "the marriage supper of the Lamb" (Revelation 19:9), of which the eucharist is seen as a foretaste in the present. The Second Vatican Council spoke of the eucharist as a "foretaste of the heavenly banquet," where John Wesley (1703–91) had earlier referred to it as a "pledge of heaven". The basic theme is that heaven is to be a place of rejoicing and plenty, into which those who worship on earth at present shall be welcomed in the future. The celebration of the Lord's Supper in the present is thus both an important reminder of what happened in the past (the death and resurrection of Christ) but also an assurance of what will happen in the future (being welcomed and received into the presence of the living God). This point is made particularly clearly by the great patristic writer Theodore of Mopsuestia (c. 350–428), who wrote as follows (note the echoes of the "awesome mysteries" of faith):

> Every time that the liturgy of this awesome sacrifice is performed, which is the clear image of the heavenly realities, we should imagine that we are in heaven . . . Faith enables us to picture in our minds those heavenly realities, as we remind ourselves that the same Christ who is now in heaven is [also present] under these symbols. So when faith enables our eyes to contemplate what now takes place, we are brought again to see his death, resurrection and ascension, which have already taken place for our sakes.

For Theodore, the eucharist allows worshipers to look both *backward* and *forward*. Retrospectively, they are reminded of Christ's death and resurrection for us; prospectively, they can begin to imagine themselves in heaven, where Christ can be seen in all his glory. The Christ who is seen dimly through the sacramental symbols will then be revealed in all his glory and wonder. Then the sign and symbol will be rendered unnecessary, when believers finally enter into the presence of the risen Christ. They are thus encouraged to look forward to that day with eager expectation.

Journeying to the Promised Land

The image of a journey is perhaps one of the most important way of stimulating the Christian imagination, and sustaining the hope of heaven. Both Old and New Testaments depict journeys, such as Abraham's journey to Canaan, or Paul's great missionary journeys. Perhaps the two most important journeys described in the Old Testament are the wandering of the people of Israel through the wilderness for forty years prior to entering into the Promised Land, and the return of the people of Jerusalem to their native city after decades of exile in the great city of Babylon. Each of these journeys has become an image of considerable importance for Christian spirituality.

It will thus come as no surprise to learn that one of the most powerful images of the Christian life is that of a journey. Indeed, the New Testament records that the early Christians initially referred to themselves as followers of "the way" (see, e.g., Acts 9:2, 24:14). Just as God led the people of Israel out of captivity in Egypt into the Promised

Land, so the Christian life can be seen as a slow process of deliverance from bondage to sin before being led triumphantly into the heavenly city.

At several points in the writings of St. Paul, a modification is introduced to the image of a journey. For Paul, the Christian life is like a race – a long and arduous journey, undertaken under pressure, in which the winners receive a crown (see Galatians 2:2, 2 Timothy 4:7–8). The image is also used in the Letter to the Hebrews, which urges its readers to persevere in the race of life by keeping their eyes focused firmly on Jesus (Hebrews 12:1–2). This image stresses the importance of discipline in the Christian life.

The theme of the hope of heaven, and especially the consummation of all things in the heavenly Jerusalem, is of major importance in Christian spirituality. In the medieval period, the Latin term *viator* (literally, a "wayfarer") was used to refer to the believer, who was envisaged as a pilgrim traveling to the heavenly city. The vision of the heavenly city was seen as an encouragement and inspiration to those engaged on this pilgrimage. Many writings of the period direct the believer to focus attention on the glorious hope of final entry into the New Jerusalem, and the rejoicing and delight that this will bring. Such thoughts were widely regarded as an encouragement, enabling believers to deal with the disappointments and hardships that were so often their lot.

The metaphor of "journeying to heaven" thus has a long history of use within the Christian tradition. Often, this is specifically linked with the idea of life as a "pilgrimage to the New Jerusalem" – as in Guillaume de Deguileville's *Pelerinage de Vie Humaine* (1330–1). Chaucer's *Canterbury Tales* can also be seen as falling into this category. Although Chaucer's witty account of an often scurrilously venal group of pilgrims traveling from London to Canterbury can be read as a stinging commentary on the social conditions of the time, the work undergoes a subtle transformation as the pilgrims near Canterbury. The bawdy tale is subverted into an other-worldly understanding of pilgrimage from exile to the New Jerusalem, as sacred and spiritual themes begin to reassert their proper place in the narrative.

The object of the Christian life is thus to arrive safely in the heavenly homeland. Anything that distracts from this task is to be seen as potentially dangerous. For this reason, many spiritual writers stress the importance of cultivating indifference to the world. In his sermon "The Christian Pilgrim," Jonathan Edwards (1703–58) stresses the importance of this point:

> We ought not to rest in the world and its enjoyments, but should desire heaven . . . We ought above all things to desire a heavenly happiness; to be with God; and dwell with Jesus Christ. Though surrounded with outward enjoyments, and settled in families with desirable friends and relations; though we have companions whose society is delightful, and children in whom we see many promising qualifications; though we live by good neighbors and are generally beloved where known; yet we ought not to take our rest in these things as our portion. . . . We ought to possess, enjoy and use them, with no other view but readily to quit them, whenever we are called to it, and to change them willingly and cheerfully for heaven.

Edwards is not in any way disparaging the world as God's good creation. His concern here is that Christians might come to value the creation more highly than the creator, and as a result settle for something that is good, but not as good as God.

Two works of Christian spirituality that focus on the theme of "journeying" have already been discussed. The central theme of the *Divine Comedy* is that of a journey from the darkness of a wood to an encounter with God in the beatific vision, in the course of which the poet achieves insight into his own identity, and the nature and means of achieving salvation. In Bunyan's *Pilgrim's Progress* Christian journeys from the "City of Destruction" to "the Heavenly City." Once more, the dominant theme is the difficulties, temptations, and encouragements which are to be had on the journey to the new Jerusalem, intended to encourage and admonish its readers.

More recently, the leading British evangelical preacher and theologian John R. W. Stott has stressed the importance of sustaining the "hope of heaven" as a means of encouraging Christians to keep going on the long journey of faith. Stott explored this theme in some detail in a series of addresses given to the Inter-Varsity Mission Convention at Urbana, Illinois in 1976. In the course of exploring the relevance of the theme of the "hope of glory" for sustaining and stimulating both individual Christians and the Christian community, Stott argued powerfully for the recovery of this leading theme of the Christian faith, and its application to every aspect of Christian life and thought.

> Lift up your eyes! You are certainly a creature of time, but you are also a child of eternity. You are a citizen of heaven, and an alien and exile on earth, a pilgrim travelling to the celestial city. I read some years ago of a young man who found a five-dollar bill on the street and who "from that time on never lifted his eyes when walking. In the course of years he accumulated 29,516 buttons, 54,172 pins, 12 cents, a bent back and a miserly disposition." But think what he lost. He couldn't see the radiance of the sunlight, and sheen

of the stars, the smile on the face of his friends, or the blossoms of springtime, for his eyes were in the gutter. There are too many Christians like that. We have important duties on earth, but we must never allow them to preoccupy us in such a way that we forget who we are or where we are going.

Stott encouraged his audience to renew their acquaintance with the "hope of glory," and begin to anticipate its wonder. Anticipation of journey's end is an important means of sustaining the pilgrim on that journey itself.

Returning to the Homeland from Exile

The Christian concept of heaven can be set out in terms of the hope of return to a homeland. The image invites us to imagine that we are coming home to a well-loved place – a place where we belong, where a joyful welcome awaits us. The image of returning from exile has long been used as a means of crystalizing this hope and expectation of return to the homeland.

One of the most pivotal events recounted in the Old Testament is the exile of Jerusalem to Babylon, which took place in 586 BC. In 605 BC, the Babylonian emperor Nebuchadnezzar defeated the massed Egyptian armies at Carchemish, establishing Babylon as the leading military and political power in the region. Along with many other territories in this region, the land of Judah became subject to Babylonian rule, possibly in 604. The king of Judah decided to rebel against Babylon, possibly encouraged in this move by a successful Egyptian counterattack against Babylon in 601, which may have seemed to suggest that

Babylon's power was on the wane. It was to prove to be a terrible misjudgment. Judah was invaded by Babylonian forces, and its armies routed. This event was interpreted by writers of the time as the execution of the promised judgment of the Lord against a faithless people and king. The king, the royal family, and the circle of royal advisors gave themselves up to the besieging forces early in 597. They were deported to Babylon, along with several thousand captives. The Babylonians placed Zedekiah on the throne as their vassal, and seemed happy to leave things like that for the present. Yet Zedekiah attempted to rebel against Babylon. The Babylonian response was massive and decisive. In January 588, they laid siege to the city; in July 586, they broke through its walls, and took the city. The defending army attempted to flee, but was routed. The next month, a Babylonian offical arrived in Jerusalem to supervise the destruction of the defenses of the city and its chief buildings, and the deportation of its people. The furnishings of the temple were dismantled, and taken to Babylon as booty. The exile of Jerusalem had begun.

The exile was a catastrophic event, which forced the exilic community in Babylon to rethink its identity and mission. Writings dating from this period show that the exile was interpreted as, in the first place, a judgment against Judah for its lapse into pagan religious beliefs and practices; and in the second, a period of national repentance and renewal, which will lead to the restoration of a resurgent people of God. Yet alongside theological reflection on the meaning of the exile, we find a heartfelt expression of the unutterable sense of loss and bereavement felt by the exilic community, as they remembered their homeland. Psalm 137 is perhaps one of the most powerful expressions of the pain of exile, and the longing for restoration.

By the rivers of Babylon –
there we sat down and there we wept
when we remembered Zion.
On the willows there we hung up our harps.
For there our captors asked us for songs,
and our tormentors asked for mirth, saying, "Sing us one
of the songs of Zion!"
How could we sing the Lord's song in a foreign land?
Psalm 137:1–4

This powerful psalm of lament for the homeland offers an organizing image for the complexities of the Christian life. Christians are to see themselves as cut off from their homeland, and nourishing the hope of return from exile, often under difficult and discouraging circumstances.

A very similar idea is also developed in the New Testament, especially in Paul's letter to the church at the Roman colony of Philippi. Philippi was founded as the city of Krenides by an Athenian exile, Callistratus. After Anthony and Octavian defeated Brutus and Cassius there in 42-41 BC, the city was refounded as a Roman colony. After the defeat of Anthony's forces at Actium 11 years later, Octavian reconstituted the colony once more. The city thus developed a decidedly Italian atmosphere, both because of the permanent presence of Italian settlers, and the large numbers of Roman troops regularly passing through the city, on account of its strategic location in Macedonia. The language, imagery, and outlook of a Roman colony would thus be part of the everyday thought-world of Paul's audience within the city. Philippi was conscious of its ties with Rome, including its language (Latin seems to have been more widely spoken than Greek) and laws. Roman institutions served as the model in many areas of its communal life.

Paul uses the image of a "colony (*politeuma*) of heaven" (Philippians 3:20) to bring out several leading aspects of Christian existence. By speaking of the Christian community in this way, he naturally encourages his readers to think along certain lines. Those strands of thought would certainly include the following. The Christian church is an outpost of heaven in a foreign land. It speaks the language of that homeland, and is governed by its laws – despite the fact that the world around it speaks a different language, and obeys a different set of laws. Its institutions are based on those of its homeland. And, one day, its citizens will return to that homeland, to take up all the privileges and rights which that citizenship confers. This image thus lends dignity and new depths of meaning to the Christian life, especially the tension between the "now" and "not yet," and the bitter-sweet feeling of being outsiders to a culture – being in the world and yet not of that world. Christians are exiles in the world; citizens of heaven rather than of any earthly city.

This image of "exile" was developed within Christian spirituality, particularly by writers of the medieval period. While the basic theme of exile was taken from the history of Jerusalem, it was interpreted and developed in a particular manner. Drawing on Paul's image of Christians as "citizens of heaven," and the Christian hope of finally entering the new Jerusalem, such writers argued that life on earth was to be thought of as a period of exile from the heavenly Jerusalem. The world is not our homeland; it is the place to which we have been exiled. During the long period of exile from heavenly realms, believers keep alive the hope of returning to the homeland.

Once more, this theme was expressed in the church architecture of the medieval period. An excellent example of this tactile theology was once to be found on the north portal of the abbey church of Notre-Dame of Bourg-Dieu of Déols. This building fell into disrepair after the French Revolution of 1789, and was eventually demolished in 1830. However, some fragments of the portal remain in the Musée Bertrand in Châteauroux, from which it can be established that the following words greeted visitors to the abbey:

> *Qui captivaris miser in misera regione,*
> *Ad patriam reditus per me patet ex Babylone.*

(You miserable person, who is held captive in a miserable place, the way back from Babylon to your homeland lies through me.)

An excellent example of this approach can be found in the writings of Peter Abelard (1079–1142), especially his hymn *O quanta qualia sunt illa sabbata*. In this hymn, Abelard contrasts the present situation of Christians as exiles in Babylon with the hope of return to Jerusalem:

> *Nostrum est interim mentem erigere*
> *Et totis patriam votes appetere,*
> *Et ad Jerusalem a Babylonia*
> *Post longa regredi tandem exsilia.*

(In the meantime, it is ours to direct our minds and to seek in prayer the native land, and after a long exile finally to return to Jerusalem from Babylon.)

A related approach can be found in the "Prayer to Christ" of Anselm of Canterbury (c.1033–1109). In this prayer, Anselm wrestles with his longing to be with Christ in heaven. The thought of being with Christ simultanously heightens his sense of sadness at not yet being with Christ, and offers him hope and encouragement that he one day will be in this presence. Again, the image of exile controls his thoughts at this point:

> All this I hold with unwavering faith
> And weep over the hardship of exile.
> Hoping in the sole consolation of your coming
> Ardently longing for the glorious
> contemplation of your face.

On the basis of this model, medieval spiritual writers began to develop a series of insights that illuminated the status of Christians, and offered them guidance as to how they should behave in the world. For example, they stressed the importance of cultivating the hope of return to the homeland. Many writers of the period offered powerful visual images of the heavenly Jerusalem, in order to encourage their readers to set their hearts firmly on heaven. The Old Testament indicates that some exiled inhabitants of Jerusalem actually came to prefer Babylon, and chose to stay on in that city when others returned home. Bernard of Clairvaux (1090–1153) and others discerned a similar danger in the Christian life – that Christians will come to prefer their place of exile to their homeland, and in effect choose to remain in exile.

In the face of this threat, medieval spiritual writers offered another powerful incentive to their readers. To keep alive the hope of returning to the heavenly homeland was the prospect of seeing God face to face. What greater beauty or joy could anyone hope to experience? As we bring this work to a close, it is appropriate to explore the role of this beatific vision in Christian spirituality.

The Christian hope is often expressed in terms of seeing the face of God directly, without the need for created intermediaries. In the Old Testament, divine favor is indicated by the face of God being turned toward an individual, just as disfavor is signaled by that face being averted. In cultic petitions of this period, worshipers might invoke God not to turn his face away, as a means of securing the acceptance of the sacrifices or prayers being offered (Psalm 27:9, 132:10). If the face of God were "hidden" or "turned away," the believer had no hope of finding divine acceptance (Deuteronomy 31:17; Ezekiel 7:22).

Yet the image of the "face of God" concerns far more than the notion of the divine pleasure and favor; it evokes the possibility of an encounter with the living God. To "see the face of God" is to have a privileged, intimate relationship with God – seeing God "as God actually is" (1 John 3:2), rather than having to know God indirectly, through images and shadows. Now we see God "as through a glass, darkly;" but we shall finally see God face to face (1 Corinthians 13:12). The Book of Revelation affirms that this will be the privilege of those in heaven, where the saints will finally "see God's face" (Revelation 22:4).

This hope of seeing the face of God was developed extensively in the Christian tradition. In his *Letter 92*, Augustine of Hippo wrote to Italica, a noble widow, who had some questions concerning the hope of heaven. Augustine responded by fleshing out the brief biblical statements concerning "seeing God." While we are in exile on earth, we are not "fitted" or "adapted" to beholding the full glory of God; it is only when we ourselves are raised to glory and transformed that we may hope to see the radiance and glory of God in all their fullness.

> We see God according to the measure by which we are adapted to him . . . no matter how far we may advance, we still fall short of that perfection of likeness which is fitted for seeing God, as the apostle says, "face to face." . . . When you read, "Now we see through a glass darkly, but then face to face" (1 Corinthians 13:12), learn from this that we shall then see God face to face by the same means by which we now see him through a glass darkly. In both cases alike, the vision of God belongs to the inner person, whether while we walk in this pilgrimage still by faith, in which it uses the glass and the shadow, or when, in the country which is our home, we shall perceive by sight, a vision denoted by the words "face to face."

For Augustine, the vision of God possesses a unique capacity to satisfy human desire, utterly surpassing the ability of any created being or thing in this respect. Such a vision is the *summum bonum*, the supreme good, the "light by which truth is perceived, and the fountain from which all blessedness is drunk."

Augustine develops this idea further in the *City of God*, arguing that the vision of God in heaven sustains believers throughout their pilgrimage of faith:

> God himself, who is the Author of virtue, shall be our reward. As there is nothing greater or better than God himself, God has promised us himself. What else can be meant by his word through the prophet, "I will be your God, and you will be my people" than "I shall be their satisfaction, I shall be all that people honourably desire – life, health, nourishment, satisfaction, glory, honour, peace, and all good

things?" This, too, is the right interpretation of the saying of the apostle "That God may be all in all." God shall be the end of all our desires, who will be seen without end, loved without cloy, and praised without weariness.

The nature of the vision of God enjoyed by the saints in heaven was the subject of no small debate throughout the Middle Ages. Pope John XXII provoked a particularly vigorous controversy through his argument that the saints who are now "under the altar" – a phrase deriving from Revelation 6:9 – are able to find consolation through contemplation of the humanity of Christ; after the resurrection and final judgment, however, they will finally be able to enjoy the full and perfect joy of seeing God directly. His successor Benedict XII tried to dampen down the somewhat heated exchanges that John had provoked by arguing that those who were already purified were able to enjoy the vision of God before the end of time; others, however, would have to wait until history ended before the full revelation of the glory of God. But, he insisted, it would be worth waiting for.

The Psalmist set out his longing to see God in these words:

> One thing I ask of the Lord,
> This is what I seek;
> That I may dwell in the house of the Lord
> All the days of my life,
> To gaze upon the beauty of the Lord. (Psalm 27:4)

The Christian vision of heaven affirms that what the Psalmist longed for all his life will one day be the common privilege of the entire people of God – to gaze upon the face of their Lord and Savior, as they enter into his house, to dwell in peace for ever. It is no accident that Dante's *Divine Comedy* reaches its climax when the poet finally, after his epic journeys through hell and purgatory, emerges to behold "The love that moves the sun and the other stars."

That is where Dante's wandering reaches its final goal, and it is fitting to end a brief history of heaven at this same point. As John Donne put it: "No man ever saw God and lived. And yet, I shall not live till I see God; and when I have seen him, I shall never die."

Works Consulted

Auffarth, Christoph (1991) *Der drohende Untergang: Schöpfung in Mythos und Ritual im Alten Orient und in Griechenland am Beispel der Odyssee und des Ezechielbuches*. Berlin: Walter de Gruyter.

Armaud, Barton Levi St. (1977) "Paradise Deferred: The Image of Heaven in the Work of Emily Dickinson and Elizabeth Stuart Phelps." *American Quarterly* 29: 55–78.

Backscheider, Paula R. (1984) *A Being More Intense: A Study of the Prose Works of Bunyan, Swift, and Defoe*. New York: AMS Press.

Batson, E. Beatrice (1984) *John Bunyan, Allegory and Imagination*. London: Croom Helm.

Bauckham, Richard (1993) *The Theology of the Book of Revelation*. Cambridge, UK: Cambridge University Press.

Beretta, Ilva (1993) *"The World's a Garden": Garden Poetry of the English Renaissance*. Uppsala: University of Uppsala.

Bietenhard, Hans (1951) *Die Himmlische Welt Im Urchristentum Und Spätjudentum*. Tübingen: Mohr.

Braden, Gordon (1979) "Claudian and His Influence: The Realm of Venus." *Arethusa* 12: 203–32.

Brantley, Richard E. (1999) "Christianity and Romanticism: A Dialectical Review." *Christianity and Literature* 48: 349–66.

Burns, Norman T. and Christopher Reagan (1976) *Concepts of the Hero in the Middle Ages and the Renaissance.* London: Hodder and Stoughton.

Bynum, Caroline Walker (1991) "Personal Survival and the Resurrection of the Body: A Scholastic Discussion in Its Medieval and Modern Contexts." In *Fragmentation and Redemption: Essays on Gender and the Human Body in Medieval Religion.* New York: Zone Books, pp. 239–97.

Bynum, Caroline Walker (1997) *The Resurrection of the Body in Western Christianity, 200–1336.* New York: Columbia University Press.

Cabasilas, Nicholas (1960) *A Commentary on the Divine Liturgy.* London: SPCK.

Caird, George B. *The Language and Imagery of the Bible.* London: Duckworth.

Campbell, K. M. (1978) "The New Jerusalem in Matthew 5:14." *Scottish Journal of Theology* 31:335–63.

Cantor, Paul A. (1992) "Blake and the Archaeology of Eden." In Paul Harris and Deborah F. Sawyer (eds.), *A Walk in the Garden: Biblical, Iconographical, and Literary Images of Eden.* Sheffield, UK: JSOT Press, pp. 229–43.

Cardman, Francine (1984) "Fourth-Century Jerusalem: Religious Geography and Christian Tradition." In Patrick Henry (ed.), *Schools of Thought in the Christian Tradition.* Philadelphia: Fortress Press, pp. 49–64.

Clarke, Elizabeth (1997) *Theory and Theology in George Herbert's Poetry: "Divinitie and Poesy Met".* Oxford: Clarendon Press.

Comblin, José (1968) *Théologie de la ville.* Paris: Éditions universitaires.

Cornelius, Izak (1988) "Paradise Motifs in the Eschatology of the Minor Prophets and the Iconography of the Ancient near East." *Journal of Northwest Semitic Languages* 14: 41–75.

Corp, Ronald (1993) *Spirituals of the Deep South.* London: Faber Music.

Crosby, Sumner McKnight and Pamela Z. Blum (1987) *The Royal Abbey of Saint-Denis: From Its Beginnings to the Death of Suger, 475–1151.* New Haven, CT: Yale University Press.

Darr, Katheryn Pfisterer (1987) "The Wall around Paradise: Ezekelian Ideas About the Future." *Vetus Testamentum* 37: 271–9.

deSilva, David A. (1994) "At the Threshold of Heaven: The Preaching of John Donne as Sacrament of the Word." *Anglican and Episcopal History* 43: 5–34.

Edwards, Michael (1992) "C. S. Lewis: Imagining Heaven." *Journal of Literature and Theology* 6: 107–24.

Egginton, William (1999) "On Dante, Hyperspheres and the Curvature of the Medieval Cosmos." *Journal of the History of Ideas* 60: 195–216.

Emmerson, Richard K. (1998) "Apocalyptic Themes and Imagery in Medieval and Renaissance Literature." In John Joseph Collins, Bernard McGinn, and Stephen J. Stein (eds.), *The Encyclopedia of Apocalypticism*. New York: Continuum, pp. 402–41.

Erffa, Hans Martin von (1989–95) *Ikonologie der Genesis: Die christlichen Bildthemen aus dem Alten Testament und ihre Quellen*, 2 vols. Munich: Deutscher Kunstverlag.

Evans, J. Martin (1968) *Paradise Lost and the Genesis Tradition*. Oxford: Clarendon Press.

Evans, Joan (1960) *English Mediaeval Lapidaries*. London: Oxford University Press.

Farrer, Austin (1949) *A Rebirth of Images: The Making of St John's Apocalypse*. London: Dacre Press.

Fritz, Volkmar (1995) *The City in Ancient Israel*. Sheffield, UK: Sheffield Academic Press.

Gardner, Eileen (1989) *Visions of Heaven and Hell Before Dante*. New York: Ithaca Press.

Giamatti, A. Bartlett (1969) *The Earthly Paradise and the Renaissance Epic*. Princeton. NJ: Princeton University Press.

Godman, Peter (1987) *Poets and Emperors: Frankish Politics and Carolingian Poetry*. Oxford: Clarendon Press.

Grimm, Reinhold R. (1977) *Paradisus Coelestis – Paradisus Terrestris. Zur Auslegungsgeschichte des Paradieses im Abendland bis um 1200*. Munich: Wilhelm Fink Verlag.

Gundry, Robert H. (1987) "The New Jerusalem: People as Place, Not Place for People." *Novum Testamentum* 29: 254–64.

Haag, Ernst (1970) *Der Mensch am Anfang: Die Alttestamentliche Paradiesvorstellung nach Gn 2–3*. Trier: Paulinus-Verlag.

Hammond, Mason (1972) *The City in the Ancient World*. Cambridge, MA: Harvard University Press.

Hunt, John Dixon (1986) *Garden and Grove: The Italian Renaissance Garden and the English Imagination 1600–1750*. London: Dent.

Jeremias, Joachim (1974) *Jerusalem in the Time of Jesus: An Investigation into Economic and Social Conditions during the New Testament Period*. London: SCM Press.

Karavidopoulos, John (1988) "Jerusalem in the Orthodox Theological Tradition." *Greek Orthodox Theological Review* 33: 89–200.

Landy, Francis (1979) "The Song of Songs and the Garden of Eden." *Journal of Biblical Literature* 98: 513–28.

Lewalski, Barbara Kiefer (1979) *Protestant Poetics and the Seventeenth-Century Religious Lyric*. Princeton, NJ: Princeton University Press.

Lincoln, Andrew T. (1981) *Paradise Now and Not Yet: Studies in the Role of the Heavenly Dimension in Paul's Thought with Special Reference to His Eschatology*. Cambridge, UK: Cambridge University Press.

Lucchesi, Enzo (1977) *L'usage de Philon dans l'œuvre exégétique de Saint Ambroise: Une "Quellenforschung" relative aux commentaires d'Ambroise sur la Genèse*. Leiden: E. J. Brill.

Lys, Daniel (1968) *Le plus beau chant de la création: Commentaire de "Cantique des Cantiques"*. Paris: Editions du Cerf.

Markschies, Christoph (1995) *Gibt es eine "Theologie der gotischen Kathedrale"? nochmals: Suger von Saint-Denis und Sankt Dionys vom Areopag*. Heidelberg: Universitätsverlag C. Winter.

Markus, R. A. (1970) *Saeculum: History and Society in the Theology of St Augustine*. Cambridge, UK: Cambridge University Press, 1970.

McDannell, Colleen and Bernhard Lang (1988) *Heaven: A History*. New Haven, CT: Yale University Press.

Menken, M. J. J. (1992) "Paradise Regained or Still Lost? Eschatology and Disorderly Behaviour in 2 Thessalonians." *New Testament Studies* 38: 271–89.

Michaels, J. Ramsey (1996) "Going to Heaven with Jesus: From 1 Peter to Pilgrim's Progress." In Richard N. Longenecker (ed.),

Patterns of Discipleship in the New Testament. Grand Rapids, MI: Eerdmans, pp. 248–68.

Moorman, Charles (1967) *A Knyght There Was: The Evolution of the Knight in Literature.* Lexington, KY: University of Kentucky Press.

Morgan, Alison (1990) *Dante and the Medieval Other World.* Cambridge, UK: Cambridge University Press.

Mumford, Lewis (1961) *The City in History: Its Origins, its Transformations, and its Prospects.* New York: Harcourt Brace & World.

Nagy, Gregory (1999) *The Best of the Achaeans: Concepts of the Hero in Archaic Greek Poetry,* rev. edn. Baltimore, MD: Johns Hopkins University Press.

Nussbaum, Martha Craven (1986) *The Fragility of Goodness: Luck and Ethics in Greek Tragedy and Philosophy.* Cambridge, UK: Cambridge University Press.

Nussbaum, Martha Craven (1993) "Beatrice's Dante: Loving the Individual?" *Apeiron* 26: 161–78.

Nussbaum, Martha Craven (2001) *Upheavals of Thought: The Intelligence of Emotions.* Cambridge, UK: Cambridge University Press.

O'Donovan, Oliver (1980) *The Problem of Self-Love in St. Augustine.* New Haven, CT: Yale University Press.

Patch, Howard Rollin (1970) *The Other World According to Descriptions in Medieval Literature.* New York: Octagon Books.

Pelikan, Jaroslav (1986) *The Mystery of Continuity: Time and History, Memory and Eternity in the Thought of St Augustine.* Charlottesville, VA: University of Virginia Press.

Peterfreund, Stuart (1994) "Blake and the Ideology of the Natural." *Eighteenth-Century Life* 18: 92–119.

Peters, F. E. (1986) *Jerusalem and Mecca: The Typology of the Holy City in the Near East.* New York: New York University Press.

Preston, Peter and Paul Simpson-Housley (1994) *Writing the City: Eden, Babylon and the New Jerusalem.* London: Routledge.

Raya, Joseph M. (1978) *Eyes of the Gospel.* Denville, NJ: Dimension Books.

Rössner, Michael (1988) *Auf der Suche nach dem verlorenen Paradies: Zum mythischen Bewusstsein in der Literatur des 20. Jahrhundert.* Frankfurt am Main: Athenäum.

Russell, Jeffrey Burton (1997) *A History of Heaven: The Singing Silence*. Princeton, NJ: Princeton University Press.

Russell, Robert D. (1994) "'A Similitude of Paradise': The City as Image of the City." In Clifford Davidson (ed.), *The Iconography of Heaven*. Kalamazoo, MI: Western Michigan University Press, pp. 146–61.

Smith, Mark S. (1988) "'Seeing God' in the Psalms: The Background to the Beatific Vision in the Hebrew Bible." *Catholic Biblical Quarterly* 50: 171–83.

Soskice, Janet Martin (1998) "Resurrection and the New Jerusalem." In Stephen T. Davis, Gerald O'Collins and Daniel Kendall (eds.), *The Resurrection: An Interdisciplinary Symposium on the Resurrection of Jesus*. Oxford: Oxford University Press, pp. 41–58.

Startzman, L. Eugene (1987) "Wisdom and Beauty: Two Principles in Paradise Lost." *Christianity and Literature* 36: 26–39.

Stevens, Ray (1991) "Scripture and the Literary Imagination: Biblical Allusions in Byron's Heaven and Earth." In Wolf Z. Hirst (ed.), *Byron, the Bible, and Religion*. Newark: University of Delaware Press, pp. 118–35.

Strong, Roy C. (1998) *The Renaissance Garden in England*. London: Thames and Hudson.

Swanston, H. F. G. (1983) "Liturgy as Paradise and Parousia." *Scottish Journal of Theology* 36: 505–19.

Thurman, Howard (1955) *Deep River; Reflections on the Religious Insight of Certain of the Negro Spirituals*. New York: Harper.

Wengst, Klaus (1994) "Babylon the Great and the New Jerusalem: The Visionary View of Political Reality in the Revelation of John." In Henning Reventlow, Yair Hoffman, and Benjamin Uffenheimer (eds.), *Politics and Theopolitics in the Bible and Postbiblical Literature*. Sheffield: JSOT Press, pp. 189–202.

Whitehill, Walter Muir (1968) *Spanish Romanesque Architecture of the Eleventh Century*. London: Oxford University Press.

Wyatt, Nicolas (1990) "'Supposing Him to Be the Gardener' (John 20, 15). A Study of the Paradise Motif in John." *Zeitschrift für die neutestamentliche Wissenschaft* 81: 21–38.

Wybrew, Hugh (1989) *The Orthodox Liturgy: The Development of the Eucharistic Liturgy in the Byzantine Rite*. London: SPCK.

Yourcenar, Marguerite (1974) *Fleuve profond, sombre rivière: Les negro spirituals*. Paris: Gallimard.

Yu, Anthony C. (1980) "Life in the Garden: Freedom and the Image of God in Paradise Lost." *Journal of Religion* 60: 247–71.

Index

Note: Page references in *italics* indicate illustrations.

Marx, Karl   146–7, 149, 159
Medici, Lorenzo de   58
Methodius of Olympus   34–5,
    49–50
millennium, as paradise   52–4
Milton, John
    Paradise Lost   39, 40, 58,
        70–2, 78–9, 90, 114
monasticism
    and attitudes to the world
        19–20
    devotional literature   20,
        21–3
Muggeridge, Malcolm   112
music, in worship   167–8
mysticism, Christian   142

nakedness   15–16, 24, 34
nature
    as anticipation of heaven
        113–16
    and heaven as garden
        39–40, 73, 152
    and longing for heaven   78,
        111, 112, 124–30
    and Romanticism   124–9
    secularization of   124–5, 128
    in Traherne   123–4
Neale, J. M.   21–2, 82–3
New Testament
    and the heavenly body   33
    and Jerusalem   6, 10–13,
        17, 75
    and New Jerusalem   6,
        10–12, 24, 26–8, 31, 75,
        138–9

and paradise   43, 46–7
    see also Paul, St.; Revelation
Notre-Dame of Bourg-Dieu
    church   179
Nussbaum, Martha   117–19

Old Testament
    and face of God   181
    and images of God   4
    and Jerusalem   6, 7–10
    and paradise   41–2, 43–6
    and worship as heaven on
        earth   166–7
Origen, and resurrection body
    33–4
Orthodoxy
    and icons   2
    and worship as heaven on
        earth   166, 168

Palestrina, Giovanni Pierluigi
    da   168
paradise
    access through Christ   46,
        50–1, 76, 87
    allegorical interpretation   51
    and Augustine of Hippo
        15–16, 51–2
    church as   65–7
    classical images   70
    in early church   47–52
    heaven as   39–74
    in medieval literature   54–64
    millennium as   52–4
    in New Testament   43,
        46–7

Compiled by Meg Davies
(Registered Indexer, Society
of Indexers)

The Service Leaders Club

Bill Byham and his DDI colleagues have taken the art of the business fable to new heights with *The Service Leaders Club.* Customer service leaders in every industry will enjoy and learn from the insightful and very relevant experiences of Don, Maureen, Stan, and Tom.

Ron Zemke
Coauthor of *Coaching Knock Your Socks Off Service*

The Service Leaders Club

Dazzling Your Customers Through Service

By William C. Byham, Ph.D., with Ray Crew and James H.S. Davis

Published by DDI Press, c/o Development Dimensions International, World Headquarters—Pittsburgh, 1225 Washington Pike, Bridgeville, Pennsylvania 15017-2838.

Manufactured in the United States of America.

Library of Congress Cataloging-in-Publications Data:

Byham, William C.
The Service Leaders Club

1. Business
2. Self-Help
ISBN 0-9623483-7-6

10 9 8 7 6

To my father, Edgar W. Byham,
a model of customer service,
dedication, and skills from whom
I learned the principles
described in this book.

Praise for *The Service Leaders Club*

The Key Principles defined here provide the keys to
successful relationships with coworkers, family, and friends.
When we become wise enough to teach this parable in every
school across the land, the world will become a better place,
and everyone will live happily ever after.

> **Raymond E. Miko**
> Vice President
> Corporate Training and
>   Organization Development
> Ricoh Corporation

A very entertaining and educational book! What a great
reinforcement that organizational leaders cannot "Dazzle"
customers without first "Zapping" their employees. Being a
member of the Service Leaders Club may not be easy, but this
book helps us understand that the rewards are worth the
effort.

> **Amie Hedley**
> Director, Organizational Capability
> MedTrans (a division of Laidlaw, Inc.)

An excellent story that breaks down the definition of the
Golden Rule into understandable principles. We should all
use our internal LISAs more!

> **Connie Tolleson**
> Vice President, Human Resources
> HomeBase

A simple story with a poignant message! We managers often forget the part we play in delivering service excellence. The story hits home. When can I order the book for my management team?

Susan K. Skara
Vice President, Human Resources
Apria Healthcare

We have spent so much of our energy and resources on transforming strategy and structure. *The Service Leaders Club* reminds us of the behaviors that will be required in the new millennium.

Donald E. Stapp
Senior Manager—Marketing and
    Business Alliances
Training Services Group
Deloitte and Touche LLP

The Service Leaders Club is a clearly understood explanation of the five Key Principles of service leadership that is presented in a hybrid format between a short story and a case study.

William Shilling
Vice President, Human Resources
Laidlaw Transit

The Club That Created the Club

At Development Dimensions International we help organizations create customer loyalty by working with them to develop service cultures that are linked to business strategies and built on a foundation of interaction skills. Over the years we've learned that leadership is the key to customer loyalty. In fact, the way leaders act can have a greater impact on customer loyalty than any other factor. As you'll see in this book, leadership based on training, trust, and partnership results in repeat business.

DDI's award-winning training programs help leaders and frontline employees develop the skills and strategies they need to consistently dazzle customers, and dazzled customers are loyal customers.

Continuing that tradition of training excellence is *The Service Leaders Club,* a fable about how a group of service leaders discovers those skills and strategies. It is also the result of a collaboration between authors who have extensive expertise in the areas of leadership, employee involvement, and service quality.

William C. Byham, Ph.D., is president and CEO of Development Dimensions International, a leading provider of programs and services designed to help organizations create effective service cultures. Dr. Byham has written 17 books on leadership and employee involvement, including the international best-sellers, *Zapp!® The Lightning of Empowerment, HeroZ™—Empower Yourself, Your Coworkers, Your Company,* and *Empowered Teams.*

The Service Leaders Club is a business novel. The *Wall Street Journal* has identified Dr. Byham as a pioneer of this new genre that uses engaging stories and characters to make concepts more memorable and more accessible to a wide audience.

For the past 25 years Dr. Byham has written, lectured, and consulted extensively in three major areas: the use of empowerment to motivate and energize a workforce, the importance and viability of empowered work teams, and the improvement of employee selection and promotion decisions.

Ray Crew develops training programs at DDI. He has been a communications and service quality improvement consultant for more than 15 years. A pioneer in the use of engaging, story-based training, he has written, produced, and directed numerous films and videotapes. He also has developed service quality improvement programs for clients in many industries, including banking, utilities, telecommunications, and manufacturing. His films have been honored by the American Marketing Association and the Florida Motion Picture and Television Association. This is his first business novel.

James H.S. Davis, a Development Dimensions International vice president and service culture practice leader, has 25 years of experience in developing, marketing, and implementing service quality programs. He is a recognized expert in combining selection, training, and management support to create service quality. He consults with numerous organizations throughout the world and is sought after as a consultant and speaker.

About Development Dimensions International

At DDI we help our clients create satisfied, loyal customers. Since 1970 DDI has served more than 16,000 clients worldwide, spanning a diverse range of industries and including more than 400 of the *Fortune* 500 companies.

DDI is the only major human resource solution provider in the world to fully integrate the three elements essential to the development of an effective service culture: organizational change consulting, assessment and selection systems, and training and development programs.

DDI's corporate headquarters and distribution facilities are located in Pittsburgh, Pennsylvania. We maintain 71 offices around the world, including regional training centers in Atlanta, Chicago, Dallas, Denver, Los Angeles, New York, and San Francisco as well as operations in Argentina, Australia, Brazil, Canada, Chile, China, Finland, France, Germany, Hong Kong, Indonesia, Japan, Korea, Peru, the Philippines, South Africa, Spain, Switzerland, and the United Kingdom. DDI's programs are available in 19 languages.

Chapter 1

Y ou probably picked up this book because
you're thinking about joining the Club. I'm
not surprised. A lot of successful people like
you are already members. But you should
know what you're getting into, right? Well,
that's what this story is about. That's why you
should read this book.

It's no secret that long before the

original members of The Service

Leaders Club stumbled onto it, other

people had discovered the primal force

now known as Zapp. They knew about

the tremendous energy Zapp released in

people and how that energy resulted in

better job quality and productivity and,

best of all, greater job satisfaction.

History tells us that Zapp was discovered by Ralph Rosco in the mid-80s. Using the primitive technology available at the time, Rosco had to enter a parallel dimension to observe the effects of Zapp. I researched the phenomenon and wrote about it. I thought I knew pretty much all there was to know about Zapp and what it could do, but as I have since learned, other people were finding their own roads to the power of Zapp and new uses for it as well.

You often hear Rosco referred to as the Ben Franklin of Zapp. The analogy is fitting—Franklin discovered the primal force of electricity. But it was Thomas Edison who figured out how to use that force to light a filament in a glass bulb. And with Zapp, it was the members of The Service Leaders Club who pioneered some of its most powerful uses.

For one thing, they discovered that Zapp has an amazing by-product, named Dazzle by the club members, that produced delighted customers. They worked tenaciously to learn the secrets of this Zapp-induced phenomenon, finally harnessing it to create loyal customers for their organizations and eventually for organizations around the world.

But I'm getting ahead of the story. It's best to start with first things first. That's something my good friend Stan taught me.

Some people credit me with making The Service Leaders Club the force it is today, but the fact is their story began long before I ever met Stan or any of the other club members. And that's a story worth reading. When you've finished this book, you'll know how the club you're about to join came to be and what it stands for. So, if you'll just go to the next page, we can get started.

Chapter 2

They ate lunch at **The Home Plate** every day, and they didn't know why. It wasn't because they had no choices. There were plenty of other eateries in Nearville competing for their business. There was even another restaurant in The Home Plate chain about a block closer to all of them.

It's not that they all had the same tastes or were creatures of habit either. Don, Maureen, Stan, and Tom were as different from one another as four people could be. Don was branch manager at the bank. Maureen was a nursing supervisor at the hospital. Stan managed a group of customer service representatives at the power company, and Tom oversaw the Order Fulfillment

Laverne

Department at the Federated Framis plant. The only thing they had in common was that each was a leader in his or her organization.

Yet, every day at precisely six minutes after noon, they would all walk through the door of The Home Plate and sit at the same table by the window. Laverne, their waitress, knew it was their favorite, so she always saved it for them. In fact, Laverne knew their likes and dislikes so well they hardly had to order. Things went on like this for years until one rainy Tuesday when the routine changed forever.

At six minutes after noon on that particular day, Don, Maureen, and Stan walked through the door looking like they had lost their best friend.

"Where's Tom?" Laverne asked as she reflexively plucked four menus from a stack and led them to their table.

"You didn't hear?" Don asked solemnly.

"Didn't hear what?"

"Tom's gone," Maureen said, her voice quavering.

Now it was Laverne's turn to sound solemn. "You mean he's . . . "

"Laid off," Stan finished the sentence. "Federated Framis shut its doors yesterday."

"Why?" Laverne asked, still holding the unnecessary fourth menu.

Don shrugged. "Too many people decided to buy their framises from the competition."

"Why?" Laverne asked again.

"Customers are fickle," Stan sighed. "There's just no pleasing them anymore. They get it in their heads that they don't like you, and they take their business someplace else."

"You can say that again," Maureen said sadly.

Don looked over the top of his menu. "You work in a hospital. Where else are sick people going to go?"

"We're not the only hospital in town, you know," Maureen shot back. "And besides, people are different these days. They're more selfish. Don't you think so?"

"No doubt about it," Don said as he handed the menu to Laverne. "All they do is complain. My people have to listen to it all day long. 'The service charges are too high.' 'The interest rates are too low.' 'The lines are too slow.' 'Everything takes too long.' I love the ones that come into the bank with 10 minutes left on their lunch hour and get mad because we can't solve all their problems and get them back to work with time to spare."

Stan nodded. "They're the same people who act like you're killing them if you ask them to be at home to wait for a repairman. And half of them are the deadbeats who never pay their bill. They string us along as long as they can, and then they move or change their name, and the whole thing starts all over again."

Laverne listened sympathetically as she brought them their drinks and rearranged the silverware to accommodate Don, who was left-handed. "I'm real sorry to hear about Tom," she said sadly. "What'll you folks have?"

"The usual," they replied in unison. Laverne retreated to the kitchen.

Maureen picked up the lemon slice Laverne always gave her and squeezed it into her water glass. "If you really want to see people at their worst, just come to the hospital when a whole floor of patients buzzes the nurses' station at the same time. One's complaining because the room is too hot. Another one's mad because the room is too cold. They all hate the food, and they're convinced that the nurses never give their messages to the doctors."

Stan stirred the cup of decaf after pouring in the cream and two sugars Laverne had put in front of him when they sat down. "I don't know how your nurses handle the stress, but a lot of my people are getting so fed up they're quitting and leaving."

"You're lucky," Don said sarcastically. "A lot of my people are quitting and staying."

"What's that supposed to mean?" Maureen asked.

"Maybe it's different at the hospital, but at the bank I feel like I'm managing the living dead," Don answered. "My tellers have been downsized, reorganized, and computerized so many times they're like zombies."

Maureen shook her head sadly. "It's no different at the hospital. I have fewer nurses and more patients who demand more. My nurses might have started out to become Florence Nightingales, but they've turned into stressed-out clock watchers who can't wait till their shifts are over."

Stan nodded. "None of my people are excited about their jobs anymore either. It's like they've only got enough energy to do what they have to do, and when they get a tough customer on the line, they transfer the call to me. If they get too many tough customers, they quit!"

"So, how are we supposed to motivate people?" Don asked no one in particular.

"You can't," Stan intoned glumly. "And that's exactly what did in poor Tom."

Don picked up and studied the diet soda with no ice that Laverne brought him every day. "You know," he said after taking a sip, "the way things are going, we'll all end up like Tom."

As Don spoke, Stan scribbled something on his napkin. "If we do end up like Tom, here are the reasons why," Stan said. He showed the napkin to his friends.

Maureen sighed as she finished reading the message. "And there's nothing we can do about it."

"Not necessarily," Stan said with a faraway look in his eyes.

"What do you mean?" asked Maureen.

> Customers are more demanding. We have fewer people to handle them. Our people have been so downsized, reorganized, and computerized they've become demoralized, and we can't motivate them.

A smile spread across Stan's face. "Maybe we can't do anything about our people being downsized, reorganized, and computerized. Maybe we can't make their jobs any easier. But there might be a way to help them prepare for the really tough customers."

"How?" Don asked.

"With an early warning device," Stan said as he jumped up and grabbed his coat. "I'll show you. Here. Tomorrow." He ran to the door, leaving behind the liverwurst on rye with two onion slices, horseradish, and brown mustard that Laverne brought to the table.

Chapter 3

The next day **Stan arrived** in front of The Home Plate, where Don and Maureen were waiting. Stan was wearing dark glasses and a trench coat with the collar pulled up. He carried a mysterious black leather case.

"What's in there?" Maureen asked.

"Not so loud!" Stan croaked in a hoarse whisper. He looked over one shoulder, then the other. "For the past year," he whispered, "our Research and Development Department has been trying to invent something that would measure the electro-magnetic energy coming from damaged power lines. A few months ago they came up with these." Stan opened the case. Inside

Stan

were three identical boxes. Each looked like a small television with a satellite dish on top. Stan handed two of the boxes to Don and Maureen.

"Here," he said. "Compliments of the power company."

They examined their contraptions. "Do they work?" Maureen asked.

"Not exactly," Stan replied.

Don looked puzzled. "Who cares if they work or not. What do these things have to do with preparing people to deal with tough customers?"

Stan cast another worried look over his shoulder before answering. "It turns out they don't measure what comes from power lines very well, but they seem to be able to measure what comes from people."

"Huh?" Don and Maureen said.

"In other words," Stan continued, "these machines pick up the different types of radiation that come from people when they're happy or sad or angry or aggravated. Since the difficult customers we were talking about yesterday are definitely aggravated, these devices should be able to identify them and act as sort of an early warning system."

"What do you call this thing?" Don asked as he ran a finger over a row of dials and buttons.

"It's a Linear Infrared Spectral Analyzer," Stan replied. "We just call it LISA."

"Well, at least she, I mean 'it' has a pretty name," Maureen said, still holding her machine as if it might explode at any second.

Don gave Stan a long look. "What's with the spy outfit?"

"I'm not exactly supposed to have these machines," Stan said.

"You didn't steal them, did you?" Maureen practically shouted.

"Shhhh!" Stan hissed. "No, I did not steal them. I got them out of the trash. The power company's not exactly proud of LISA. I don't think they want anybody to know about it."

"How does LISA work?" Maureen asked.

"Let me power her up, and I'll show you." Stan flipped a toggle switch on the back of his machine. LISA began to hum and the screen glowed. "All you have to do is aim this parabolic reflector in the direction of the person you want to get a reading on." Stan swiveled the open end of the satellite dish toward some people on the other side of the street.

Maureen squinted as she peered at the screen. "Everybody's outlined in green."

"That's normal," Stan replied. "When people look green on the screen, it means they aren't happy or upset. They're just kind of neutral." Stan examined the screen. "By the looks of things, I'd say most of the pedestrians in this part of Nearville are pretty neutral."

"Wow, look at how blue the diner is!" Don shouted. He had turned on his LISA and was pointing the reflector toward The Home Plate.

"We found that the color blue indicates happiness and satisfaction," Stan explained.

"So, does that mean the diner's happy?" Maureen asked.

"No," Stan said patiently. "It probably means the people inside are."

"What would happen if they weren't?" Don asked.

"The diner would look red," Stan answered.

"I wonder what color the bank is," Don said as he walked rapidly in the direction of his office. Stan and Maureen followed, but Don outpaced them and disappeared around the corner. When they caught up with him, he was pointing LISA toward the bank building.

"What does this mean?" Don sounded baffled. Stan and Maureen looked over his shoulder at the screen; the bank glowed a sickly pink.

"Pink," Stan said slowly, "is a light shade of red."

"So?" Don demanded.

"So," Stan continued diplomatically, "it looks as though the people in the bank are . . ." He searched for the right words.

"Are what?" Don asked.

"Are mildly unhappy," Stan said at last.

"This is awful," Don groaned, still staring at the screen.

"Don't feel bad," Stan consoled. "The power company looks a lot redder."

Maureen decided that she had no interest in pointing LISA at the hospital, at least not right now.

The three friends walked slowly back to the diner. They sat at their usual table. Laverne hurried past, balancing two trays of food. "The usual?" she asked. They nodded silently. Don stared accusingly at his machine.

"Are you sure this thing is working right?" he asked,

looking up at Stan. Before Stan could answer, the front door of The Home Plate swung open with a determined whooosh! Don looked up to see who had come in, then tried to hide behind Stan.

"Uh-oh," he said in a small voice.

"What's the matter with you?" Maureen chided as Don sunk lower in his seat.

"Do you see the lady who just came in?" Don asked, practically under the table.

"What about her?" Maureen looked toward the door. "She looks like a nice little old lady to me."

"Looks can be deceiving," Don said. "That's Glennis Groanington."

"Why are you hiding?" Maureen asked mockingly.

"She had a run-in with one of my tellers this morning," Don whispered. "I don't want her to see me. If this LISA thing really works, she should look fire-engine red on the screen."

"Let's see," Stan said as he pointed his machine's reflector at Mrs. Groanington, who at that moment was impatiently tapping her foot as she waited for a table. LISA's steady hum wavered for a moment and the screen dimmed.

"What's happening?" Don asked.

Stan looked puzzled. "I'm not sure. I think she's overloaded." Just then LISA's screen turned to a bright, blinding red.

"Whoa!" Stan shouted. "I'd better turn the gain down." He turned a dial beside the screen until it was possible to distinguish Glennis Groanington's red outline.

"Now what's happening?" Don asked, completely under the table.

"You were right," Stan replied. "She's on fire."

"I knew it!" Don croaked, hitting his head on the table in his haste to see the screen. "Uh-oh," Don said suddenly. "Laverne's walking over to her. Boy, is she in for it."

"Poor Laverne," Maureen sounded worried. "Shouldn't we warn her?"

Stan braced himself. "Too late," he said.

"I can't watch." Maureen put her hands over her eyes.

Mrs. Groanington had not had a good day, and her visit to the bank earlier in the morning was the capper. A new teller who didn't recognize her had refused to cash her check until she showed him her driver's license.

"That little upstart treated me like I was a crook," she fumed to herself as she waited for her table at The Home Plate. She was startled out of her reverie by Laverne's pleasant voice.

"Welcome to The Home Plate," Laverne said with a smile. "Would you like a table in our smoking section or in our nonsmoking section?"

"I quit smoking years ago," Mrs. Groanington said haughtily.

"Now, that was a good idea," Laverne said, undaunted. "You're smarter than a lot of people I know, and I bet you have more willpower too." Mrs. Groanington was momentarily flustered.

"Well, yes," she said finally. "I guess when I put my mind to something, I can be pretty determined."

Meanwhile, Stan was puzzled by what he saw on LISA's screen. "That's odd," he said.

"What's odd?" Maureen asked, peeking out through the fingers of one hand.

Stan shook his head. "The colors are changing. She's not as red anymore. As a matter of fact, she's turning pink."

"Maybe these machines really don't work!" Don said hopefully.

Stan shook his head again. "I don't think so. According to LISA, your Mrs. Groanington isn't as unhappy as she was when she walked in." Stan followed Mrs. Groanington and Laverne with the parabolic reflector as they walked through the restaurant.

"Is this your first visit?" Laverne asked when they reached the table.

Mrs. Groanington was surprised by the question. "Why, ah, yes, as a matter of fact it is."

"I thought so. I would have remembered you. And your outfit? It looks great. Did you pick it out yourself?"

A broad smile crossed Mrs. Groanington's face as she told Laverne her shopping secrets.

Stan, Don, and Maureen couldn't believe their eyes. LISA's screen showed that Mrs. Groanington was turning from pink to green.

"I think she might be turning a little blue around the edges," Stan observed.

"How did that happen?" Don asked.

"Laverne must have done something," Stan said as he

looked up from the screen.

They stared at the screen, lost in their own thoughts. Don finally broke the silence. "Do you know what this means?" He answered his own question. "If customers like Mrs. Groanington can be satisfied, then maybe there's hope after all."

Stan stood up and said, "Let's ask Laverne what she did." He walked toward the kitchen window where Laverne was picking up an order. Don and Maureen followed.

Laverne seemed surprised to see them. "Did I forget the ketchup again?"

"What did you do to that customer over there?" Stan asked loudly, pointing at Mrs. Groanington, who was engrossed in her menu.

Don pulled down Stan's pointing arm gently but firmly and whispered, "What he means is, would you mind telling us what you said to Mrs. Groanington a moment ago?"

Laverne looked at them suspiciously. "Why?" she whispered.

"We noticed how unhappy she looked when she came in," Maureen explained.

"Yeah, she was really bright red," Don exclaimed. He winced as Stan elbowed him sharply in the ribs.

"We couldn't help noticing how fast her mood improved," Maureen continued. "We just wondered what you did."

Laverne glanced at Mrs. Groanington, who apparently still hadn't decided what to order. Then, she pushed open the door to the kitchen and beckoned for the trio to follow.

"I figured she wasn't having a good day as soon as I came

up to her," Laverne explained when they were inside the kitchen. "So, I said a couple things to help her feel good about herself."

"That's all you did?" Don asked skeptically.

Laverne thought. "That's all," she confirmed.

"You sort of built her self-esteem?" Don still couldn't believe what he was hearing.

"If you say so," Laverne said, pulling her order pad and a pen out of the front pocket of her apron. "If you'll excuse me, I think she's ready to order. I'll have your lunches out to you in a few minutes."

Don, Maureen, and Stan followed Laverne out of the kitchen. When they were seated again, Stan said, "If our people handled difficult customers the way Laverne does, maybe there wouldn't be so many to handle."

"Right. But how do we get them to do it?" Maureen said.

Don glanced over at Mrs. Groanington, who was smiling as Laverne wrote down her order. He shook his head. "Why couldn't my teller have done that? Everybody at the bank is trained to be nice to people."

"I don't know," Maureen said. "Everyone at the hospital is trained to be nice too, but training programs don't create people like Laverne."

Meanwhile, Stan was swiveling LISA's parabolic reflector around the diner. He noticed that all The Home Plate's employees were good at turning red customers green and even blue. Then, he saw something he couldn't explain. He was following Laverne with the parabolic reflector as she raced to the kitchen with the order. When she passed her boss, Otto, she stopped and said something to him. As he answered her, the picture on LISA's screen broke up and the machine made a loud crackling sound. When the screen cleared, Laverne was glowing so brightly that Stan had to turn down the brightness.

"What was that?" asked Maureen, startled by the sound.

Stan looked worried. "I don't know."

"I tell you there's something's wrong with these things," Don whined.

Stan continued to stare. The image broke up again, and LISA crackled even louder.

"No, I think it's Otto," he said.

"You mean Laverne's boss Otto?" Maureen asked.

Stan nodded. "Every time he says something to Laverne, LISA goes crazy and Laverne gets brighter on the screen."

Whatever Otto was doing, it wasn't just with Laverne. Don and Maureen watched as Stan followed Otto with the reflector. Otto walked by a dull red busboy who was struggling to clean a big table for a group of waiting customers. Otto put his hand on the young man's shoulder and smiled as he said something to him. At this LISA's screen broke up so violently they didn't even see Otto help the busboy clean the table. When the screen cleared, the busboy now glowed a light blue.

"Whatever Otto's doing, it sure makes a big difference in his people," Maureen said. "Look at how much energy they have."

She was right. They'd never really paid attention before, but even without LISA, they couldn't help noticing that all The Home Plate employees were energized and enthusiastic.

"No wonder Otto can get his people to build customers' self-esteem," Maureen said.

"It looks like Otto can get his people to do anything," Don added.

Stan was writing on his napkin. When he finished, he showed it to his friends.

A wild look came over Stan. "If we can figure out what Otto's doing, our problems will be solved," he said dramatically. "And LISA's going to give us the answer."

Even difficult customers can be satisfied if they are handled right. Energized, enthusiastic employees are able to satisfy difficult customers. There is a way to energize people and make them enthusiastic about their jobs.

"Couldn't we just ask Otto?" Maureen wondered.

Stan didn't answer. Instead he quickly scooped up all three machines and put them back in the case.

"Hey, I thought you said we could keep them," Don protested as Stan put on his dark glasses.

"I'll bring them back tomorrow," Stan called over his shoulder while hurrying toward the door.

Chapter 4

The rest of that day Stan couldn't think of anything else but how to get LISA to reveal Otto's secret. At quitting time he hurried home, where he barely acknowledged his wife and kids before locking himself in his workshop. All through the evening he tinkered and adjusted and thought and tinkered some more. Sometime after midnight he gave up and emerged from his workshop.

Weary and discouraged, he collapsed into his easy chair and turned on the television. He picked up the remote control and started surfing mindlessly through the channels as a thunderstorm rumbled outside in the darkness.

Suddenly there was a blinding flash outside the window followed by a crashing boom so loud Stan nearly dropped his remote control. As rain began drumming on the roof, Stan noticed something happening on the television screen. With each flash of lightning, the picture on the screen broke up the same way the image on LISA's screen broke up when Otto spoke to his employees.

Stan jumped out of his chair. "That's it!" He ran back to his workshop, where he worked throughout the night.

Don and Maureen arrived at The Home Plate the next day to find Stan waiting for them. His dark glasses hid the circles under his eyes but not his enthusiasm. LISA was on the table in front of him, its screen glowing. The reflector was pointed toward the cash register, where Otto was listening to an obviously upset cashier.

"Have a look," he said. As the three of them stared at the screen, they saw a bolt of lightning pass from Otto to the cashier, and LISA made a faint zzzapp sound. Maureen gasped. Don closed his eyes, certain that when he opened them, he would see the poor cashier lying on the floor, smoldering and dead. Instead he saw her smiling and glowing with a bright light.

After Otto left, the cashier turned to a customer. Sparks passed from the cashier to the customer, who glowed a bright blue.

"What was that?" Don asked, awestruck.

"I call it Zapp and Dazzle," Stan replied.

"Zapp and Dazzle?" Maureen repeated.

"Every time you see a lightning bolt on the screen, LISA makes a

He tinkered.

noise that sounds like Zapp, and the way customers glow and shimmer just made me think of the word Dazzle," Stan explained. "I've been watching it happen for over an hour, and it's always the same. First, Otto says or does something that Zapps an employee. The employee glows. Then, the employee says or does something that Dazzles a customer, and the customer starts glowing a happier, more satisfied shade."

"How come we can see it now?" Don asked.

"I turned the master gain control down so Zapp doesn't overload LISA, and I turned the spectral attenuator up so she's sensitive enough to see Dazzle," Stan explained. "I made the same adjustments to your machines."

Don looked skeptical. "Does this Dazzle magic work on really tough customers?"

Stan nodded.

"Amazing," Don whispered as he watched more Zapping and Dazzling on the screen.

"Apparently, it works on everybody," Stan explained. "But the really amazing part is that the glow employees get when Otto Zapps them doesn't dissipate when they Dazzle a customer. It actually gets brighter."

"Very interesting," Don said, "but we still don't know what Zapp and Dazzle are."

"That's not entirely true," Stan said. "I think what Laverne did with Mrs. Groanington yesterday was Dazzle."

"But we still don't know what Otto did to Zapp Laverne," Don insisted.

"Don's right," Maureen said. "All the colors and lightning

bolts and sparks are very pretty to look at, but they don't give us any clues about what to do."

"Let's just ask Otto what this Zapp business is all about." Don said resolutely.

"I said that yesterday," Maureen reminded him. Don and Maureen were out of their seats and headed for the kitchen.

"Wait," Stan shouted. They turned back to where he was sitting. "Let's not mention LISA and the lightning bolts, OK?"

A moment later the three of them came up behind Otto.

Otto

"Could we see you for a minute?" Don asked.

Otto looked concerned as he turned to face them. "Is there something wrong?"

"No, not at all," Maureen reassured him. "We just wanted to ask you something."

Otto looked at them expectantly, but none of them could quite put the question into words. Finally, Don blurted out, "There's something going on here, and we want to know what it is."

"What?" Otto looked alarmed. "Has someone been hurt? Should I call the police?"

"No, it's nothing like that,"

Maureen said. "What Don meant to say was all your people seem so . . . so . . ."

"Energized," Stan filled in the missing word.

"Right," Maureen continued. "They all seem so energized. They care about their jobs and they're great with customers."

"You must have your pick of some excellent people," Don said. "Which employment agency do you work with?"

"I don't use one. When I need to hire someone, which isn't often, I just put an ad in the paper like everyone else."

"You must really pay them well," Stan offered.

"I wish I could. They're all worth more than they make, but I can only pay as much as the corporation will let me."

"The company must have really trained you well?"

Otto laughed. "Oh, yeah. After one day with the regional manager, I attended the 'school of sink or swim.'"

"Then what are you doing to get your employees to do such a good job?" Don asked.

Otto thought for a moment. "Well, it's only partly what I do. I think my people do most of it themselves. I just do my best to keep people feeling good about themselves and the jobs they do."

The faces of his three inquisitors told him they were expecting more.

"Otto, telephone for you," the cashier shouted over the din.

"Duty calls," he said. "I'm sorry I couldn't tell you more."

"Thanks for your time," Maureen called as Otto headed for the phone.

They walked back to their table and sat in silence for a moment.

"Let's look at what we know so far," Stan said at last. "Otto makes his people feel good about themselves and their jobs. His people make customers feel good about themselves and about doing business with The Home Plate. What Otto does seems to Zapp his people. What his people do seems to Dazzle customers."

Stan began writing on his napkin. "So, based on what we've observed, we can make these conclusions." He finished writing and passed the napkin across the table to his friends.

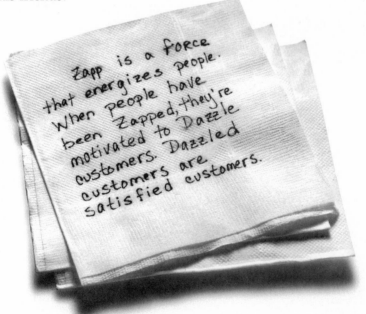

Zapp is a force
that energizes people.
When people have
been Zapped, they're
motivated to Dazzle
customers. Dazzled
customers are
satisfied customers.

Don looked up. "And the trick is making everybody feel good."

Stan started to disagree, but Don slapped his hand down on the table so hard the silverware jumped an inch in the air.

"That's it!" he declared. "From now on, every teller is going to feel good about themselves and their jobs, and our customers are going to feel good about themselves and about banking with us!"

He stood up and pumped Stan's hand. He held his LISA triumphantly in the other. "This is one great machine! Thanks to you and LISA here, my problems are solved."

"Just don't tell anybody where you got that!" Stan called as Don raced for the door, nearly knocking over Laverne, who was carrying a tray with his bologna on white bread with mayo.

Maureen was no less enthusiastic as she left. "I've got work to do!" she shouted, grinning from ear to ear.

When he was alone, Stan stared at what he had written, wondering how he could make it happen at the power company.

Chapter 5

That night Maureen baked cookies:
chocolate chip cookies and sugar cookies
and raisin cookies and macaroons. The next day
she left the cookies on the
counter at the nurses' station on
her floor with this note
attached: "You're all very
important and very special,
and you make a real
difference."

Maureen hid in her
office and peeked through
the blinds as one nurse
after another discovered
the cookies. Happily she
noted that each one got a
little brighter on LISA's
screen when they read the
note. But the longer she
watched, the dimmer each
nurse became. In fact, by the
end of the day they were just

Maureen

as dim as they'd been before Maureen went on her baking spree.

That same morning before the bank opened for business, Don met with his staff.

"I have an announcement to make," Don began. Everybody stopped breathing, certain that some awful news was going to follow. "You are all very important. The bank couldn't stay in business without you. You should all feel very good about yourselves."

The staff breathed again, but after a second their relief was replaced by confusion.

"Oh, by the way," Don added, "if you all do your best to make our customers feel good about themselves, they'll be happier and your jobs will be easier. I know you can do it. I have complete confidence in you all. Any questions?"

No one spoke for a moment. Finally, Gina, the newest teller, raised her hand. "How do we do that exactly?"

"Do what?" Don asked.

"Make people feel good about themselves."

"It's easy," Don replied slowly, suddenly realizing he hadn't thought about how to do it. "All you have to do is . . . ahhh . . ."

"Compliment people?" Agnes, another teller, offered.

"Right!" Don said, relieved. "And be sure you let customers know how important they are! OK. Let's get to it!"

The staff dispersed, still not sure about the "it" they were supposed to get to. Confident that his inspirational meeting had gone well, Don whistled a little tune as he walked toward his office. On the way he passed Frank, one of the senior tellers. Feeling inspired and motivational, Don put his arm around Frank's shoulder.

"That is one sharp tie you're wearing," Don said.

"Uh, thanks," Frank replied. He'd worn the same tie one day a week for the past five years.

"Oh, by the way," Don said as he and Frank headed in opposite directions, "I noticed your balance was off by three dollars last night. Keep a closer eye on it from now on."

If Don had been watching this on LISA's screen he would have seen all the light and color draining from Frank. For his part Frank was imagining wrapping his "sharp" tie tightly around Don's neck.

After completing some paperwork, Don emerged from his office carrying LISA under his suit jacket. He walked quietly toward a dimly lit corner of the bank, where he hid behind a potted plant. He took LISA from under his coat and scanned the teller lines. Finally, he swiveled the parabolic reflector in the direction of a customer who was walking up to Agnes' window. On LISA's screen the customer glowed a dull red. "Typical lunchtime customer," Don thought. "Now I'll see what happens when Agnes enhances his self-esteem."

Sure enough, after just a second or two at Agnes' window, Don saw a few dim sparks pass from Agnes to the customer. The customer changed from a dull red color to faint green. For a brief moment he was a medium shade of blue. Suddenly, Don felt LISA vibrate in his hand. On the screen he saw something startling. The sparks were replaced by a dark shape that looked like a vacuum cleaner hose. The hose sprouted from Agnes, wrapped itself around the customer, and drained the color and brightness from him until he was a dull red again.

Don was incredulous. "What's wrong?" he practically shouted to himself. The customer left Agnes' window, dragging the hose with him.

Don swung the reflector toward Gina. Her customer, a young mother with two small children in tow, wasn't red when she stepped up to Gina's window—just a pleasant shade of neutral green.

"Good afternoon," Gina said pleasantly.

"Hello," the young woman said as she fumbled in her infant's diaper bag for her checkbook while trying to stop her four-year-old from knocking a stack of brochures off the counter.

"That's a nice outfit you're wearing," Gina offered.

The young woman looked down at her baggy sweatshirt and old jeans and then back at Gina as if she had lost her mind. "Thank you," she said with a question in her voice.

As Don watched, Gina suddenly sprouted a vacuum

"Typical customer," Don thought.

cleaner hose that started to drain the light from the customer.
Don had to find out what was going on. He put LISA down,
slipped out from behind the plant, and casually walked by
Gina's window, trying to look inconspicuous.

After the customer wrote out her check, the infant began
crying.

"You have such well-behaved children," Gina said
sincerely.

The woman pulled the four-year-old back from the counter
and put a pacifier in her infant's mouth. "You don't have to
be sarcastic," she snarled at Gina. "And could you please
hurry? What's taking so long? I just need you to cash that
check."

Shocked by this outburst, Gina forgot about offering
compliments and gave the woman her money. "Have a nice
day," Gina called as the woman dragged her two children out
the door.

Don shuffled zombie-like back to his office. If he had taken
LISA outside and pointed her at the bank, he would have
seen the building's pinkish glow grow redder and redder.

Meanwhile at the power company, Stan wasn't sure what
to do to Zapp his people. He had brooded all night about it.
By morning he wasn't any closer to knowing what to do.

He was still brooding when Ellen, one of his customer
service reps, walked by his desk. Seeing Ellen reminded him
of a letter he'd gotten from a customer earlier in the week.

"Hey, Ellen, got a second?" he called to her.

"What's up?" she replied.

"I got a letter from a Mrs. Morrison about you."

Ellen looked confused for a moment.

"Mrs. Morrison? Oh, yeah. What'd she have to say?"

"She actually thanked me for hiring you and told me to thank you for taking the time to solve her billing problem. If you hadn't stuck with her and unraveled the problem, she might have had her service turned off. So, on behalf of Mrs. Morrison, thank you. And on behalf of myself, I want you to know you set a great example for all of us. I'm going to put this letter on the bulletin board so everyone can read it."

Ellen positively beamed as she walked back to her desk. Stan had a hunch. He quickly took LISA out of his bottom drawer and pointed the reflector at Ellen. She glowed so brightly that Stan had to squint.

"Zapp!" he whispered happily.

Chapter 6

"This Zapping business is a lot harder than I thought," Maureen complained at lunch the next day. "I stayed up half the night baking cookies and writing a nice note. They ate the cookies and read the note, but nothing changed."

"Cookies and a note aren't enough," Don chided her. "I told everybody they were important. I complimented them. I told them to do the same thing to the customers."

"Did that help?" Maureen asked.

"Uh . . . no . . . not really," Don mumbled.

"We must be missing something."

Don

Don turned to Stan. "By the way, what's the creepy vacuum cleaner hose all about?"

"Based on the laws of physics," Stan answered, "it stands to reason that Zapp and Dazzle have opposite counterparts."

"Opposite counterparts?" Maureen repeated.

"Yes. I call them sapp and fizzle," Stan said. Don and Maureen nodded, though they had no idea what he was talking about.

"I think I Zapped one of my people yesterday," Stan said after a moment.

Don and Maureen leaned forward. "You did? How?"

Stan told them about what had happened with Ellen.

"So," Don said when Stan finished his story, "you spoke to one person and gave her positive feedback that was job related."

"And," Maureen added, "you singled her out and talked about something she did."

"And you were specific about what you were praising," Don continued. "We've got this self-esteem thing nailed!"

"I thought so too," Stan said. "But when I tried to do the same thing with some other people, I found out it's not as simple as I thought."

"What do you mean?" Maureen asked.

"All day I went out of my way to build people's self-esteem," Stan recounted. "I made it a point to say something constructive to each one of my people, and sometimes it didn't Zapp them. In fact, sometimes it sapped them."

"That doesn't make sense," Don protested.

Stan nodded. "I thought so too at first, but as I analyzed what happened, I realized that when I sapped somebody, it was because I wasn't really sincere about the praise or they just didn't deserve it. But you know what really surprised me?"

"What?" Don and Maureen inquired in unison, leaning in closer.

"At the end of the day, I had to talk to a customer service rep about a complaint. Ordinarily this rep is great with customers, but I guess he was having a bad day or something, and the customer got me on the line to complain that he was rude to her. When I talked to him, I tried my best not to make him feel inferior or put him down. In fact, I made it a point to say that ordinarily he was able to handle the toughest customers.

"The talk went well, although I figured he'd probably still feel bad about the negative feedback. But when I pointed LISA at him when he walked away, I found out he was a nice shade of blue, and I could still see some lightning passing between us."

"OK," Don said. "So, to Zapp people, you have to do more than just say complimentary things about them."

"And you have to do more than bake a few cookies," Maureen added.

"Right," Stan agreed. "I think that what Zapps people— what really maintains and enhances their self-esteem—is offering praise to people who deserve it about specific, job-related things that they've done well. And even when you have to tell somebody something negative, you can still Zapp them by recognizing something positive."

Stan wrote on his napkin. "I think we can safely say that we know at least part of what makes Zapp happen."

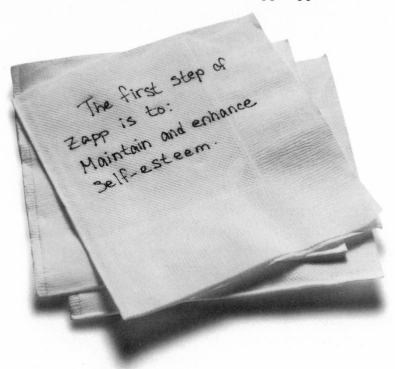

The first step of Zapp is to: Maintain and enhance self-esteem.

Just then Otto walked by. He started to say something when the kitchen door swung open, hitting the wall with a bang so loud it made everyone jump. Laverne came running out. She looked shell-shocked as she approached Otto.

"Is everything all right?" he asked.

Laverne shook her head. "No," she said. "I can't believe I was so stupid."

Stan took LISA out of its case and surreptitiously aimed it at Otto and Laverne.

"You know that chamber of commerce group in the meeting room?"

Otto nodded.

"I set up the lunch menu over the phone last week. They wanted 22 orders of the Tomato Surprise. Well, when I wrote it down, I abbreviated it. Lenny read it wrong, and now I have 22 orders of tomato soup! I should have remembered that Lenny was new. It's too late to make the right orders. We don't even have five tomatoes left in the kitchen!"

As she spoke, Otto nodded and listened intently. On LISA's screen Stan noticed something interesting. Small but intense sparks of lightning were passing from Otto to Laverne. This puzzled Stan. As far as he could see, Otto wasn't doing anything.

"I understand why you're upset," Otto told Laverne. "I felt the same way when it happened to me."

Laverne's face brightened a little. "This happened to you?"

As the sparks became more intense, Laverne glowed a soft blue and LISA emitted the loud, crackling noises it always made in the presence of strong amounts of Zapp. Stan switched LISA off to avoid detection.

Otto continued. "My handwriting's worse than yours. I still remember the looks I got from that group of rabbis when those ham dinners came out of the kitchen."

Laverne managed a little chuckle.

Otto stood up. "So, what would you like to do about the chamber of commerce?"

Laverne thought for a moment. "Could we give them a free dessert and a 20 percent discount coupon they could use the next time they come in?" she asked.

Otto nodded. "Great idea!"

As Otto and Laverne moved out of earshot, Stan told Don and Maureen what he'd observed on the screen. "It appears that another way to Zapp people is to listen to them."

"That sounds too easy," Maureen said.

"I'm an excellent listener," Don added, "but I haven't seen much Zapping going on at the bank."

"Look," Stan said to his skeptical friends, "all I know is what I saw. LISA doesn't lie, so there must be something *enzapping* about listening."

They mulled this over.

"The problem," Don eventually declared, "is that we can't really be sure what works because we can't observe ourselves."

"You're right!" Stan said excitedly. "Our data is too limited to be conclusive."

"But," Maureen added, "if we observe each other, we'll get a better idea of what works and what doesn't. If you guys come over to the hospital at lunchtime tomorrow, you can observe me, and I'll treat you to lunch in the cafeteria."

"Hospital food?" Don wrinkled his nose.

"We must make sacrifices in the cause of science," Stan concluded dramatically.

Chapter 7

The next day after lunch in the hospital cafeteria, Don and Stan hid in Maureen's office with LISA. From this vantage point they were able to watch the results of her attempts at Zapping through listening.

Carol was one of the senior nurses on Maureen's floor. She was very professional and very thorough—and not very easy to listen to. Carol spoke in a slow monotone and repeated herself. Maureen tried to pay attention, but as soon as she heard that monotone voice, her mind would wander. By the time Carol finished a sentence, Maureen had forgotten how it had started. Maureen usually cut her off by turning away and pretending she had something pressing to do.

Maureen was hoping Don and Stan would observe her listening to Carol.

"She's the acid test," Maureen thought to herself. "If I can Zapp her by listening, I can Zapp anybody."

Maureen wasn't disappointed. Soon, Carol approached her, carrying a patient's chart and looking worried.

Meanwhile, back in Maureen's office Don and Stan had to look twice to see if Carol was even there. "I've never seen anyone so dim," Stan commented.

"I'm having trouble with Mrs. Huffnagle again," Carol began tonelessly. "She won't take her medication until she sees the doctor, but the doctor won't be in until tomorrow morning. I told her that, but she's insisting that . . ."

Maureen was very conscious of letting Carol know she was being heard. She stood in front of her. She looked her in the eye. She focused her full attention on Carol. She nodded her head at all the appropriate times.

LISA revealed some dim flickers passing between them.

". . . and so," Carol concluded, "I called Mrs. Huffnagle's son, who's coming in later. Maybe he can talk her into taking it."

When Carol finished, Maureen found to her surprise that she was able to summarize what Carol had just told her. The flickers got a little stronger, and for a moment Carol looked a little brighter on the screen. "She's doing it!" Don whispered.

Maureen was feeling very pleased with herself as she left Carol and walked back to her office. Stan told her what they had seen on LISA's screen.

"Yes!" Maureen raised a triumphant fist in the air.

"But," Stan said, cutting her celebration short, "as soon as you walked away from her, the flickering stopped, and she got as dim as she was before."

"That didn't happen with Otto and Laverne did it?"

Maureen asked, though she knew the answer.

"No. As a matter of fact, Laverne got even brighter," Stan confirmed.

"Maybe I just need more practice."

While Don and Stan watched LISA's screen, Maureen practiced her best listening skills for almost an hour. She found that by focusing on what her people were saying, she was able to keep her own thoughts silent. When she noticed her mind wandering, she would make a mental list of what the other person was saying. Soon, Maureen was pretty good at restating what she'd heard, and if she missed a point or misunderstood something, her summary gave the other person an opportunity to clarify it.

Still, the Zapp Don and Stan saw was weak at best. In some cases the mild Zapp even turned into a sapp.

Maureen was exasperated. "I give up!" she said at last. "Whatever magic Otto's got, I don't have it!"

Stan thought about what Otto had done. "Maybe there's more to this than just paying attention. Otto did more than listen to Laverne. He let her know he

"She's the acid test," Maureen thought.

heard her and that he understood."

"So did I!" Maureen insisted. "I've nodded so much in the last hour that my nurses must think I've got a spring in my neck!"

"He also let Laverne know he was going to help her with her problem," Stan noted.

"I always do something about the nurses' problems," Maureen protested.

"Do you tell them what you're going to do?" Stan asked.

"Sometimes," Maureen replied, a little less sure of herself.

"Something else Otto did was acknowledge how Laverne felt," Don said. "Remember?"

"I remember."

"Have you been doing that?" Stan wanted to know.

"No, but I'm going to try right now," Maureen said resolutely.

Out on the floor she found Carol, who was still worrying over Mrs. Huffnagle's chart. "Carol, I know how frustrating it is when patients won't let you help them. Calling her son was the right thing to do. Just in case he can't talk her into it, I'll see if I can get Dr. Burroughs to talk to her."

Carol smiled, which made Maureen realize that smiling wasn't something Carol did very often. On LISA's screen bright bolts flickered from Maureen to Carol. As Maureen walked back to the office, Carol glowed brightly.

The next day at The Home Plate the three friends reviewed what they had learned.

"So, it's not enough to just actively listen to people," Maureen summarized. "We've got to empathize with them."

"I think we have enough data to make that conclusion," Stan agreed. He wrote this new finding on a napkin.

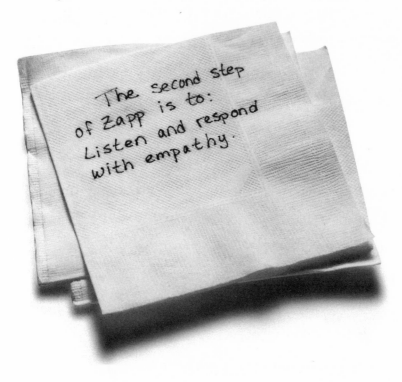

The second step
of Zapp is to:
Listen and respond
with empathy.

Chapter 8

In the weeks that followed, Don, Stan, and Maureen got better at the art of Zapping. They made every effort to listen to people. They paid attention not just to their words but to their facial expressions and body language too. By doing this they found that they were able to respond to the whole message their employees were sending: the feelings as well as the facts. The three leaders got so good they Zapped their employees even when they weren't able to solve a problem or do what was wanted—the employees knew they'd been heard and that their bosses empathized with them.

Occasional LISA readings confirmed that there was more Zapping at the bank, the power company, and the hospital. The three friends even observed some individual cases of customer Dazzle.

"I bet if we pointed LISA at the power company now, it'd be just as bright a blue as The Home Plate," Stan bragged as they walked to the diner one day.

"Maybe," Don replied quickly, "but the bank would be brighter."

"Not as bright as the hospital," Maureen chimed in.

"There's only one way to find out." Stan turned and walked back toward the power company, with Don and Maureen following close behind. After Stan retrieved LISA from his office, they hid behind a repair truck in the parking lot.

"I don't know about the rest of the building, but my floor should be bright blue," Stan said, confidently pointing LISA's reflector at a row of third-floor windows.

They stared expectantly at the screen. The power company building glowed a sickly pink except for the section where Stan's department was located. There, a light bluish-green glow radiated from the windows. Stan jiggled the reflector a few times, but nothing changed.

"That's it?" he asked.

"Maybe we should get closer to the building," Maureen suggested.

"That won't make any difference," Stan replied sadly.

"Maybe the building is too big," Don offered.

"Yeah, and so the color is diluted." Stan brightened and quickly packed LISA into its case. "Let's check the bank. It's a lot smaller."

At the bank they hid behind some bushes across from the drive-through window. They pointed LISA at the building and looked at the screen. It was as dull and as green as the third floor of the power company.

Don was crestfallen. "I don't get it."

They walked quickly to the hospital, pointed LISA at Maureen's floor, and got the same result.

"What are we doing wrong?" Maureen asked later as they stood in front of The Home Plate.

"We're doing everything Otto does," Don whined.

Stan pointed LISA's reflector at the diner, and as before, it glowed bright blue. "We must be missing something," he said evenly.

Inside The Home Plate Laverne was even more enthusiastic than usual as she led them to their table.

"I've got a surprise for you," she gushed, handing them bright new menus. "Open 'em up," she urged as they sat down.

The new menus not only featured The Home Plate's traditional offerings, but they also featured Laverne's picture along with pictures of all the other waiters and waitresses.

Next to each picture was a lunch or dinner special. The "Laverne," for instance, was a pastrami on whole wheat with cole slaw and a bowl of French onion soup.

"Whattaya think?" she asked after they had a moment to look at the menus.

"Whose idea was this?"

"Laverne, this is neat," Maureen said.

"You're famous," Don added. Laverne blushed.

"Whose idea was this?" Stan asked.

"Mine," she blurted out. "Well, ours really. All of ours."
She swept her arm to indicate the rest of the staff. Laverne
explained that Otto had asked each of them to come up with
a menu item that they thought customers would like. He
encouraged them to get input from customers and from the
kitchen staff. He worked with them to set the price.

"Remember when I was asking you all those questions last
month?" she reminded them. "You thought I was just being
nosy, but it was part of my survey."

"Well," Don said, "in honor of this occasion, I say we all
order a round of Lavernes!"

Laverne walked proudly back to the kitchen.

"What a great idea," Maureen said as she looked at the
new menu.

Stan looked at the crowded restaurant and had a hunch.
He turned LISA on and swiveled the reflector around.
"There's a lot more Zapp in here than usual and a lot more
Dazzling going on too."

"That's no surprise," Maureen said. "Look at how
pumped up Laverne is. I don't need LISA to know there's a
lot of new energy in here."

"No wonder this place glows so bright," Don said. He
studied the new menu enviously. "I wish I could do
something like this at the bank."

"Why don't you?" Maureen asked.

Don arched his eyebrows. "I don't think my bosses would look too kindly on 'Agnes' Free Checking' or 'Gina's Retirement Account.'"

"I don't mean you should do exactly what Otto did," Maureen said, "but at least you could try something like it."

Don shook his head. "Banking is too regulated."

"Not as regulated as health care," Maureen replied. "Almost everything a nurse does is ordered and charted. I'm sure they have lots of good ideas, but there's not much I can do with them."

Don pushed the new menu across the table. "All I know is there are a lot more rules and regulations about money than pastrami sandwiches."

"We have lots of rules and regulations at the power company too," Stan said as they studied the happy mayhem of the lunchtime rush.

Don sighed deeply. "Rules and regulations can't create this."

Maureen shook her head. "We've done our best with Zapp and Dazzle, but we can only do what we can do."

Stan noticed that his friends were more depressed than he'd ever seen them. "Look," he said, trying to sound encouraging, "I know this new menu is having a big effect here today, but there are other things we can do."

"Like what?" Don asked.

Stan couldn't think of a reply.

The three of them didn't talk much about Zapp and Dazzle in the weeks that followed. Don and Maureen resigned themselves to the fact that despite their best efforts, they'd never be able to create the bright blue energy they saw at The Home Plate.

Stan tried to forget the problem too, but he couldn't. He thought long and hard about how to use his employees' ideas and involve them, just like Otto. He thought about putting a suggestion box in his department, but that had been done before and none of the suggestions were ever seen or heard from again.

He was about to ask his boss if he could run a contest for the most creative solution to a problem in his department, but then he remembered that had been done before too. He met the winner of that contest at a company picnic once. When Stan congratulated her, she said, "Don't remind me! I saved the company a million dollars—and I got fifty bucks and a certificate in a plastic frame."

Stan finally gave up thinking about employee involvement and turned his thoughts to improving LISA instead. It bothered him that the only way he could measure Zapp and Dazzle was by carrying LISA around and watching lightning bolts, hoses, and colors. It was hard to gather data that way, and the data he gathered was hard to quantify.

"I'm a numbers guy," Stan often said of himself, "because numbers don't lie."

After many nights in his basement workshop and a dozen trips to the hardware store, Stan found a way to plug LISA into his computer. After many more nights he came up with a program that converted the lightning bolts, hoses, and colors to numbers. He called them "Zapp-sapp" and "Dazzle-fizzle" levels. After a little more tinkering and a little more programming, he gave LISA a memory so he could measure the levels when it was undocked from the computer.

Stan took the new LISA computer combo to work and placed it behind a plant in his office. He pointed the reflector toward his door. With this setup he could monitor the Zapp-sapp and Dazzle-fizzle levels in his department continuously. Stan also offered to attach Don's and Maureen's LISAs to their computers, but they weren't interested in Zapp and Dazzle anymore.

Undaunted, Stan conscientiously measured the levels day after day. He tried to build his employees' self-esteem, and he listened and tried to respond with empathy. The levels rose and fell a little but not much. Zapp got as high as 31, and on one memorable day Dazzle peaked at 42. Stan knew things were better in his department than before, but when he compared his levels with those he measured at The Home Plate, he got discouraged. There he recorded Zapp and Dazzle levels of 200 and higher. Stan also noticed that when he was out of the office, his levels plummeted. He might have given up on the whole thing if the storm hadn't hit.

Chapter 9

It started raining just before midnight.
By the time Stan got to work, the winds were
picking up, and by lunchtime the rain was
blowing in horizontal sheets across the
windows.

At first the trouble calls were routine.
Lines were down here and there.
Lightning (not the Zapping kind) was
striking transformers. Then, the storm
sewers backed up, the roads began to
flood, and the repair trucks couldn't get
through. Soon the phone lines were
jammed. Stan's people were answering
calls from customers without power as
fast as they could and entering the
information about the outages into the
master computer.

Stan was racing from the customer service
reps on the phones to the dispatchers on the
radios to a big map on the wall, where the
areas without power were outlined in red.
Everybody was coming to him with their
problems. He was solving them one after
another and loving every minute of it. He

pictured himself as a general in a war room making brilliant snap decisions. At first it was fun. He felt important and challenged. At 3 p.m. the first real crisis hit.

Libby, a customer service rep, was finishing up what must have been her seventieth call of the day.

"Yes, sir," she said staring at her computer screen. "We're aware of that problem. Please understand, but I can't tell you specifically where our crews are or when they'll get to your area. Yes, sir. I will. Thank you for calling."

Libby took a deep breath and punched another blinking button on her console. "Nearville Power, this is Libby. How can I help you?"

The man's voice on the other end of the line was weak. "Nearville Power?"

"Yes, can I help you?" Libby tried not to sound impatient.

"I just saw one of your trucks go past," the voice continued.

"Yes," Libby barked. Then she heard a sharp gasp on the other end of the line. A bolt of fear shot through her. "Sir, are you all right?"

"No." His voice was weaker now. "I'm having chest pains . . . trouble breathing."

Libby tried to keep the panic out of her voice. "Have you called an ambulance? Do you want me to call an ambulance for you?"

"Called already," he choked. "I live in Mountainview . . . in a cabin. Take 'em an hour to get here in this weather . . . and their helicopters are grounded. I was hoping that truck of yours could give me a lift."

Libby's mind began to swirl. She looked around for Stan. "I'm not able to speak with the repair crews myself, but I can give the message to our dispatcher. What's your name?"

"John Sutton," he replied, almost in a whisper.

"And your address?" Libby asked. He did not reply. "Mr. Sutton, I need your address." The silence on the other end was broken by the sound of the phone hitting the floor.

Libby's blood ran cold. "Mr. Sutton?" she asked plaintively. Libby tore off her headset. "Stan!" she screamed. Everything in the room stopped. Stan rushed over to her, and she breathlessly explained what had happened.

Everyone's eyes were on Stan. He felt a little panicky at first, but he quickly got himself under control. In fact, with this crisis Stan felt a new exhilaration.

"Run a computer search on the last name. There can't be that many Suttons out in Mountainview," Stan commanded calmly. He followed Libby back to her computer. She typed in "John Sutton." They waited for the list to appear on the screen. A list of Suttons flashed on the screen, then everything in the room went dark.

"There goes our power," said a voice in the darkness. Just as suddenly the lights flickered on, but the computer screen was maddeningly blank.

Libby's blood ran cold.

"Computers are down," another voice reported.

Stan felt as if he was floating. He looked at the expectant faces all around him.

"What's the matter with these people?" he thought to himself. "This guy could be dying, and they're all just standing there."

Stan's mind was blank. After what seemed like an eternity, he heard himself say, "Does anybody have any ideas?" Nobody replied for a long moment. They weren't used to being asked for ideas, especially in a crisis. Finally Fred, the dispatcher, spoke up.

"I can find out which truck is closest to Mountainview and get it to reverse its route."

"Great idea," Stan said, sending out a powerful first-level Zapp.

Patty, a customer service representative, held up a phone book. "I can look up his address," she shouted triumphantly.

"Yes!" Stan shouted. "The phone book. Excellent!"

"I'll get the hospital on the line," Ellen said. "If the driver doesn't know CPR, they can give him instructions!"

Stan stood back and watched the team swing into action. He didn't feel like a general anymore. He just felt relieved.

Mr. Sutton was found. The driver of the repair truck administered CPR and got him to the hospital in time. After he was admitted, he ended up on Maureen's floor.

A few days later, after the newspaper stories stopped and the local TV news turned its attention elsewhere, Stan remembered that LISA had been running during the crisis.

He hadn't thought about Zapp during the excitement. When Stan checked what LISA had recorded, he found that the Zapp level had not only been higher throughout the storm, but that it had escalated steadily from the moment he asked for help with Mr. Sutton. At the height of the crisis, LISA recorded levels of over 150.

"Incredible," Stan said to himself. Even after everything was back to normal in the department, Zapp levels remained high, and when LISA was pointed at customers, Dazzle showed a definite increase. "It's self-sustaining," Stan thought excitedly.

When he told Don and Maureen about what he'd observed, their curiosity about Zapp and Dazzle was renewed. But Don remained skeptical.

"What you did was life-and-death stuff. No wonder everybody got Zapped for a while."

"But they stayed Zapped," Stan reminded him. "And I don't think the seriousness of the situation caused that. Remember what Otto did? He asked for people's ideas about the new menu, and he got them involved in creating it. When I didn't know what to do for Mr. Sutton, I did the same thing."

"And we can do that even though we're regulated?" Maureen asked.

"If I can do it, you can do it," Stan concluded. He picked up a napkin and started writing. "I think it comes down to this." He pushed the napkin toward his friends.

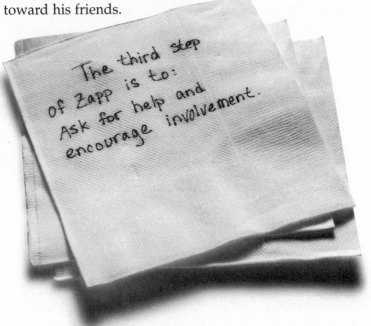

Don read the napkin. "Are you still willing to soup up our LISAs and plug them into our computers?" he asked Stan.

Stan nodded.

"All right then," Don declared. "Let's get to work."

Chapter 10

Stan was eager to keep up Zapp's momentum in his department. "I need to get people's ideas and involve them on a regular basis," he thought.

In that spirit one morning he called a team meeting. "How can we improve things so we'll be better prepared the next time we have a big storm?" he asked, after they were all seated around the table.

No one spoke at first. They looked around or at the table. They still weren't used to being asked what they thought. He decided to throw out a well-deserved Zapp. "Thanks to your hard work and quick thinking, we handled the storm really well last week. We even helped save a man's life. I know you have some ideas about how to improve the way we do things."

Finally, Libby spoke up. "Well," she began timidly, "it would save a lot of time if the customer service reps could call the repair crews directly."

"That's the dispatcher's job," Fred objected.

"I know," Ellen chimed in, "but we could respond to emergency trouble calls a lot faster if we didn't have to go through you guys."

"But you don't know who to call," Fred insisted. "And besides, you can't call the trucks on the phone. You have to use the radio."

Pretty soon everybody was throwing out ideas about how to improve response time. Stan threw out more Zapps by listening to each of their ideas and writing them down. The list of ideas was narrowed as the meeting progressed.

"We need to develop some guidelines for when customer service reps should be able to contact repair crews," Libby concluded. "And it shouldn't just be in emergencies."

"And," Fred added, "we need to figure out a way to tie in your headsets to the radio."

"You're right!" Stan said. "I think that's where we should start. Thanks for your help."

Stan adjourned the meeting. "You know we should have meetings like this more often," he said as everyone went back to work.

After the meeting Stan was too excited to check on LISA. If he had, he would have seen that the Zapp level in his department first climbed above 100 during the meeting, then plummeted at the end. Instead, Stan made a list of guidelines for when customer service reps could contact repair crews. It was, he decided, an excellent list. He thought about calling someone in engineering about the headset-radio connection, but because he enjoyed tinkering so much, Stan decided to solve the problem himself in his basement workshop on his own time.

All it took was a few parts from the hardware store and a little ingenuity. "I even saved the company money," he thought proudly.

Stan was so taken with himself that he didn't notice the blank stares on everyone's faces when he implemented the new system. And he was completely baffled when no one used it. None of the customer service reps bothered to learn how to use the radio—not even Libby. Dispatch still did all the talking to the repair crews. When the next storm hit, response times were no better than they had been before.

But what bothered him more was that LISA told him Zapp levels were low and getting lower. During lunch at The Home Plate, he told Don and Maureen what had happened.

"I don't understand," Stan whined. "I asked everybody for their ideas. I used their ideas. They could've been involved in making the ideas work, but they didn't want to be for some reason."

Don looked puzzled. "I had the same kind of meeting at the bank, and my Zapp levels are through the roof, not to mention Dazzle."

This didn't make Stan feel any better.

"What did you do exactly?" Maureen asked Don.

"One of our biggest problems at the bank was getting customers in and out fast at peak times, like at noon or at the end of the day on Fridays. That's what I asked for ideas about."

Chapter 11

Don's team had no trouble coming up with ideas for how to move customers more efficiently through the teller lines during peak times. They had lived with the problem for a long time; they all had ideas for how to solve it. They enjoyed the discussion, and their Zapp level went up on the new and improved computerized LISA that Don had pointed through his office doorway and into the conference area where the meeting was held.

After a lot of discussion, Agnes summed up the problem. "If customers ask us to do anything more complicated than make a deposit or a withdrawal, we have to leave the window to do it."

Gina nodded. "That's not a problem when things are slow, but it is a problem between noon and one."

"And all day on Friday," Agnes added.

"That's when the lines are long to begin with," Gina added, "and the longer it takes us to do things, the longer the lines get."

"We need to be able to do more things at our windows," Agnes said. "And we could if we had better access to account information. For example, if someone wants a loan payoff amount, we should be able to pull it up on our computers instead of going to someone in Customer Service."

Everyone nodded enthusiastically, especially Don. "Great idea!" he exclaimed. "Thanks, everybody. I'll take it from here." He didn't know it, but the Zapp level at the bank began plummeting at that moment.

Don walked happily back to his office, eager to get started. He sat at his desk and took out a piece of paper and wrote "Account Information Tellers Need" across the top. He stared at the paper a long time. His last words at the meeting—"I'll take it from here"—kept ringing in his ears. After a while he realized he couldn't "take it from here" or anywhere else for that matter. He didn't know what kinds of new account information tellers needed because he hadn't been a teller for years.

The next day Don called another meeting. "I adjourned our meeting too soon yesterday," he began. "You came up with a great idea for how to get customers in and out faster, but I don't know what kinds of account information you need."

During the meeting Don let his employees take the lead in coming up with a list of what they needed. When they had finished, Don said, "Now I think we're really getting somewhere. Just let me know what I can do to help."

Meanwhile, in his office LISA hummed atop the computer and recorded a sharp jump in Zapp. In fact, it was a little too much Zapp for some of the people at the meeting. They were used to being sapped, and this new energy was a little intimidating. Some tried to deflect it back at Don or to other people who could handle it better.

Don said some things to build their confidence and their self-esteem, and he let them know that he would stand behind them as they implemented their solution. As he got up to leave, he was asked if the team could stay together for a while and get started. He happily granted the request.

Back in his office Don looked at LISA's readings. The screen glowed with a new, blue intensity. Lightning bolts passed from one person to another.

"In other words," Maureen asked, "your people are responsible for solving the problem?"

"With my help," Don added. "I arrange for people to have time off their regular jobs to plan. I make sure they have access to the information they need. Stuff like that."

Maureen turned to Stan. "Maybe you should try that."

"No," Stan protested. "Solving problems is *my* job. I think it's great to get employees' ideas and involve them, but they don't know what I know. They can't do what I do, and they don't see the big picture."

"Maybe not," Maureen said. "But it's just human nature that people don't care about things they don't have a stake in."

"But my people have a stake in solving the response time problem," Stan protested. "It'll make their jobs easier."

"Sure," Don replied. "But if you come up with the solution and take all the responsibility for it, then *you* own it—not them."

"So, what's the bottom line?" Stan asked.

This time it was Maureen's turn to write on a napkin. "I think this sums it up," she said.

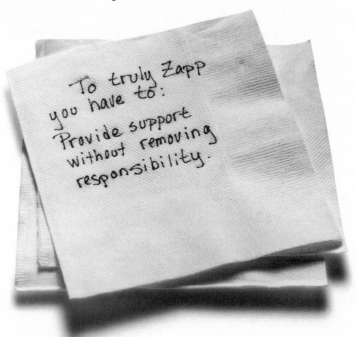

To truly Zapp you have to:
Provide support without removing responsibility.

The next day Stan called another meeting. He started out by ripping up and throwing out his list of guidelines. After that his team got to work on coming up with some guidelines of their own. Like the people at the bank, Stan's employees threw more and brighter lightning bolts back and forth as they worked on their ideas.

Not that things were perfect with either Stan's team or Don's team. Both teams made a few false starts, but the two leaders offered their help and got the resources their people needed to succeed. Maureen learned from the experiences of her friends, and soon the nurses on her floor at the hospital were tackling their own problems and doing things they never thought they'd be able to do.

Meanwhile, LISA recorded higher and higher Zapp levels, and the Dazzle levels weren't far behind. The three friends had discovered the secrets of Zapp and Dazzle. Some days the power company, the bank, and the hospital glowed with a blue intensity that rivaled The Home Plate itself.

Chapter 12

As time passed, the power of Zapp worked its magic. Employees were happier and more energetic. As they got better at Dazzling customers, the customers became happier too. These happier customers did more business with Don's bank, felt better about paying their power bills after dealing with Stan's customer service reps, and recommended the hospital to their friends after a stay on Maureen's floor.

In fact, if you had to stay in a hospital, Maureen's floor was a great place to be. It radiated Zapp and Dazzle. You could see it on the faces of the nurses. Even the normally dour Carol seemed to be smiling all the time.

Yet, Maureen was scared. She knew Zapp did a lot of good, but she didn't trust it. She didn't want to take responsibility away from the nurses on her shift, but she knew that in the end, she was responsible for the consequences of their actions.

Despite her doubts, Maureen admitted that things did seem to be going a lot better on her floor. For one thing, she almost never heard patients complain about their meals anymore because now the nurses always tried to get what their patients liked.

The nurses developed a Food Preference Profile (or FPP as it was called) based on the likes and dislikes of each patient. Every day a nurse compared the profiles to the next day's menu selections. If a day's menu didn't include something a patient liked, the nurse would send the kitchen a special order for something he or she did like.

It seemed like a good idea. In the beginning Maureen offered suggestions about how and when to get information for the profile, but after that she left the rest up to the nurses. She was afraid that if she stayed too close, she would sapp her nurses.

The nurses started with a rush of enthusiasm. When they went to Maureen about something, she usually would nod and say, "Use your best judgment" or "Whatever makes the patient happy" or words to that effect. As far as the nurses could see, Maureen didn't really care what they did.

The nurses seemed happy and the patients seemed happy, so Maureen couldn't see a reason to be unhappy. Then Adele, her boss, gave her one.

Adele appeared at Maureen's office door one day with fire in her eyes and a memo in her hand. "This is a hospital, not a gourmet restaurant!" she said through clenched teeth.

Maureen couldn't argue with that. "What's up?" she asked calmly.

"Costs are up!" Adele shouted. In a very loud voice she explained that she was upset because all the special meal orders were putting her over budget. The director of Nutrition Services was upset because the extra work to make the custom meals was driving up payroll costs—and besides, meal planning was their job. The hospital administrator was upset because he had a budget meeting with the corporate board next week, and he knew they would be upset.

"I don't know what's going on around here," Adele concluded, "but it's got to stop!" Maureen was about to explain about Zapp and Dazzle and how happy the patients were, but Adele turned on her heels and stalked toward the elevator. Now it was Maureen's turn to be upset. Soon the nurses on her floor would be upset too.

"The Food Preference Profile has got to stop," read the memo Maureen sent to her staff. "Effective immediately the only special meals allowed will be those ordered by doctors for their patients. NO EXCEPTIONS."

Sapp!

Maureen didn't need to check with LISA to know that Zapp all but disappeared from her floor. The familiar patient complaints were back. Carol was her old frowning self again, and Maureen wasn't very happy either.

At lunch a couple days later, she told her friends what had happened. "Since the memo went out, everybody's been in the pits," she moaned.

"What are your Zapp levels like?" Stan wanted to know.

Maureen was annoyed by the question. "What do you think?" she asked. "They're awful. The nurses walk around like zombies. All I do is handle patient complaints all day, and nobody is doing one thing more than they have to do, just because something didn't go their way. If you ask me, they're all acting like spoiled brats!"

"My Zapp levels have their ups and downs too," Don said, trying to sound sympathetic.

Maureen was incredulous. "This is more than ups and downs! Look, Zapp is fine as far as it goes, but I never did trust it—and now I know why. I don't have a problem with being nice to my nurses and listening to them and asking for their ideas and letting them take responsibility. But when things go wrong, I'm the one who gets the blame. And if too many things go wrong, I'll be the one who gets fired. If that's the price of Zapp, I'm not willing to pay it!"

Don and Stan both nodded. They knew Maureen had a point. In fact, they both had their own doubts about how far Zapp and Dazzle could really go in that place people commonly refer to as "the real world."

"Does this mean," Don asked, "that the first time we have to make a hard decision or do something people don't like, Zapp goes down the tubes?"

"I don't know," Stan said quietly. He looked around him at the usual happy hubbub of The Home Plate. "It never seems to go down the tubes here, and I don't think Otto's got it any easier than us."

Don turned to Maureen. "Didn't your nurses have any ideas about how to handle the food complaints and stay within budget?"

"Well, no," she answered slowly. "I didn't tell them about the budget part."

"What reason did you give for the change?" Don asked.

"I didn't exactly give them a reason," Maureen answered.

Don raised his eyebrows. "Why not?" Maureen couldn't think of an answer.

"It isn't Zapp you don't trust," Stan answered for her. "It's your nurses."

"Wait a minute . . . ," Maureen said defensively.

Stan held up his hand. "No offense," he said. "The fact is sometimes I don't really trust my people either. In fact, trust may be the hardest part of this whole Zapping business. Your nurses took some detours that caused a problem, and you got the blame. You took an action they didn't like, and now you don't trust them enough to tell them why."

"Trust has nothing to do with it!" Maureen protested. "I can't always tell them the reasons behind my decisions."

"That's true," Stan agreed. "Neither can I. But if we can share them and if the information will benefit people, then we should do it. The way things are now, your nurses don't trust you because they think you don't trust them."

No one spoke for a while. "It's a vicious cycle, isn't it?" Maureen asked.

Stan nodded. "But if we can break that cycle, we might be able to save Zapp after all."

"What should I do?" Maureen asked.

"I think telling the nurses about the problems the Food Preference Profiles caused is a good first step," Stan said.

"They may not like the decision you made, but at least they'll understand why you made it," Don added.

Chapter 13

The next day Maureen sent another memo. She explained about the budget and the food costs and the overtime and the board. She stayed in her office most of the day and did paperwork. Every now and then she checked LISA for the Zapp numbers. As the nurses read this follow-up memo, the numbers went up a little. But there was no renewed energy. Carol still frowned. As far as Maureen could see, not much had changed.

"So much for sharing the rationale for my decision," Maureen said disgustedly after she told her friends what had happened.

"I really thought it would help," Stan said.

"What did they say when you told them you're as unhappy as they are about the way things turned out?" Don asked.

"Well," Maureen replied quietly, "I didn't exactly tell them that."

"What did you tell them about what you're thinking and feeling?" Stan wanted to know.

"Nothing," Maureen admitted. Don and Stan looked surprised. "Look," she said, "I had a business decision to make, and I made it. It had nothing to do with how I felt. Talking about feelings isn't me. It's just not my style!"

"You're a nurse!" Don said. "You take care of sick people. You deal with their feelings every day."

"I deal with *their* feelings," Maureen shot back, "not mine! Look, I'm very good at keeping my feelings out of what I do for a living. I can't just change over night, and frankly, I'm not sure I want to!"

"It's hard to know how to handle this feeling stuff," Stan conceded. "When you're the boss, you have to maintain some distance between yourself and your people. You can't share how you feel about everything, but if you don't share how you feel about some things, your people will never trust you because they won't know what you're thinking or why."

"And without trust," Don added, "they'll never be willing to go that extra mile, to try something new, to do the extra things it takes to satisfy your patients."

Maureen sighed deeply. "This isn't going to be easy for me," she said, "but I'll try."

The next day Maureen held a meeting with the nurses on her shift. As she began the meeting, the nurses stared at her blankly, their faces revealing nothing.

"I know how hard you all worked on the Food Preference Profiles," she said evenly. "And I know how much the patients appreciated what you did. I'm sorry we had to discontinue them."

No one said anything during the uncomfortable silence that followed. Maureen was surprised at how much disappointment she really did feel. It was as if she hadn't disclosed her true feelings even to herself.

"Was there anything else?" Carol asked at last. Maureen nodded. She was about to adjourn the meeting when she realized she was blowing it. "They still don't know how I really feel!" she thought. The nurses were getting ready to leave.

"Wait," Maureen said suddenly. They all turned toward her.

Maureen took a deep breath. "Look, I want you to know I take responsibility for what happened." She felt their eyes on her. Her heart was pounding as she continued. "I think the Food Preference Profile was a wonderful idea, and I feel proud to work with a group of people who work so hard to do what's right for patients.

"Wait," Maureen said suddenly.

"Unfortunately," she continued, "the preference profiles caused more problems than they solved. What I'm trying to say is, I'm not just sorry that the idea didn't work out. I'm sorry I let you down, and I'm sorry for not telling you how I felt earlier. I guess I just didn't think it through."

Zapp!

As soon as she said those words, it was as if a dam broke.

Carol smiled warmly. She reached out and touched Maureen's hand. "We all could have thought it through a little more," she said. "Thanks for supporting us the way you did."

Maureen shook her head. "But I didn't support you the way I should have. If I'd been in closer touch with what you were doing, I could have helped you avoid problems."

"Maybe," Carol replied. "But you trusted us." She looked around the table at the other nurses. "The fact is, we're sorry we let you down."

The bad feelings that had been sapping the staff suddenly crumbled, and a new energy seemed to come from everyone. Back in Maureen's office LISA hummed as the Zapp levels shot abruptly skyward.

"Isn't there something else we could do?" asked Patty, one of the younger nurses.

"Something else?" Maureen asked, still a little shell-shocked.

"Just because our first idea didn't work out, it doesn't mean we can't think of something better," Patty explained.

"Sure," another nurse chimed in. "We're smart enough to think of something better."

"Maybe it would help if we knew more about the budget and the way things work in Nutrition Services," Carol said. "That's a great idea!" Maureen said enthusiastically. "And this time let's really work together to make sure we don't make any mistakes."

Soon everyone was talking about a new solution to the menu problem. As the lightning bolts flew around the room, the whole floor resumed its former glow on LISA's screen.

The glow got brighter the day Maureen referred Carol to Victor in Nutrition Services. Maureen asked her to ask Victor how his department worked and to report back to the rest of the group.

The glow got even brighter when Maureen asked Adele to explain the budgeting process at a nurses meeting.

The glow got brighter still when Maureen asked Carol and Patty to lead the new Daily Dietary Initiative, or DDI, as it came to be called. She met with them once a week so she knew enough about their progress to help them get what they needed and avoid pitfalls.

When it came to approaching Adele about asking the hospital administrator for more money, Maureen knew she'd have to do that herself.

Adele had her doubts, but she encouraged Maureen to present her case directly to the hospital administrator. Maureen asked if Carol and Patty could accompany her, and Adele agree. On the big day Maureen watched with pride as her two nurses made a convincing presentation.

Zapp and double Zapp!

"I knew it would work!" Stan said triumphantly at The Home Plate when Maureen told her friends how the board approved the nurses' recommendations.

"It's ironic," Maureen said. "At first I thought I had to abandon my control to Zapp people, but because I didn't know what was going on, I stopped trusting people. Then, when things went wrong, I over-controlled and sapped everyone. Now I think I understand that the only way I can truly Zapp people is to really share responsibility with them—to trust them, but at the same time know what's going on and help out with the things only I can do."

"I don't think keeping track of what's going on sapps people," Don said. "People only seem to respond negatively to control when they think it's inappropriate.

"When you share responsibility, the staff knows you trust them," Don continued. "And if you share your thoughts, feelings, and rationale for doing things, people will trust you to exercise control where you have to."

"I guess we can add a few more things to our list of what makes Zapp work," Stan said.

He took a napkin and wrote this:

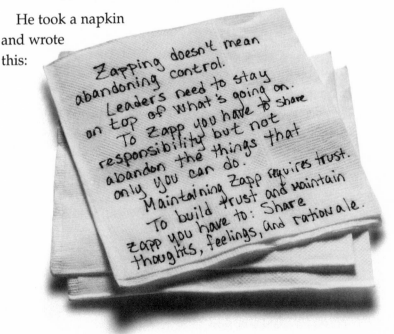

Zapping doesn't mean abandoning control.
Leaders need to stay on top of what's going on.
To Zapp you have to share responsibility but not abandon the things that only you can do.
Maintaining Zapp requires trust.
To build trust and maintain Zapp you have to: Share thoughts, feelings, and rationale.

Chapter 14

Don, Maureen, and Stan put all they had learned into practice. They Zapped their people consistently. As a result, more and more customers were Dazzled by the treatment they received from the energized people they came into contact with.

Some things had changed a lot since that first day when LISA began to reveal the secrets of Zapp. But other things were still the same.

Employees at the bank, the power company, and the hospital were energized when they were changing those things that made their customers unhappy. They knew they were doing something important. But they still didn't feel very important. In addition, when they weren't pumped up about making changes or solving problems, they were back at what Ellen at the power company referred to as "the same old dull job." Ellen never called her job dull in front of Stan, but he probably wouldn't have disagreed with her. Some days he thought his job was pretty dull too.

It was the same at the hospital and the bank. Everybody had a title and a job description that told them what to do and what not to do. Agnes summed it up best when she told a customer, "I'm just a teller."

But, of course, Agnes and everyone else knew that's the way it was in the real world. As Patty at the bank said, "You can't fight city hall."

None of this bothered Don, Stan, or Maureen very much. According to their LISAs, Zapp and Dazzle levels were about as high as The Home Plate's, and that was good enough for them.

Tom

One day, at just about six minutes after noon, Laverne came out of the kitchen at The Home Plate carrying a tray of food. She looked over at the table by the window where Don, Stan, and Maureen usually sat. She stopped dead in her tracks and stared. What she saw nearly made her drop the tray.

"You look like you've seen a ghost," Otto said. He followed her gaze to the table by the window and saw the ghost she was looking at.

Tom was back. Tom, who had left Nearville when the Federated Framis plant closed, was at his old table looking at a menu as if he'd never left. Just then the diner's door swung open and in walked Don, Stan, and

Maureen. When they saw their old friend, they stopped and stared along with Laverne and Otto.

Tom felt all those pairs of eyes staring at him. He looked up, smiled, and said something that broke the silence.

"Hi," he said. A round of handshaking, backslapping, and hugging followed.

Tom told his friends that he'd found a job at Farburg Framis Fabricators and that he was living in one of Farburg's near suburbs. He'd taken a few vacation days and decided to come back to Nearville for a visit.

"I really miss you guys," Tom said, "but getting laid off may have been the best thing that ever happened to me. Farburg Framis is a great place to work!"

"What makes it so great?" Stan wanted to know.

"It's kind of hard to explain," Tom said, "but basically everyone at Farburg Framis owns their job."

"They own their jobs?" Don asked.

"I know it sounds weird," Tom said, "but that's the best way I can describe it."

"By the way," Stan said, "what job do you own there?"

"I'm a team leader," Tom replied proudly.

Don, Stan, and Maureen exchanged puzzled glances. "Well, that's different," Maureen said.

"It sure is," Tom gushed, "and it took me a while to get used to it." Tom explained that the team he led was responsible for fulfilling customer orders for industrial-strength framises. He told them that the team members schedule their own work, prioritize what they work on, and decide who does what. When a customer has an unusual or out-of-the-ordinary need, the team finds a way to meet the need.

Don let all of this sink in for a moment. "If they do all of that on their own, what do you do?"

"I help them figure out what they should be doing and I give them the support they need to be successful. But they're pretty independent, which gives me the time to do all the things I never seemed to have had time for in my old job."

"What kind of things?" Stan asked.

"The long-range, big picture stuff," Tom replied. "I analyze market data, look for new product ideas, figure out ways to help my people develop their knowledge and skills."

"And they pay you for this?" Don blurted out. Maureen jabbed him sharply in the ribs.

"What are your Zapp and Dazzle levels like?" Stan asked suddenly. Now it was Tom's turn to look puzzled.

"Oops. I forgot. You don't know about that." Stan explained LISA and Zapp and Dazzle. Tom was instantly enthusiastic.

"That's fantastic!" he exclaimed. "If you guys ever get a day

"And they pay you for this?"

off, you should come out to Farburg, and we'll see what LISA has to say about Zapp and Dazzle at my place."

Don and Maureen didn't want to spend one of their vacation days at a framis plant, but Stan's curiosity was piqued. He had to see if all the stuff about people owning their jobs would make the Zapp and Dazzle levels at Farburg Framis higher than the levels they were creating.

Based on his observations at The Home Plate, the bank, the hospital, and the power company, 200 seemed to be the upper limit of Zapp, and 165 was as high as Dazzle ever got.

The day before he left for Farburg, Stan expressed his skepticism to Don and Maureen. "Our people are already working in teams to solve problems," he said. "As for everything else, well, it sounds good, but I'll believe it when I see it."

When Stan arrived at Farburg Framis the next morning, he drove his car to a remote corner of the parking lot and took LISA out of its case. He pointed the reflector at the building and checked the screen. What he saw took his breath away.

Chapter 15

On LISA's screen Farburg Framis glowed with such bright, deep blue intensity that Stan had to shield his eyes. Even with the gain turned all the way down, he could look at the image for only a few seconds at a time.

When he was able to look, he saw something he'd never seen on LISA's screen. Bright circles of sparks whirled behind the glass in every window in the building. But that surprise was mild compared to the shock Stan felt when he checked the numbers on LISA's computer monitor. Zapp was running at a steady 517, and Dazzle was in the low 600s!

Until that moment Stan didn't think levels that high were possible. He'd also never seen Dazzle higher than Zapp. He'd always thought Dazzle was a kind of echo of Zapp and for that reason would always be less intense.

Completely intrigued and a little intimidated, Stan packed LISA away, parked his car, and went inside.

Tom greeted his friend warmly and took him on the "nickel tour." Everywhere he looked, Stan saw energized people working together—designing, building, selling, and shipping framises.

At Tom's department Stan met the members of the order fulfillment team. Most of them were on the phone with customers, but each one took a moment to shake Stan's hand and welcome him to their department.

In Tom's cubicle Stan told Tom what he'd observed using LISA.

"The place looks pretty impressive, huh?" Tom asked with pride.

"That's putting it mildly," Stan said. "Do you mind if I take a reading of your department?"

"Not at all," Tom said. "Let's have a look at this LISA."

Stan took LISA out of the case and pointed the reflector through the cubicle opening toward Tom's people, all of whom were busy on the phones.

"Don't look directly at the screen," Stan cautioned. "As bright as the building looked from the parking lot, it could be blinding in here at close range."

"I've got some welder's dark safety glasses around here somewhere," Tom said as he rummaged through his desk drawers. "Here they are," he said, handing a pair to Stan.

They put on the glasses and gazed at LISA's screen. Through the bright, deep blue, they saw a cyclone of Zapp bolts spinning around the people on the phones. Their headsets and computer terminals sparkled with Dazzle.

"Wow!" Tom said.

Stan nodded, "That's what I said."

"What's making all that lightning? And why are the phones and computers sparkling like that?"

"The lightning is the energy we call Zapp," Stan explained. "I know what makes it go from one person to another, but I have no idea why it's spinning around like that. The sparkling is Dazzle. That's the positive energy that Zapped people pass on to customers."

"Even over the phone?" Tom asked, a little overwhelmed by what he was seeing.

"Over the phone, face-to-face—it doesn't seem to matter," Stan explained. "I haven't been able to prove it yet, but theoretically, customers can even be Dazzled with a letter."

Tom nodded, his eyes locked on the screen.

"I've never seen Dazzle as strong as it is here," Stan went on. "In fact, it's stronger than Zapp, and I used to think that was impossible."

"My people are all pretty high energy to begin with," Tom said, still transfixed by the image on LISA's screen. "And since they started working as a team, they're even more energized."

"My people work as a team too," Stan said, "but they don't look anything like that." He glanced down at the numbers on LISA's computer monitor. "And they don't generate these Zapp and Dazzle levels."

"It could be because my team is empowered," Tom explained.

Stan looked skeptical. "Now there's a word that gets thrown around a lot. What do you mean by empowered?"

"Well, empowered means a lot of things," Tom replied. "One of the things it means is that the team is in charge of working with customers."

"How so?" Stan asked.

"The staff in this department is closer to customers than anyone else in the company," Tom explained. "They're in the best position to make decisions about what makes customers happy, so they're the ones that make most of those decisions."

"That could explain the high Dazzle levels," Stan said. "But don't you worry that they'll make the wrong decision?"

"I used to," Tom admitted. "But I make sure everyone understands what we have to accomplish and what the decision-making limits are, and they pretty much take it from there. It took me a while to get used to letting go of most of the decision making, especially after what I went through when the plant in Nearville closed. After all, I lost my job because the customers deserted us in droves. So when I got here, I wanted to make sure I did everything I could to keep customers happy."

"Well, that was understandable," Stan said.

Tom smiled and shook his head. "Understandable, but wrong. At first I tried to do everything myself. Everything came across my desk, and I tried to make every decision personally."

"I've made that mistake myself," Stan said ruefully.

"Then you probably won't be surprised to learn that the reward for all my hard work was that I was exhausted, the staff hated me, and our customer satisfaction ratings were in the cellar."

"So, you let go of some things, right?" Stan asked.

Tom nodded. "And that's when things got better. First, I worked with the team to create a shared vision."

"A shared vision of what?" Stan asked.

Tom thought for a moment before he answered. "A shared vision of exactly what our service needed to be like to help the company succeed. I made sure everyone on the team understood the role they had to play. Now my job is to make sure they have the knowledge, the resources, and the authority they need to perform their roles successfully and make the vision a reality."

"And what happens when your shared vision becomes a reality?" Stan asked.

Tom looked surprised by the question. "Our customers will be delighted, of course. And when they're delighted on a regular basis, they'll become loyal."

Chapter 16

Don practically choked on his decaf when Stan told his friends about his trip to Farburg the next day at The Home Plate. "Zapp and Dazzle were how high?" he asked in disbelief after he stopped coughing.

"Between five and six hundred or so," Stan repeated.

Don shook his head. "What is Tom doing over there?"

"That's what I've been trying to figure out," Stan said, pulling some scribbled notes from his top pocket. "I've been thinking about what Tom's doing that's different from what we're doing. We've experienced the most Zapp and Dazzle when we've had a crisis to get through or a problem to solve or a really difficult customer. After the crises are over and the problems are solved, Zapp and Dazzle decrease.

"Tom's people, on the other hand, seem to be in a permanently Zapped state. I'm sure they have their crises and problems too, but they also seem very involved in what they do and in the organization. They have a vision of what they have to do for the company to succeed, and Tom makes sure they have what they need to get the job done."

"Is that what he meant when he said people own their jobs there?" Don asked.

"I think so," Stan replied.

"But why are the Zapp and Dazzle levels so high?" Maureen wanted to know.

"I'm not sure," Stan replied. "The Zapp and Dazzle I saw on LISA looked like some kind of perpetual motion machine. Tom may have provided the initial Zapp that started it, but now the energy seems to feed on itself—and it gets stronger with time, not weaker."

Stan stared out the window. "You know, the Dazzle I saw there was so strong, I bet Tom's customers never think about buying a framis from another company."

"That's very interesting, Mr. Science," Don said, "but how do *we* make it happen?"

Stan stood up. "Our people need to be totally involved. They need to own their jobs," he said like a politician on the stump. "They need to know their role in making our organizations successful! They need a shared vision!"

"A shared vision of what?" Maureen asked.

Stan looked surprised. "Of what it takes to satisfy customers, of course."

Back at his office that afternoon, Don dug up a copy of the bank's most recent annual report. He thumbed through the glossy pages filled with pictures of beautiful buildings and smiling faces until he found what he was looking for.

There, on the inside cover, was the bank's vision statement.

He ran his finger over words like "world-class" and "value" and "integrity" until he found the sentence he was looking for. "Meeting or exceeding customer expectations is our number-one priority."

At a staff meeting the next morning before the bank opened, Don wrote those words on a flip chart in the front of the room.

"I know we all have different titles," he began, "and we play different roles around here, but we all have the same job. Our job is to make sure this happens," he said, pointing to the flip chart, "not just in a crisis or when there's a problem, but every day. The reason I asked you to come in early today is to ask for your ideas about how we can do it."

Everyone studied the words on the flip chart.

"Well, I think we all know what customers expect," Agnes volunteered. Everyone nodded.

"What do they expect?" Don asked, walking over to a blank flip chart.

Frank answered first. "The big depositors expect a break on service charges."

Don wrote it on the flip chart. "Good," he said. "What else?"

"All the customers expect to park in the lot across the street for free if our lot is full," Gina offered.

Don wrote that too. "Both ideas are good," he said.

"When customers call, they expect the phone to be answered right away," Frank said.

"And they expect whoever answers to be able to help them," Elsie added.

"They don't want to wait more than a couple of minutes in line!" Gina sang out.

Everyone had ideas. For nearly an hour they brainstormed a list of the customer expectations they should be meeting or exceeding.

"This is quite a list," Don said as the hour wound down.

"How are we going to do it all?" Agnes asked.

"We can't do it all at once." Frank said.

"That's true," Don said, studying the flip charts he had posted around the room. "Which ones do you think will have the most impact on customers—and are the most important to them—yet will require the least effort and cost?"

They narrowed the list to a handful of things they believed fit the criteria. Before adjourning the meeting, Don pointed to the shortened list. "If we do these things, the bank will succeed," he said. "Now let's get out there and do them!"

They enjoyed some small successes right away. The rest of that week, there were lots of smiling faces at the bank. Customers were happier and the staff was happier. Meanwhile, Don monitored Zapp and Dazzle on LISA. His levels were up. They weren't as high as Tom's readings, but they were the highest Don had ever measured at the bank.

On Friday afternoon Don passed Frank on the way to the vault. "So, how am I doing?" Frank asked.

Don wasn't sure how to respond. "Ahh, great Frank. You're doing great."

Frank nodded. He wasn't smiling. "Thanks," he said.

"Keep up the good work!" Don called as Frank walked away. Later, when Don was in his office, Agnes stuck her head in the door.

"Did we have a good week?" she asked with an expectant smile.

Agnes had never asked a question like that before. "Sure," Don said uncertainly. "We had a fine week."

"Oh," Agnes said, her smile fading. "Well, have a nice weekend."

As she walked away, Don glanced down at where LISA was hidden under his desk. Zapp had plunged 50 points. "What's going on?" Don whispered.

Monday at lunch Don, Stan, and Maureen looked glum. When Don told them what had happened to him on Friday, Maureen sighed. "The same thing happened to me."

Stan raised his hand. "Ditto," he added.

"What are we doing wrong?" Don complained.

"I don't know," Stan said, "but I know who will."

Chapter 17

Later that week the three friends drove to Farburg together. "This is a real reunion," Tom said as he greeted them in the lobby of Farburg Framis.

"Thanks for taking the time to talk with us," Maureen said. "I hope we're not taking too much of your time."

"Don't mention it." Tom led them to his office. "You'd do the same for me."

"We did what you did," Stan summarized. "We worked with our people to create a service vision." Don and Maureen nodded. "Now they have a mission as a group and as individuals. We've supported them, given them authority and resources."

Don and Maureen nodded more vigorously. "But it's not working," Stan said.

"It started to work but then it stopped," Don corrected him.

"How do you know it stopped?" Tom asked.

"Because our Zapp levels are in the tank!" Maureen blurted out.

Tom stroked his chin. "I'm not sure I understand this Zapp and Dazzle stuff, but if you did what you said you did, your people should be pumped up and well on their way to meeting and exceeding customers' expectations."

Tom got up from his desk and walked over to the window. He stared out at his own team for a moment. "How are your people measuring their progress?" he asked.

Don, Maureen, and Stan exchanged uneasy glances.

"Well," Maureen began, "we . . . ahhh . . ."

"We do a customer survey once a year at the bank!" Don exclaimed.

"That's good," Tom said diplomatically. "But you need to measure a little more often than that—like every day or at least every week. And it's important for your people to do the measuring themselves."

"Remember," Tom said, now back at his desk, "when you control the measures of your job success, you control your job."

Stan's face brightened. "And when you control your job, you own your job!"

"Right!" Tom agreed. "I couldn't have said it better myself."

The next day Don met with his team. As the team members filed in, they noticed that the list of customer expectations they were supposed to be meeting or exceeding was taped to the wall behind Don. "I have some good news and some bad news," he began.

The team exchanged uneasy glances.

"The good news is that I think we're making progress," he said. "The bad news is none of us knows how much progress we've made. I have to find a way." He stopped and smiled. "I mean you have to find a way you can measure your progress. That way, you won't need to ask me how you're doing. You'll know. In fact, I'll start asking you how you're doing."

He pointed to an item on the list that read, "Customers should wait in line only a few minutes."

"How are you doing on this one?" Don asked.

There was an uneasy silence. "Better," Gina said at last. "I think."

"How can we make it easier for you to know?" Don asked.

"For one thing," Frank said, "we should be more specific about what we mean by a few minutes."

"Good idea!" Agnes agreed.

"What do you think, Gina?" Don asked.

Gina thought before answering. "I think two minutes ought to be tops. And we can have the security guard time how long people are in line."

"Keeping the waits under two minutes means doing more than just working faster," Frank added. "One way to make the lines shorter is to make sure people are using the ATMs as much as possible. We also need to help customers, particularly our older customers, to overcome their fear of the ATMs. Maybe we can put one in the lobby and help people learn how to use it."

"Yeah," Elsie added. "A lot of people still don't know they can do almost everything with it. If we tell every customer who comes to the window with a transaction that it could have been done at an ATM, we could really make the lines shorter."

"Let's all make a record of how many customers we tell," Agnes added. "That way, we can track the number of customers that are getting the information and how long customers are waiting in line. Maybe we can get info on the number of new ATM users too. That really would measure whether or not we're making any headway."

Everyone agreed that this was a good idea.

They had similar discussions about the other customer expectations on their list. By the end of the meeting, Don's team had turned the customer expectations into a set of measurable objectives that they could track themselves.

During the next few weeks everyone began to feel differently about their jobs, though they couldn't put the feeling into words. As Tom had told his friends, the staff now owned their jobs, and that felt great.

Don suspected it was happening, and LISA confirmed it. Zapp levels were up. Customers were being Dazzled every day as their expectations were met and exceeded.

One day at his desk, Don saw all the evidence he needed on LISA's screen. A ring of lightning bolts was spinning around the bank's employees. It was nearly as bright as the Dazzle that sparkled and crackled around each customer.

Stan and Maureen were having similar success. Over lunch at The Home Plate, they tried to figure out what they had learned.

"It starts with having a vision," Maureen said.

"It starts with knowing what your organization's vision is," Stan corrected.

Maureen nodded. "Right, but the next step is to figure out exactly what your people have to do to make that vision a reality."

"And that," Don added, "becomes their vision. But it's different from the big, organizational vision because it specifies the actions they need to take."

"It's sort of a day-by-day vision," Stan said. "An operational vision or, in our case, an operational service vision."

"And to make that vision a reality," Maureen said, "you have to turn it into a set of objectives that are achievable and measurable. But the most important part is to make sure the people who have to achieve the objectives are in charge of measuring their own progress. They don't have to do all the measuring, but they should have input and see the results of the measurement."

"That's how you build Zapp into everybody's job," Don summarized. "And that's how people come to own their jobs."

Stan had been taking notes on yet another napkin. When he was done, he showed it to his friends. "So," he said. "It looks like this is the recipe for spirals of Zapp and blinding Dazzle."

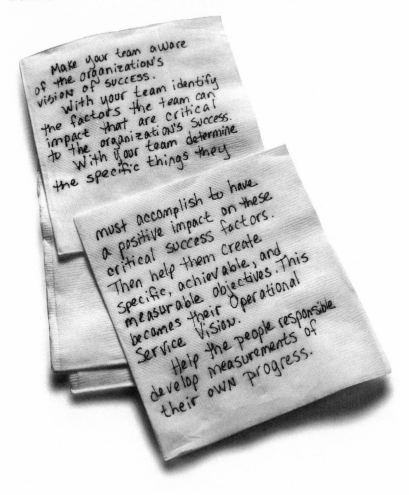

Make your team aware of the organization's vision of success.

With your team identify the factors the team can impact that are critical to the organization's success.

With your team determine the specific things they must accomplish to have a positive impact on these critical success factors.

Then help them create specific, achievable, and measurable objectives. This becomes their Operational Service Vision.

Help the people responsible develop measurements of their own progress.

Chapter 18

The spirals of Zapp and the sparks of Dazzle grew stronger and brighter at the bank, the power company, and the hospital. While Don, Stan, and Maureen hadn't quite achieved Tom's levels at Farburg Framis, they were sure they were well on their way.

Stan conscientiously recorded the Zapp and Dazzle levels in his department, and from time to time, he took LISA to the parking lot and pointed it at the building. He was glad to see the intense blue glow, but it troubled him to see that the rest of the building was so dull.

Maureen noticed the same thing from the hospital parking lot. Spirals of Zapp spun behind the Dazzling blue windows on her floor, but the windows in the rest of the hospital were a dark and dingy red.

When Stan looked at a graph of the Zapp and Dazzle levels at the power company, he realized that they had, to use his phrase, "topped out."

"Look," he said as he spread a long computer printout on their table at The Home Plate. "They get to about 300, and then they drop back again."

Don tried to look on the bright side. "That's twice as high as they used to get."

Stan was unimpressed. "But it's half as high as the levels at Farburg Framis."

"That's not a fair comparison," Maureen said. "Farburg Framis was already pretty Zapped before Tom got there. He doesn't have to deal with what we have to deal with."

"Like what?" Stan asked.

"Like my home office," Don replied. "I have something to say about what happens in my branch, but headquarters still makes rules I have to enforce, and that doesn't make Zapp and Dazzle any higher."

Maureen was not to be outdone. "Do you have any idea how bureaucratic a hospital can be?" she asked. "We Dazzle patients all day long on my floor, but as soon as they get on the elevator, the patients are at the mercy of another department that we can't control.

"Sometimes," she continued, "patients don't even have to leave the floor for some rule or regulation to turn their Dazzle to fizzle in a heartbeat, pardon the expression. Look, I wouldn't trade Zapp and Dazzle for anything, but they can't change the way things are in the real world."

Stan brooded darkly, staring at the flat graph spread on the table. "Then we'll have to change it," he said.

"Change what?" Don asked.

Stan looked up. "The real world."

Stan didn't realize it then, but the real world had taken notice of what was happening in his department.

Milton was the power company's second assistant vice president for Consumer Relations. He was also Stan's boss.

Milton was accustomed to getting letters from customers— not that the letters were sent to him personally. Most of the letters were simply addressed to the power company and most contained a complaint about some unnamed rude, arrogant, uncaring so-and-so who had treated the writer badly. The letters almost always ended with a reminder that the writer was paying the salary of the offending party plus a promise that the writer would be there the next time the power company went before the Public Utility Commission to request a rate increase. Some even warned that the power company would pay the consequences when competition comes to the electric utility business.

Milton

Milton usually responded by having his secretary sign his name on a form letter thanking the writer for his or her ideas about how the power company could better serve its customers.

But when Milton began to get letters addressed to him personally or to Stan (which were then forwarded to him), he knew that something was up, as he would later testify. These letters were about power company employees the writers seemed to know by their first names. They were written to thank Stan, Milton, or whoever in the power company hired people like Libby or Patty or Ellen or Fred. These letters usually included a story about how Libby, Patty, Ellen, or Fred had gone the extra mile to do something nice.

Milton didn't know Stan or his people very well, but after the letters got to be a regular occurrence, he figured it was about time he did.

"Hi, Stan, Milton here," said a voice on Stan's phone mail one day. "Drop by the office when you get a chance so we can have a little chat." Stan swallowed hard as he hung up the phone. He was not accustomed to having little chats with Milton or for that matter any other vice-presidential type.

At first he couldn't imagine what Milton would want to talk to him about. He ran through a mental checklist of the possibilities, but nothing made sense. Then he looked down at LISA, hiding in its customary spot under his desk.

Stan felt his stomach drop to his shoes. He swallowed hard for the second time that day. Had Milton found out about LISA? Did Milton know he had rescued three LISAs from the trash, altered them, and then given two of them to people outside the power company? Stan quickly reached the paranoid conclusion that his goose was cooked.

As he walked to Milton's office later that day, he felt like a condemned man taking that last long walk with the warden and the chaplain. Milton's receptionist told Stan that Milton would be with him in a minute.

"Have a seat," she said. Stan turned from her desk, and for a moment he imagined the high-backed leather chair in the reception area turning to wood and sprouting ankle straps on its legs and a metal cap from its back.

Stan sat down shakily. His palms were sweating, and his heart was pounding like a jackhammer. A moment later an impeccably dressed Milton was standing in front of him, his hand held out in greeting.

"Good to see you," Milton beamed. "Come on into the office."

Stan mumbled a reply, thinking to himself, "Is he this nice to everybody he fires?"

"Let me get right to the point," Milton said when they were seated. "I've got to know what's going on in your department."

Stan saw his life pass before his eyes. "This is it," he thought. He was about to admit to everything and throw himself on Milton's mercy, but Milton cut him off.

"This is it," he thought.

"These letters are amazing," Milton gushed. "People just don't write letters like this to power companies."

Stan became dimly aware of the fact that he wasn't in trouble. In fact, Milton was complimenting him.

"Whatever you're doing, it's very

powerful, and we've got to share it with the rest of the company."

In his mind Stan heard the warden telling him that he'd just gotten a call from the governor.

"So tell me," Milton said. "What's your secret?"

Stan started to answer. He was going to tell Milton about Zapp and Dazzle and spirals and The Home Plate and Farburg Framis, but he stopped himself. "I'm really not the best one to tell you," Stan said. "With your permission I'd like to have my team tell you the secret."

"Your team?" Milton's smile faded and was replaced by a look of bewilderment.

"If it would be all right?" Stan asked.

Milton stared at Stan, a quizzical look on his face. Stan started to think that maybe the governor had called back and the execution was on after all.

Then Milton broke into a big grin. "I'll be looking forward to it," he said. "Set something up with my secretary."

Chapter 19

Stan agonized for days over whether to tell Milton about LISA. He knew that rescuing the machines from the trash was technically wrong. He knew that souping up the rescued machines by hooking them to personal computers also was technically wrong. He knew that giving the units to Maureen and Don was just plain wrong.

Yet, Stan reasoned, it was because of these "wrongs" that a "right" happened. Because of what LISA helped them see, he, Maureen, and Don had done good things.

"So, that makes it OK, right?" he asked his friends a few days later at The Home Plate.

"No," Maureen shook her head. "It doesn't make it OK, but it . . . it . . ." She struggled for the right word. "It . . . justifies it, sort of."

That wasn't the kind of reassurance Stan was looking for. "That's it!" he shouted, throwing up his hands. "I can't stand all this ethical ambiguity. I'm just going to come clean. Milton can do what he wants to me!"

"Let's just throw the things out," Don suggested. "That way they end up back in the trash where you found them, and you won't have anything to come clean about."

Stan was horrified at the idea. He knew he could never do it. "That won't solve anything," he insisted. "And it won't change what I did. Besides, we still need LISA, and so will other managers who try to create Zapp and Dazzle. I've got to confess everything and hope for the best."

"Well," Maureen sighed, "whatever happens, we're all in this together, right?" She looked at Don, who had taken a sudden interest in his menu. "Right?" she asked again, kicking Don sharply in the shins.

"Right!" he winced. Rubbing his sore leg under the table, he turned to Stan. "But right now Milton wants to know what your team is doing differently that's making customers so happy. So, make sure your confession doesn't steal the show and end up becoming more important than all the work the team has done."

This made Stan stop and think. He knew the team's efforts should be the main focus. He also knew he had to tell the truth about LISA if he wanted to see the power of Zapp and Dazzle pushed beyond the boundaries of his department. He knew that couldn't happen without the cooperation of people like Milton. After all, it was people like Milton who made the real world the way it was. They determined the policies and procedures. They set the rules and directed the creation of the systems and the processes that got things done.

Stan knew that if those systems didn't change—if they weren't redesigned to focus on the customer—the organization would never reach its customer service goals.

He still wasn't sure how and when to reveal the truth

about LISA, but Stan wisely decided that because the members of his team were the ones Dazzling the power company's customers, they should make the presentation.

When he asked them for their help with the presentation, they were even more Zapped than normal. He provided them with some coaching, but he let the team decide what to present and how to present it.

On the big day Stan introduced Libby, Patty, Ellen, and Fred to Milton. He explained the concept of Zapp and how it created Dazzle. He also talked about the opposites of Zapp and Dazzle—sapp and fizzle. Milton looked skeptical as he wrote the strange-sounding words on his legal pad.

Each member of the team shared a story of what Zapp had done for him or her and how it enabled the team to Dazzle customers. As he listened, Milton's skepticism melted away. The team's enthusiasm was contagious. When they told him how Zapp had helped them save Mr. Sutton's life, Milton had to brush away a tear.

"This is amazing!" he declared at the end of the presentation. "We have to make sure everybody in the company gets Zapped right away."

Suddenly Milton got a wild look in his eyes. "We can corner the market on Dazzle!" he shouted. "Our customers will love us. We can sell our secret to other companies for a hefty profit!"

Stan tried to tell him that Zapp wasn't exactly a secret, but Milton was too excited to listen. He quickly ushered Stan and his team from his office and instructed his secretary to set up a meeting with his fellow executives that very afternoon.

The executives sat around the long table in the boardroom

and listened attentively to Milton as he preached his new-found gospel of Zapp. Everybody agreed it sounded like a good idea, but after the meeting they kept doing things the way they'd always done them.

A few weeks passed and, except for the customer letters praising Stan's team, Milton didn't detect any new outpouring of customer affection for the power company.

"Maybe our customers are Dazzled, but they're just not telling us," he reasoned. To find out, he commissioned a customer survey.

The survey's results told Milton what LISA had been telling Stan: There was no additional Zapping going on at the power company.

Stan had been trying to set up a meeting with Milton for weeks but to no avail; so, he was understandably surprised when Milton called him one afternoon. Stan didn't get a chance to ask how his boss was doing. Milton jumped in first.

"What are we doing wrong?" Milton wanted to know.

"I think it's time you and I had a talk," Stan said.

A few minutes later Stan arrived at Milton's office. Milton was pacing back and forth. "Why does Zapp work for you and not for anybody else?" Milton asked accusingly.

Stan patiently explained that to create Zapp, a person has to use Zapp. Looking at all the notes he, Don, and Maureen had written on the napkins, Stan realized that they boiled down to five key principles. Together these key principles formed a kind of "How to Zapp" instruction guide. Stan explained to Milton that the keys to making Zapp work were:

- Maintain or enhance self-esteem.

- Listen and respond with empathy.

- Ask for help and encourage involvement.

- Share thoughts, feelings, and rationale.

- Offer help without removing responsibility.

The five Key Principles are copyrighted by Development Dimensions Int'l, Inc., MCMXCVII.

Stan also told Milton about creating an operational service vision; why it was important to set specific, measurable goals; and why it was important to make people responsible for measuring their own progress.

"All right, then," Milton said. "We'll all start doing these things. I'll have copies made of your instructions and distribute them to everyone."

"Those are great first steps," Stan said, "but if you really want Zapp to spread through the company and Dazzle our customers, there are some things that will have to change."

"What things?" Milton sounded suspicious.

Stan cleared his throat. "Over the years a lot of the policies and procedures we've put into place have turned into barriers that have kept us from meeting customer expectations."

Milton wrote a lot of those policies and procedures. He didn't like hearing them called "barriers."

"We do things the way we do them for good reasons," Milton said defensively.

Stan was now very nervous, but he pressed on. "I know you used good judgment in developing our policies and procedures," he said, maintaining and enhancing Milton's self-esteem. "And I know they all meet a real need, but some of them meet our needs at the expense of the customer."

There was a long, uncomfortable silence. "What are you suggesting?" Milton eventually asked.

"I'm suggesting that we can only create so much Zapp in individual departments while our corporate policies and procedures create sapp. I'm suggesting that there's a limit to the amount of Dazzle people can create if the system is designed in a way that creates fizzle."

"And the alternative is?"

"The alternative is for the company to start doing things in a way that puts the customer first. We have to create work processes and systems that focus on meeting customers' expectations more than on meeting our own internal needs. It means redesigning backward from the customer instead of the other way around."

Milton fixed Stan with a steely gaze. "That sounds pretty risky to me. If we take all the time and trouble to make our work processes and systems supposedly more customer focused, how will we know it's working? How will we know it's worth it? How will we know we're doing it right?"

Stan considered himself to be very insightful, but he didn't claim to be a management consultant. "I don't know exactly how we'll know," he said. "But I guess we'll need to decide on the things that are really important and then measure them. Meanwhile we can use LISA."

A split second after he had spoken the words, Stan realized what he'd said. For a moment he hoped that maybe Milton hadn't caught his remark about LISA. His hope was in vain.

Chapter 20

"**W**ho's Lisa?" Milton wanted to know. "Does she work in your department?"

Stan felt his face turning red. "Ahhh, sort of."

Milton rolled his eyes. "What do you mean 'sort of'? Look, if this Lisa can tell us if we're on the right track, I want to know who she works for. I want her on this full time."

Stan felt the room spinning. "Well, she's already on it full time, except that she's an *it*."

"Whatever, we're an equal opportunity employer," Milton rolled on. "If we need Lisa to keep us on track, then we should—" Milton suddenly realized what Stan had said. "What do you mean she's an *it*?"

Stan had an out-of-body experience. He hovered somewhere near the ceiling and watched himself spill his guts to Milton. While the senior executive listened in dumbfounded silence, Stan told him the whole story. He told him about taking three LISAs out of the dumpster, rebuilding them in his basement, and giving one to Don and one to Maureen. He concluded by describing how the three of them had been using the machines to measure Zapp and Dazzle ever since.

"Do you have one of these things here in the building?" Milton asked sharply.

Stan nodded. He dragged himself back to his office, plucked LISA from its hiding place, and carried it back to Milton's office.

"Isn't this one of our Linear Infrared Spectral Analyzers?" Milton asked as he slowly circled the contraption.

"With a few enhancements," Stan replied modestly.

"And these enhancements, you made them all yourself?"

Stan nodded.

Stan told the whole story.

"Well," Milton said, "this changes everything." Stan began calculating how many bills he could pay with an unemployment check. He quickly concluded that he'd have to sell one of his children.

"Yes, this changes everything," Milton continued. "Helping us reproduce LISA will just have to become your top priority for a while."

He ran his hands admiringly over a row of dials. "Why couldn't the R&D people have come up with this?"

"You mean you're not going to fire me?" Stan blurted out.

"Fire you?" Milton said. "I can't fire you. I need your help to make this whole Zapp and Dazzle thing work."

Stan was incredulous. "But . . . but what about the machines I gave to Don and Maureen?"

"I can't fire them either. They don't work for me."

"You don't mind that they have company property?"

"They don't compete with us, right?"

Stan nodded.

"Then, it's simple," Milton said. "If having these things means we'll all get better service at the bank and the hospital, that's fine with me."

Stan and Milton went on to discuss the processes and systems that could be changed to better focus on customers. Milton still wasn't convinced that anything should change. He also didn't want to attract a lot of attention in case changing things led to failure rather than success.

"Let's conduct an experiment," Milton said. "If you had to pick one process to change, what would it be?"

Stan didn't need to think long. "There's got to be a more customer-friendly way for people to initiate new service. Now, when customers call to open an account, they're on the phone for at least 20 minutes. First, we have to enter information into seven computer screens. Then, we have to put them on hold and call Credit. If their credit's OK, they stay on hold while we call Scheduling. If it's service for a new building, we have to call Dispatch. By the time we get back on the line, some customers have hung up, and the ones that haven't sure aren't happy."

Milton nodded as he took notes on his yellow pad. "OK, you and your team make some recommendations for streamlining the process, and we'll make some changes." Stan smiled in triumph. "But only in your department."

Stan started to object, but Milton cut him off. "Remember, this is an experiment. If LISA shows us that it's a success in your department, we'll do it throughout the rest of the company. Meanwhile, I'm going to take a crack at our performance management system. If we're going to Dazzle customers, we have to make it important to people, right?"

Stan nodded.

"And if you reward somebody for doing something, they'll probably do it again, right?"

Stan nodded again.

"Well, if we want Dazzled customers, we should base the performance management of anyone who deals with customers on how high their Dazzle levels are."

Stan started to remind Milton of how important it was to make people responsible for measuring their own performance, but Milton cut him off, pointed to LISA, and said, "Take this down to R&D and tell them what you did to it so they can figure out how to make more. We're going to need a lot of LISAs around here before we're done."

Stan picked up LISA and headed for the Research and Development Department. He felt relieved, confused, and excited. His head was swimming. He didn't know exactly what was going to happen next, but he knew that the experiment had begun.

Chapter 21

Research and Development could work fast when they had to. Milton wanted LISA copied and reproduced in a hurry, and in just a few weeks the building was full of them. Parabolic reflectors silently monitored Dazzle anywhere a group of power company employees worked with customers.

Not that there was much to measure.

Milton had sent everyone a memo explaining how important it was to Dazzle customers. In the same memo he announced that the performance management system was being changed so that everyone who worked with customers would be judged by their Dazzle levels.

Big-time Sapp!

The employees weren't sure exactly what Dazzle was. They didn't understand what all those weird-looking contraptions were that seemed to be watching them from every corner. But everyone agreed that these were signs that bad things were happening.

After a few days the rumors were spinning fast and furious. "Those machines are going to replace us," said someone in Dispatch. "I don't know about that," replied someone from Billing, "but you can bet there'll be layoffs."

"They're selling the company!" declared someone in Shipping. "It's a plot!" cried another.

"I'm going to write a letter to the editor of the newspaper!" the receptionist in the lobby decided.

There was none of this hysteria in Stan's department. Relieved not to have to hide LISA, he gladly told everyone in his department what it was and what it did. Since his thoroughly Zapped people were already producing healthy amounts of Dazzle and were already in charge of measuring their own performance, they agreed with Stan that the machine would be a good tool.

They also were too busy to pay attention to rumors. Everyone worked on developing the streamlined process for opening new accounts. Milton approved it with very few changes. Now the team was enthusiastic about the new heights of Dazzle the process would help them achieve.

"Now the process is as focused on satisfying customers as we are!" Ellen said on the day it went into effect.

But Dazzle wasn't climbing to new heights. In fact, it was dropping as fast as fizzle was rising, and the people on Stan's team were having problems they'd never experienced before. Even though the new process enabled them to do things once done by other departments, they still needed to work with those departments, and that's where they were having problems.

Libby liked having direct access to credit records on her

computer when a customer called to open a new account. Before, she had to ask the Credit Department for that information, and that took a lot longer. She missed talking to her friend Martha in Credit though. In fact, one day when she saw some credit codes she didn't recognize in a customer's file, Libby was glad for the opportunity to give Martha a call.

"Martha, what do the letters DBC mean in a credit file?" she asked her friend.

"I'm sorry, but I'm not able to share confidential information with unauthorized personnel," Martha replied coldly.

Libby thought she was kidding. "Yeah, right. Listen, honey, I'm not unauthorized personnel. I'm Libby, remember?"

Martha's voice showed no sign of humor. "I know who you are," she said. "If you'll have your supervisor submit a request in writing, I'll give you the information as soon as the request is approved."

"But . . . but I've got a customer on hold," Libby sputtered.

"I'm sorry," Martha said, not sounding sorry at all. "I'll call you back as soon as I receive the approval."

"But . . . wait," Libby said as the dial tone buzzed in her ear.

Fred had a similar conversation with Eunice in Dispatch, and no one in Billing would return Ellen's calls.

As they watched Dazzle levels sink lower and fizzle levels soar higher, the team started to panic. So did Stan.

Stan shared his woes with Don and Maureen at The Home

Plate. "I'm doomed," he said. "The experiment is failing. When Milton sees how low Dazzle is, there's no way he'll change processes throughout the company. And since it was my idea, guess who gets the blame?"

"You're doomed," Don agreed.

Maureen looked puzzled. "Why is your department the only one that's using this new process?" she asked.

"We're the guinea pigs," Stan explained. "Milton said if we succeed, he'll support making work processes more customer focused throughout the rest of the company. But we can't succeed because we can't seem to work with other departments. Until we can, our work processes won't really be customer focused."

"Which is why Zapp and Dazzle haven't spread," Maureen added.

Stan nodded. "Right. That's why I talked to Milton about changing our processes and systems in the first place. What's happening now is making things worse. It's not just that Zapp and Dazzle aren't spreading outside my department— they're dropping inside my department and everywhere else."

"Why?" Don was alarmed.

"For one thing, this new performance management system isn't supporting Dazzle like Milton thought it would. Instead, it's sending fizzle levels through the roof."

"Why?" Don asked again.

"Except for the people in my department, no one really understands what Dazzle is or how to make it happen," Stan explained.

"Which means," Maureen said slowly, thinking as she spoke, "that the new performance management system is sapping people."

Stan nodded, adding, "Because they don't know how to control what's being measured, and they aren't in control of how it's being measured."

"There's the problem!" Maureen declared.

"Where?" Don asked looking around.

Stan shook his head. "I know what the problem is. I already tried explaining all of this to Milton, but he wouldn't listen."

"Maybe you need to explain it differently," Maureen offered.

Stan threw up his hands. "I'm all ears."

They were all silent for a minute. "Maybe what you need to tell Milton is more basic than Zapp and Dazzle and controlling performance measurement," Maureen said. "Maybe you need to tell Milton that the company needs to work on the two Ts first."

"The two Ts?" Stan asked.

Maureen nodded. "Training and trust."

Her friends fixed on her with puzzled stares.

"Don't forget how long it took us to learn the secrets of Zapp and Dazzle," she said. "We learned by watching people who were good at it, like Otto and Laverne, and then we went through a lot of trial and error. We learned some other things from Tom, and then we went through more trial and error. How can we expect other people to be as good at Zapp and Dazzle as we are without some kind of training?"

"We can't," Don answered. "It takes a lot of interpersonal skills to Zapp employees and Dazzle customers."

"But if we take what we learned and turn it into some kind of training program, people will have a way to learn the skills they need to succeed," Maureen said enthusiastically.

"That's a good idea," Stan said as he made some notes on his napkin. "If I can get Milton to go along with it. But what about the other T? Where does trust come in?"

"The new performance management system is sapping everybody because Milton didn't disclose any of his thoughts, feelings, or rationale when he introduced it."

"That's one of the reasons," Stan agreed.

"People won't trust Milton or the new system if he doesn't trust them," Maureen continued. "I learned that lesson the hard way."

Stan jotted a few more notes. "So, if we can turn what we know about Zapp and Dazzle into a training program that gives people the skills they need, and if I can somehow get Milton to buy into it and share his thoughts, his feelings, and the rationale behind the new performance management system, then we may be able to turn things around."

Stan sighed deeply and looked at what he had written. "This might work, if it's not too late."

"The two Ts," Maureen said with a triumphant smile. "They're the answer."

"They're part of the answer," Don corrected. "You forgot the P."

"The P?" Stan and Maureen asked in unison.

"Partnerships. Training people is a great idea, and without

trust you can't have Zapp. But trust between managers and employees isn't enough. Departments have to trust each other too."

Stan started writing on his napkin again. "And how do we make that happen?"

"Simple—partnerships," Don answered. "No single person or group can Dazzle customers alone. They need to know who they need to work with to make Dazzle happen, and they need to know how to work with them."

Stan rolled his eyes. "I know that, but how?"

"Partners have to set mutual goals, share information, and work together to resolve problems," Don said. Stan started writing again.

"And partners have to stop stereotyping each other and guessing at each other's motivations." Don was on a roll. "Partners have to keep their commitments and admit mistakes and stop blaming each other and . . ."

"OK, OK, I get it!" Stan shouted, writing furiously.

"Partnerships," Don said catching his breath. "It won't work without 'em."

Stan looked up from his napkin. "You guys are full of good advice. Are you doing any of these things yourself?"

Don and Maureen exchanged sheepish grins. "Like you said, you're the guinea pig," Maureen whispered.

Chapter 22

Stan had been dreading the phone call he knew was coming. When Milton had a chance to look at the data all the LISAs had been gathering, he'd see just how bad things were. And Stan knew that when that happened, he'd have a lot of explaining to do.

But Stan was so inspired after having lunch with his friends that he decided to take a more proactive approach to dealing with Milton. Stan walked upstairs to Milton's office to set up an appointment, but the receptionist was out. Milton, on the other hand, was in. From the stacks of computer printouts on his desk and the slack-jawed look of shock on his face, Stan guessed that the LISA data was in too.

Stan knocked lightly on Milton's open door. "Is that what I think it is?" he asked as the executive looked up.

Milton nodded silently and went back to looking at the numbers, which told a story of rampant sapp and fizzle.

"How am I going to explain this to the Board?" he moaned. Then he looked Stan in the eye. "Come to think of it, how are you going to explain this to me? I spent good money on those stupid machines. I started changing systems and processes like you suggested, and things are worse than ever. Even your numbers are lousy. And look at these letters!" He pointed to a stack of mail on his desk. "I'm getting more complaints now than ever."

Stan took a deep breath. "This is mostly my fault," he said evenly.

This brought Milton up short. He wasn't used to people taking personal responsibility when things went wrong. "It is?" he asked in a surprised voice.

Stan nodded. "I tried to rush things," he said. "I forgot the basics, and we didn't do first things first."

"Of course," Milton agreed, not at all sure what he was agreeing to.

Stan knew that despite his faults Milton wanted good things to happen at the power company—just like he did. And Stan sensed that even though Milton was demoralized at the moment, he was more interested in finding answers than in fixing blame.

Stan sat down in front of Milton's desk. "Earlier today, two good friends of mine reminded me of the basics of Zapp and Dazzle. It'll be a lot of work, and it's going to take some time, and it's going to cost some money."

Milton winced.

"But I think we can succeed way beyond our expectations."

Milton listened as Stan explained the importance of training, trust, and partnerships. When he finished it was

Milton's turn to take a deep breath. The executive looked at the stack of computer printouts and the pile of letters. Finally he looked back at Stan.

"Let's get started," he said quietly. "We've got a lot to do."

And it was on that day, at that moment, that their success story really began.

The first thing Milton tackled was building trust. This was a bigger struggle for him than it had been for Maureen. It was hard for Milton to admit that the people who reported to him or who occupied the many rungs below him on the organizational ladder really needed to know why he made decisions and what he was thinking or feeling. He had always thought that this kind of disclosure would be interpreted as a sign of weakness. He mistakenly believed that one of the reasons for his personal success was his ability to "make the tough calls" and "stonewall it" behind his "game face."

But he soon realized he didn't need a game face. He was building partnerships through trust. He did this by sharing his thoughts, feelings, and rationale; making and keeping his commitments; admitting mistakes; asking for feedback; and testing assumptions. He was leading an enterprise with partners who had as much at stake as he did.

Milton began to meet regularly with the customer service supervisors to talk about why loyal customers were critical to the success of the company. He talked about Zapp and Dazzle with all the fervor of a recent convert. He stressed that Zapping employees made it possible for them to Dazzle customers and that Dazzled customers were loyal customers. He explained that this was why the performance management system changed, and this was why other systems would have to change as well.

One of those systems was the one used to hire and promote people. "If Zapp and Dazzle create loyal customers," he said at a Board meeting one day, "then we should only be hiring and promoting people who have the most potential to Zapp and Dazzle."

His fellow executives agreed, and soon they were working on developing a new Zapp- and Dazzle-based selection and assessment system.

"Now, we have to get serious about training," Milton said to Stan one day as they sat in his office. "We have to train everyone to Dazzle customers. After everyone's trained, just think how high our levels will be!"

Of course, when Milton said, "We have to get serious about training," he really meant that Stan had to get serious about training, and this had Stan seriously worried.

The next day he worried out loud at The Home Plate.

"How am I going to figure out a way to train everybody to Dazzle customers?" he moaned.

Maureen chewed thoughtfully on a french fry. "The only way to really learn is the way we did it."

Stan threw up his hands. "What am I supposed to do? Have everybody at the power company hang out at The Home Plate for a couple of months and watch Laverne?"

"No," Maureen said. "But you have to give people a chance to watch what effective service providers do to Dazzle their customers—what they say, how they behave. Then, they need to practice it, get some feedback, and practice some more. That's the way we learned. That's the way the people in our departments learned."

The idea sounded good to Stan, and it sounded good to Milton when Stan explained it to him. But it sounded expensive to the members of the Board.

"Training costs money!" one member declared when Milton presented the idea at a Board meeting. "And it takes time!" another complained. "And time," a third member added, "is money!"

Milton argued persuasively in the face of these objections. He pointed out that the return on their investment would be considerable, and that electric power competition is just around the corner. Eventually, after much grumbling, the Board approved the idea and purchased a training program that would provide Dazzling service skills. They were careful to buy one that had documented behavior change.

Dazzle training had begun.

It wasn't easy, and it certainly didn't work all the time, but the training got the right skills into the hands of the right people. This training was unlike anything anyone in the company had experienced before. They knew they were acquiring skills that would help them succeed at more than just providing Dazzling service to customers.

Dazzle training had begun.

The skills they were learning would help them succeed in their everyday lives.

Unfortunately they didn't succeed at creating the sudden spike of Dazzle that Milton and Stan had been expecting.

Stan tried to sound hopeful. "The numbers aren't bad," he said as they looked at the disappointing LISA readings in Milton's office.

This did nothing to cheer Milton. "They aren't good either!" he complained. "What am I supposed to say to the Board now? Where's the return on investment I promised them?"

Stan wished he knew.

So did Don and Maureen. "This doesn't make any sense!" Don protested. "After what you did, Dazzle levels ought to be going through the roof."

Maureen looked sad. "You did everything right. You trained everybody. People on the front line have Dazzle skills, leaders have Zapp skills. What else is left?"

Sometimes the simplest things are the hardest things to see. Just then Stan experienced a split second of crystal-clear vision.

"Of course!" He leaped to his feet. "You can't have Dazzle without Zapp!"

Don looked up at the rapture-filled face of his friend. "And this is a news flash to you?"

Stan hit himself in the forehead with the heel of his hand. "No—yes—I don't know." He turned suddenly and rushed toward the door. "I gotta go!"

Don and Maureen looked at each other and shrugged.

Chapter 23

S tan raced directly to Milton's office. "Remember the five key principles that were part of the 'How to Zapp' instruction guide?" he asked.

Milton still had the guide on his desk. "What about them?"

"We're not using them!" Stan declared.

Milton got defensive. "Sure we are. Wasn't all our expensive, time-consuming Dazzle training based on them?"

Stan shook his head. "Yes, but *we're* not using them—you and I and people like us aren't using them!"

It all began to dawn on Milton. "Which means we're not Zapping people very effectively. And that means . . ."

Stan nodded vigorously. He knew what that meant.

Milton was all smiles. "That means we're not giving people on the front line what they need to Dazzle customers. That means we have to train leaders how to Zapp our people so they can Dazzle customers!"

Now Milton frowned. "And that means we have to ask the Board for more time and money!"

The next day Milton told the Board that every leader at the power company needed Zapp. The spirited discussion that followed could be generously described as a "frank exchange of views." But in the end everyone came to a profound realization: If leaders didn't develop their skills, the company would never realize the full benefit of the skills possessed by the frontline people.

And so Zapp training began. As more and more leaders got better and better at using the skills, the partnerships Don had talked about began to form.

Teams from different departments began to meet with one another on a regular basis. They learned about one another's jobs. They worked together to clarify the different roles they needed to play to ensure that customers were Dazzled. They set goals together. They solved problems together, and they began to celebrate successes together.

As people monitored the data being recorded by the LISAs throughout the company, they could see that dramatic things were happening. The Zapp and Dazzle numbers got higher and higher. The LISA screens showed more and more bright spirals surrounding teams and partners.

The stacks of customer compliment letters grew higher and higher on Milton's desk. Soon his mail started arriving in large bags, but Milton took the time to read each letter and share it with the people who had done the Dazzling.

Good things were happening at the bank and the hospital too. Inspired by Stan's success, Don and Maureen took similar steps and achieved similar success. Now, when they pointed LISA's parabolic reflector at their buildings, they saw more than a blinding blue glow.

They also saw something new. Each building was enveloped in a towering spiral of sparks. Stan's research eventually revealed that the spiral was caused by the force of satisfied, loyal employees creating satisfied, loyal customers who made each business successful. This enabled each business to do more to keep employees satisfied and loyal so they could create more value for customers, which made the customers even more satisfied and loyal, and so on. Stan also discovered that it was their leadership, right in the middle of the whole thing, that made it work. The picture he drew of the process looked like this:

To put it simply, they had achieved critical mass.

What happened next started spreading Zapp and Dazzle throughout the rest of Nearville and eventually around the world.

Being in the consulting game, I'm naturally aware of new developments in the business world. I was sitting at the counter in The Home Plate one day reading an article in the *Nearville News Chronicle* about the reopening of the old Federated Framis plant by Farburg Framis. I decided to stop by the place and get to know the new general manager.

His name was Tom. He told me he used to work at the plant before it closed. We talked about the usual corporate stuff, how Farburg Framis was the industry leader, how they were glad to be bringing jobs and opportunities back to Nearville—all routine.

Then, suddenly, Tom started babbling about these powerful forces his company used to make customers loyal. Then he said that with the right machine, a person could actually see those forces in action.

Most people would've figured the guy was a few sprockets shy of a full gearbox, if you get my drift. Tom must've realized that, because he smiled and said that as crazy as it sounded, it was true, and his company wasn't the only one tapping into these forces. The same thing was going on at the bank, the hospital, and the power company. And then came the capper. He said the guy who invented the machine that lets you see this wacky stuff lived right in Nearville.

The next day I found myself sitting with Tom, Don, Maureen, and Stan at a table in The Home Plate, looking at one of those menus Laverne was so proud of.

They told me the whole story, just as I've told it to you. Of course, what they'd learned about Zapp didn't surprise me. I already knew all about that. But the Dazzle they talked about was something else.

I started researching and writing about it, and soon everybody wanted to know more about Dazzle and the four discoverers. The rest, as they say, is history. (By the way, just for the record, the four of them never called themselves The Service Leaders Club. That was my idea.)

As you probably know, they're all doing pretty well these days—senior executives, every one of them. Even LISA is prospering. Engineers kept tinkering with it over the years, devising one improvement after another. Not long ago we used LISA technology to create the handheld Zapp-o-Meter and Dazzle-o-Meter.

Even though the members of the Club are well known as experts in creating loyal customers and much sought after as speakers and consultants, they don't put on airs. They still eat lunch at The Home Plate almost every day.

The old diner was replaced a few years ago by a new one that is twice its size to handle the overflow crowds that showed up after The Service Leaders Club became famous.

Now, I can't guarantee you'll become rich and famous if you join, but it's a great first step.

That's the whole story. Now it's your turn to go out there and give me another great story to write about. To get started, fill out the membership pledge form. Welcome to the Club.

Bill Byham

The Service Leaders Club
Membership Pledge Form

Your name: _____

1. I will Zapp the people on my service team by using the five DDI Key Principles of service leadership:
   - Maintain or enhance self-esteem.
   - Listen and respond with empathy.
   - Ask for help and encourage involvement.
   - Share thoughts, feelings, and rationale.
   - Offer help without removing responsibility.

2. I will assure that all members of my service team have the job information, technical skills, and service skills to do their jobs well.

3. I will coach them in these skills and continuously reinforce their improvement.

4. I will work with my service team members to develop an operational service vision that links to the organization's overall service vision. I will help them set goals, and I will work with them to continuously monitor the team's progress toward achieving those goals.

5. I will examine the policies, procedures, and way of doing things to identify and eliminate causes of sapp and fizzle.

Your signature: _____

Date: _____

DDI is forming a worldwide Service Leaders Club. Benefits of membership will include access to information about best practices, service innovations, and current research. Members also will have an opportunity to network with other service leaders.

For more information about the club, contact the Service Culture Practice at Development Dimensions International, 1225 Washington Pike, Bridgeville, PA 15017-2838. You also can reach us via e-mail at info@ddiworld.com.

Acknowledgments

The Service Leaders Club was produced by another club, one much larger than the three people whose names appear on the cover. The membership of this club contributed ideas, support, encouragement, and attention to detail without which this book would never have been completed. The members include:

Karen Munch and Marni Cayro—Karen and Marni personify "grace under pressure." They brought a refreshing vision and boundless creativity to the design of this book, and they did it against a backdrop of ever-tighter deadlines and ever-increasing demands.

Mike Crawmer—As editor of this book, Mike always had an answer to the question, "Does this make any sense?" Most importantly, when his answer to that question was "no," he always found a way to fix things.

Anne Maers and Lynne Amatangelo—Managing the production of a book is a production in itself. Thanks to Anne and Lynne, the seemingly endless list of things to do got done.

Jim Papariello—With the eye of a master, he created the photographs that made the book come alive.

Shawn Garry, Ellen Wellins, and Andrea Garry—It's a cliché to say that Shawn, Ellen, and Andrea made sure we crossed our t's and dotted our i's, but that's what they did. And they did it with impeccable attention to detail.

Helen Moretti—If the world ran on smiles and good humor, Helen could fuel it single-handedly. As if that isn't enough, she's also a natural at the all-but-impossible task of coordinating the endless meetings that made this project a reality.

Sherryl Nufer—A maven of Zapp in her own right, Sherryl provided the empowerment and job ownership that was essential to completing this book.

The *Service Plus* Team: Diane Bock, Neil Brem, Connie Donaldson, Karen Pradines, Dyan Rachuba, and Tom Sontag—For this book to get done, this team went above and beyond the call of duty, not only by shouldering additional work but by doing it with enthusiasm and support.

Coleman Conley, Jim Drummond, Dick Duke, Pam Gardner, Dick Hunter, Corinne Sanford, Claire Werling, and Tracy Porto—Each of these people literally became one of the characters in this book and, in so doing, breathed life into each one.

Rosemary Crew—She provided the encouragement, space, and time it took to write this book, along with light and love when things got dark.

Books by William C. Byham and Others at DDI

Select the right people for your organization:

The Selection Solution: Solving the Mystery of Matching People to Jobs by William C. Byham with Steven M. Krauzer

Help job seekers land the right job:

Landing the Job You Want by William C. Byham with Debra Pickett

Build an empowered organization:

Zapp!® The Lightning of Empowerment by William C. Byham with Jeff Cox (also available on videocassette and audiocassette)

Zapp!® in Education by William C. Byham with Jeff Cox and Kathy Harper Shomo

Zapp!® Empowerment in Health Care by William C. Byham with Jeff Cox and Greg Nelson

HeroZ™—Empower Yourself, Your Coworkers, Your Company by William C. Byham and Jeff Cox (also available on audiocassette)

Create and sustain high-performance work teams:

Empowered Teams: Creating Self-Directed Work Groups That Improve Quality, Productivity, and Participation by Richard S. Wellins, William C. Byham, and Jeanne M. Wilson

Inside Teams: How 20 World-Class Organizations Are Winning Through Teamwork by Richard S. Wellins, William C. Byham, and George R. Dixon

Leadership Trapeze: Strategies for Leadership in Team-Based Organizations by Jeanne M. Wilson, Jill George, and Richard S. Wellins, with William C. Byham

Succeeding With Teams: 101 Tips That Really Work by Richard S. Wellins, Dick Schaaf, and Kathy Harper Shomo

Team Leader's Survival Guide by Jeanne M. Wilson and Jill A. George

Team Member's Survival Guide by Jill A. George and Jeanne M. Wilson

Understand how Japanese companies operate outside Japan:

Shogun Management™: How North Americans Can Thrive in Japanese Companies by William C. Byham with George Dixon

Building a Service Culture:

Service Skills in the Workplace by Paul Bernthal and James H.S. Davis

Service Boosters—Activities to Enhance Your Service Skills by Development Dimensions International

We'd Love to Hear from You!

Now that you've read *The Service Leaders Club*, we'd love to hear from you. Here are several ways to reach us.

Write to us at: Development Dimensions International
World Headquarters—Pittsburgh
Attention: The Service Leaders Club
1225 Washington Pike
Bridgeville, PA 15017-2838

Fax us at: 412-257-3916

E-mail us at: ddidirect@ddiworld.com

For more information about our training and consulting services, please call our Customer Information Center at 1-800-933-4463 between 8:00 a.m. and 5:30 p.m. (EST), Monday through Friday, or visit our web site at: http://www.ddiworld.com.

To place an order for additional copies of *The Service Leaders Club* or other books by William C. Byham and Development Dimensions International, please call 1-800-334-1514 or visit your local bookstore.

Thanks again for reading *The Service Leaders Club*.

Notes:

Notes:

Notes: